LAW AND URBAN GROWTH

ROBERT A. SILVERMAN

LAW AND
URBAN GROWTH

*Civil Litigation
in the Boston Trial Courts,
1880-1900*

PRINCETON UNIVERSITY PRESS
PRINCETON, NEW JERSEY

Library of Congress Cataloging in Publication Data will be
found on the last printed page of this book

Publication of this book has been aided by a grant from the
Paul Mellon Fund of Princeton University Press

This book has been composed in VIP Baskerville

Clothbound editions of Princeton University Press books
are printed on acid-free paper, and binding materials are
chosen for strength and durability.

Printed in the United States of America by Princeton
University Press, Princeton, New Jersey

To my Parents and Grandparents

CONTENTS

ILLUSTRATIONS ix

TABLES xi

ACKNOWLEDGMENTS xiii

PART I THE ARENA

ONE Boston and Its Trial Courts 3

TWO *Personae* 17

PART II THE ANONYMOUS MARKETPLACE

THREE Commercial Credit 49

FOUR Emoluments 67

FIVE A Place to Live 82

PART III THE DANGERS OF EVERYDAY LIFE

SIX Accidents 99

SEVEN Malice 122

CONCLUSION At the Threshold of the Law 133

APPENDIXES

A. Sources and Samples 151

B. Classification of Cases 157

C. Occupations and Enterprises 159

D. The Bench 165

NOTES 167

WORKS CITED 199

INDEX 213

ILLUSTRATIONS

MAPS

1. The City of Boston, 1880-1900   8
2. Boston and Vicinity, 1880-1900   9
3. Outline Map of Boston   85

FIGURES

1. Former Supreme Court Room of the Suffolk
   County Courthouse (Photograph by Richard
   Cheek. Courtesy Society for the Preservation
   of New England Antiquities)   18
2. Newspaper Row, Washington Street, Boston,
   July 8, 1889 (Courtesy Bostonian Society)   53
3. Trolley Accident on the Broadway Bridge,
   South Boston, June 12, 1912 (From *Brahmins &
   Bullyboys*, published by Houghton Mifflin Co.
   Copyright © 1973 by Stephen Halpert and
   Brenda Halpert. Reprinted by permission
   of the publisher)   103
4. Immigrant Youth Maimed in an Industrial
   Accident (Courtesy Commonwealth of
   Massachusetts)   111

TABLES

1. Cases between Litigants Residing or Doing Business in Greater Boston, 1880, 1900   10

2. Distribution of Male and Female Litigants, 1880, 1900   19

3. Distribution of Male and Female Plaintiffs by Subject of Litigation, 1880, 1900   20

4. Relative Importance of Debt and Injury to White- and Blue-Collar Litigants, 1880   22

5. Relative Importance of Debt and Injury to White- and Blue-Collar Litigants, 1900   23

6. Distribution of First- and Second-Generation Immigrants and Yankees among Litigants, 1880, 1900   25

7. Nationality of Litigants, 1880, 1900   26

8. Relative Importance of Debt and Injury to First- and Second-Generation Immigrant and Yankee Litigants, 1880   27

9. Relative Importance of Debt and Injury to First- and Second-Generation Immigrant and Yankee Litigants, 1900   28

10. Distribution of Jurors and Litigants by Nationality, 1900   42

11. Distribution of White- and Blue-Collar Workers among Jurors and Litigants, 1900   42

12. Judgments for the Plaintiff by Personal Characteristics of Plaintiffs and Their Lawyers, 1880, 1900   45

13. Cases Brought per 100 Dealers in Certain
    Commodities, 1880, 1900   54
14. Incidence of Wage Claims, 1880, 1900   69
15. Influence of Size of Claim on Length of
    Litigation, 1880 and 1900 Combined   71
16. Influence of Size of Claim on Recovery, 1880 and
    1900 Combined   71
17. Incidence of Fee Claims by Doctors and Lawyers,
    1880, 1900   75
18. Relative Importance of Certain Real-Estate
    Actions, 1880, 1900   84
19. Distribution of Landlord-Tenant Litigation by
    Neighborhood, 1880, 1900   94
20. Distribution by Causation of Lawsuits for
    Accidental Injury, 1880, 1900   106

ACKNOWLEDGMENTS

Originality in legal language, lawyers are fond of saying, is rarely a virtue. The same may be said of acknowledgments. There really are no words to express fully the gratitude one feels toward those who have invested the time and offered the encouragement necessary to produce a book, especially a first book. I shall, however, take this opportunity to express publicly the appreciation I have already tried to convey privately to a number of people.

Thanks for reading the manuscript in its entirety at various stages of development, for offering eye-opening criticism, and for urging me on are due Stephen Botein, Margaret E. Conners, Kathleen Neils Conzen, Gail Filion, Lawrence M. Friedman, Oscar Handlin, Stanley N. Katz, and James Kettner. Aspects or portions of this work, as well as my morale, benefited from the comments of Christopher Jedrey, Kenneth Ludmerer, Jon Roberts, and Stephan Thernstrom. Thanks are also due Morton Horwitz for his help in developing Chapter Six and for arranging research support from Harvard Law School's Mark DeWolfe Howe Fund. Funding was also provided by the National Science Foundation and the Department of History, Harvard University.

For access to, and a better understanding of, various archival materials, I am indebted to Elijah Adlow, former Chief Justice of the Boston Municipal Court, Edward Bellafontaine of Boston's Social Law Library, Joseph Keohane and his staff at Suffolk County Superior Court, and James Owens of the Federal Records Center, Waltham, Massachusetts. Jeff Cody and Donna Silverman assisted me in coding much of the data obtained from these repositories. The final product is much the better for the editorial work of C. F. Magee, Gretchen Oberfranc, and Rhoda Silver-

ACKNOWLEDGMENTS

man, as well as the informed typing of Debby Beardsley and Gale Halpern. I could not have illustrated this work without Whitney Powell, who drew the original maps, and Ellie Reichlin, who helped me to locate photographs.

Fran Silverman typed and listened tirelessly. Above all, she made my interest in this work her own.

PART I

The Arena

ONE

BOSTON AND ITS TRIAL COURTS

"OF all the mysteries of legal history, perhaps the most impenetrable is the history of law in action, law as it was lived, not as it was supposed to be." Of all the mysteries of urban history, perhaps the least understood is the action of law in urban life.[1]

Trial courts were potentially important social institutions in the cities of late-nineteenth-century America. During the period 1880-1900, a watershed for the functioning of law, "new demands of desperate urgency were made on the administration of justice," placing novel stresses on trial courts. An increasing flow of immigrants from overseas and from the surrounding countryside combined with uncertain employment opportunities to burden urban communities with newcomers of little or no means. Such people found themselves entangled in wage disputes, landlord-tenant problems, and situations involving instruments of indebtedness. New technologies, especially in transportation and manufacturing, raised the standard of living but also injured and killed an increasing number. Within a generation, "the social importance of the law of torts (of injury)" had been transformed. Novel urban habits and practices demanded legal controls over the hazards created by crowded living.[2]

Trial courts were customarily divided into two major branches—criminal and civil—each having its own clerk and supporting staff but usually sharing the same judges. The criminal branch handled prosecutions involving wrongdoing that affected the public. The civil branch heard only those actions relating to the private rights of individuals, for example, those concerning debt or accidental injury.

The civil business of trial courts has been largely overlooked; millions of actions in contract, tort, and other civil
subjects have not been seriously considered for their usefulness in understanding the history of the city or of society
in general. The sheer volume of surviving civil cases has
been a formidable obstacle to scholarly examination. Furthermore, by themselves these civil actions have seemed
removed from human activity. Dry, technical, and often
petty, individual lower-court civil actions of the nineteenth
or twentieth century display neither the intellectual gym-
nastics that enliven the records of higher courts nor the
chattiness of seventeenth- and eighteenth-century lower-
court cases. Nevertheless, the civil records of the nineteenth-
and twentieth-century lower courts can be animated with
material from various sources about participants in the litigation and linked in this way to the society that produced
them.[3]

Thus revived, the value of such lawsuits rests in their collective meaning. At the turn of the century there was one
civil suit filed annually in Boston for every twenty adults.
In dollar-and-cents terms, criminal trials in turn-of-the-
century Boston annually deprived defendants of less than
$100,000 through fines, while civil proceedings impov-
erished defendants by more than $3,000,000. Unrecorded
out-of-court settlements pushed the civil figure considerably higher. Only the property taxes levied on Bostonians
(about $14,000,000 annually in the 1890s) represented a
larger transfer of wealth under the auspices of local government.[4]

Despite the number and impact of civil actions, little
coordination existed among legislatures, high courts, and
low courts for processing them. "No one could shift judges
about as needed from a crowded to an empty docket; or
monitor the flow of litigation; or set up rules to tell the
courts how to behave." Higher courts controlled lower
ones only through the power to reverse decisions on appeal, and legislatures directed higher courts mainly

through the difficult process of constitutional amendment.[5]

Thus, the law in theory and the law in action were not necessarily the same. Roscoe Pound emphasized the dichotomy when he addressed himself to "The Administration of Justice in the Modern City" early in the twentieth century. In the metropolis, he claimed, the main problems lay not in the substantive law but rather in the "enforcing machinery, which too often makes the best of rules nugatory in action." He chided contemporary analysts of the legal system for judging it "by the output of opinions, and not by the actual results *inter partes* in actual cases." Analysis of lower-court cases began only in the 1920s; of the trial-court business that came earlier, little is known.[6]

Urbanization and the trial courts undoubtedly influenced each other. A rash of new law books appeared around the turn of the century, devoted entirely to such urban topics as electricity, elevators, apartments and tenements, street railways, and municipal corporations. They included a substantial body of fresh statutes and judicial opinions, but it is far from certain that this body of law found application in trial courts. Individuals and businesses may have taken to court some disputes generated by the urban environment, but they chose alternative means to resolve others. The courts benefited some economic and social interests, not others. Of what importance were such factors as the sex, age, race, ethnic origin, occupation, and wealth of litigants, the legal training and professional connections of counsel, the type and size of suit brought?[7]

Investigation of the role of law in Boston's growth has followed the legal historian's traditional approach: doctrine has been scrutinized, but little attention has been paid to the law applied in trial courts.[8] Recently, however, scholars have displayed a growing concern for the routine aspects of lawmaking and of urbanization, abandoning their traditional, narrower focus on great moments in the life of the law or on notable events in the lives of cities.

Urban historians, employing new sources and techniques, have gone beyond the observations of prominent politicians, reformers, and the literati to view experiences of common men and women in an effort to understand fully the nature of city development. Legal historians, too, have begun to consider what they could learn about the evolution of law by going beyond the commentaries of prominent legislators, judges, and lawyers and the landmark statutes and cases on which they built their reputations.[9]

Students of urbanization and of lawmaking, indeed, of our society generally, have before them a vast, virtually unexploited vein of information: millions of lower-court cases deposited in vaults and storerooms throughout the country. This work attempts to demonstrate the historical value of those cases by analyzing the role of civil trial-court litigation in the emergence of modern Boston.

Boston was chosen because it is already one of the most thoroughly studied cities in America. An investigation of the many causes likely to affect a lower court's role is possible only where competent histories of the local economy and social patterns are plentiful. Boston is unique in important ways and cannot be presented as typical of late-nineteenth-century American cities. Nevertheless, Bostonians witnessed social and economic changes similar to those experienced elsewhere in America, and in Europe, at about the same time.

This, then, is an exploratory case study, seeking to identify those general areas of urban development with which civil trial courts were most directly concerned. An underlying assumption here is that the business of such tribunals mirrors the social and economic life of the communities of which they are instruments.

In addition to persons residing within city limits, Boston's trial courts served plaintiffs and defendants from neighboring towns that comprised Greater Boston. Probably 10 to 25 percent of the litigants in the late nineteenth century were suburbanites. Conversely, residents of Boston appeared in the trial courts of surrounding towns and counties.[10]

The civil business of the city's trial courts represented only a large portion of all lawsuits brought in the metropolitan area. In the late nineteenth century jurisdiction was fragmented in Greater Boston. Nine trial courts operated in the city proper under authority from the Massachusetts legislature. Seven district courts functioned—in Brighton, Charlestown, Dorchester, East Boston, Roxbury, South Boston, and West Roxbury (map 1). The Boston Municipal Court served both as a citywide tribunal, drawing its litigants from every section, and as a district court for the business area and the residential neighborhoods of the central city. It shared a downtown building with the Superior Court of Suffolk County, which also served the city of Chelsea and the towns of Revere and Winthrop (map 2).[11]

These trial courts convened to hear matters of debt and injury. The superior court possessed jurisdiction in divorce and, after 1883, in equity, and it served as an appellate tribunal for decisions rendered in the district and in the municipal courts. Suits could be brought for any amount up to $1,000 in district courts, for sums up to $2,000 in municipal court, and for any amount over $100 in superior court. Several dozen district courts and the superior courts of Essex, Middlesex, Norfolk, and Plymouth counties operated in the suburbs beyond the city limits (map 2). Each district court had its own judges, but the superior court was peripatetic, sitting in every county of the state. In other words, while Suffolk County and each of the surrounding counties had its own superior court clerk and staff, they drew their judges from the same pool on a rotational basis.[12]

In addition, each county had a permanent probate court that handled matters of family law—wills, adoptions, nonsupport actions—as well as bankruptcy petitions. At the top of this state legal structure stood the Supreme Judicial

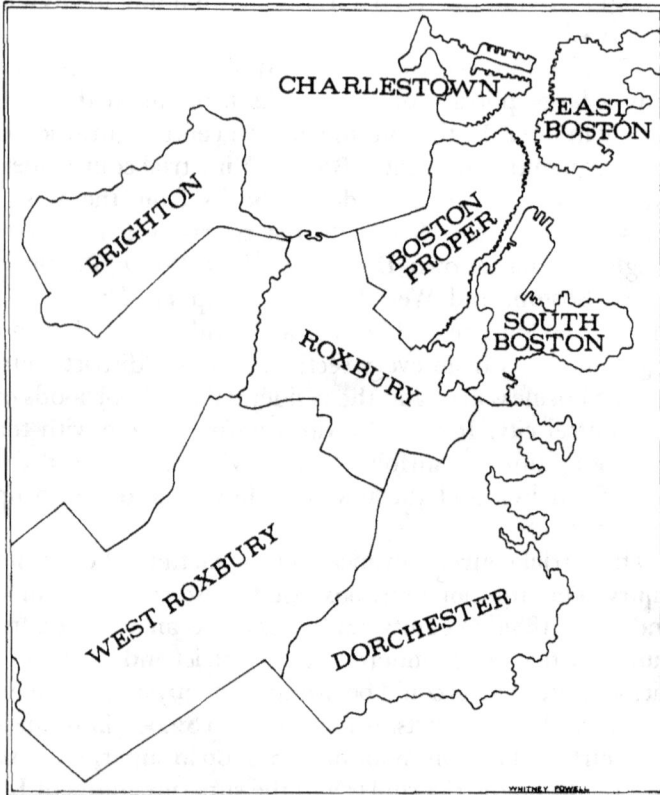

MAP 1. THE CITY OF BOSTON, 1880-1900

Court of Massachusetts, which entertained appeals from
decisions of lower courts, retaining original and concur-
rent jurisdiction with the superior court over divorce and
matters of law or equity involving $4,000 or more.[13]

Coexisting with the state judicial structure in and around
Boston were the federal courts. The United States district
and circuit courts that sat in Boston had jurisdiction over
the federal judicial district of Massachusetts in matters of
admiralty law, in cases between citizens of Massachusetts
and other states, and in any action brought under the Con-

MAP 2 BOSTON AND VICINITY, 1880-1900

ESSEX COUNTY

MIDDLESEX COUNTY

SUFFOLK COUNTY

NORFOLK COUNTY

PLYMOUTH COUNTY

ORIGINAL TOWN OF BOSTON

stitution, laws, or treaties of the United States, provided
the sum in question exceeded $500 (after 1887, $2,000).
Between 1867 and 1878, and again after 1898, federal
courts also had jurisdiction in bankruptcy.[14]

In this maze of overlapping and special jurisdictions the
Boston Municipal Court and the Suffolk County Superior
Court stood out as the chief tribunals of the city. They
heard a wide range of cases generated by conduct that occurred throughout, but normally not beyond, the confines
of Greater Boston (table 1). The jurisdiction of the district

TABLE 1. CASES BETWEEN LITIGANTS RESIDING OR DOING
BUSINESS IN GREATER BOSTON,[a] 1880, 1900

Cases between Bostonians	Superior Court		Municipal Court	
	residents	businessmen	residents	businessmen
	1880			
%	78[c]	81	73	96
N[b]	*145*	*86*	*295*	*92*
	1900			
%	90[c]	81	90	88
N[b]	*115*	*108*	*208*	*118*

[a] For the rough limits of Greater Boston, see map 2.

[b] N indicates the number of sample observations on which a statement is
based. There are, however, four separate samples of roughly the same
size drawn from four case populations of different sizes (see Appendix
A). The 2,507 superior court cases of 1880, for example, are represented
by 341 sample actions, while the 5,970 superior court cases of 1900 are
represented by 370 sample actions. Samples drawn from larger populations were weighted when used in calculations with samples drawn from
smaller populations. Sample numbers (N) from the turn of the century
represent about three times the number of actual cases as do sample
numbers from 1880.

[c] Note that the trial courts became even more concerned with lawsuits between Bostonians at the century's end. The number and proportion of
cases involving out-of-town, especially out-of-state and foreign, litigants
decreased.

courts in and around the city was far more limited in area
and in the value of cases adjudicated. The superior courts
of the surrounding counties heard a great deal of business
from rural areas beyond the boundaries of metropolitan
Boston. The Suffolk County Probate Court and the probate courts of the adjacent counties considered a narrower
range of legal issues. The supreme judicial court and the
federal tribunals entertained actions from all over Massachusetts and, except on appeal, never considered cases in
which small sums were involved.

A survey of the dockets of the municipal and superior
courts for the years between the Civil War and World War
I reveals that the annual volume of civil actions remained
remarkably stable until the early 1890s, ranging from
7,000 to 8,000 in both courts combined. Then the number
of cases filed in each court increased rapidly. Litigation
more than doubled by the century's end, reaching nearly
19,000 cases in the year 1900 and never again declining to
pre-1890 levels.[15]

Cases selected from representative years in this period
reveal changes occurring in the litigation process. Much of
what follows rests upon a random sample of 1,445 cases.
Throughout the analysis, the guiding question has been
not how many cases there were, but whose they were.[16]

Part I of this work identifies those changes in Boston that
demanded a response from the civil trial courts. Parts II
and III suggest how that response permanently altered the
process of litigation, the meaning of justice, and ultimately,
the fabric of urban life.

The Genesis of Modern Boston

For a half-century after 1790 Boston prospered through
triangular trading ventures, first with the northwest coast
of America and China, later with the West Indies and Russia. The town itself, however, produced no staple product
for trading. Its once substantial agricultural hinterland
shrank rapidly as the land gave out and other, more pro-

ductive sections of New England turned to New York for a marketplace. Lost agricultural business was replaced by a growing flow of industrial goods from the mill towns that flourished after the War of 1812. Boston ships carried shoes and textiles to the South and returned with corn and cotton, surpluses of which went to Europe in yet another triangular arrangement. Despite the lack of a staple for export and the stiffening competition from New York, Boston's merchants amassed the early Republic's largest pool of investment capital.[17]

Bostonians used these financial resources to develop Massachusetts industry. More manufacturing facilities were built in mill towns, and after some early difficulties they were connected to Boston by railroads. Raw materials for the factories came in through Boston's port, and finished products left from there for the South and Europe. Initially, Boston money did not create industry within the city, which could not meet either the water power or labor demands of early manufacturing as well as did the mill towns of the hinterland. "Boston remained in 1845 a town of small traders, of petty artisans and handcraftsmen, and of great merchant princes who built fortunes out of their 'enterprise, intelligence and frugality,' and used the city as a base for their far-flung activities."[18]

Irish immigration after 1845 changed the economic character of Boston. It provided entrepreneurs with an ample number of unskilled workers at the same time that the labor base of American manufacturing, under the pressures of mechanization, was shifting from craftsmen to factory operatives. The availability of cheap, abundant labor and, to a lesser extent, the increasing application of steam power to production made Boston the fourth most important manufacturing city of the United States by 1865. After the Civil War, improved railroad and port facilities expedited the movement of incoming leather, wool, cotton, and raw sugar and of outgoing shoes, clothing, and candy. Boston also became an important center for the manufacture of machinery, furniture, glass, and liquor. The city's railroad connections to the American interior and its shipping schedules to Europe and South America made it an important transfer point for midwestern corn, wheat, and meat.[19]

At the end of the nineteenth century Boston middlemen were still making money by trading items produced elsewhere for consumption elsewhere. Increasingly, however, the entrepôt made its own contribution to the river of goods that flowed through its terminals and warehouses, onto its wharves and sidings, and across its ledgers. Processing, storing, shipping, and record-keeping—this was the business of Boston in 1900, these were the services that the city provided the world in exchange for prosperity.[20]

The charged atmosphere of the bustling city had a magnetic effect on surrounding communities. During the nineteenth century Boston's growing population competed with entrepreneurs for available space. Land was reclaimed from bays, but not enough to accommodate demand within the boundaries of the city proper. The wellto-do surrendered their homes to commercial activities or to recently arrived immigrants and fled to nearby towns, from which they commuted to work. The introduction of street railways in the late 1850s opened suburbs to waves of middle-income people who previously had stayed in the city because of the high cost of omnibus and railroad tickets. As suburban tracts filled with transplanted Bostonians, Boston absorbed these new neighborhoods socially and economically. By 1850 sections of half a dozen neighboring towns were informally united with Boston.[21]

Political boundaries became anachronistic. In the 1850s Boston shared Suffolk County with Chelsea, North Chelsea (renamed Revere in 1871), and Winthrop (map 2). The conversion of Chelsea's waterfront from residential to manufacturing and shipping purposes and its absorption of several thousand immigrant workers at mid-century turned a once independent agricultural and resort town into an extension of Boston's North End. More remote North Chelsea and Winthrop remained detached agricultural communities until the 1880s, while the proliferating street railways made Boston's social and economic ties closer to Brighton, Brookline, Cambridge, Charlestown, Dorchester, and Roxbury in neighboring Middlesex and Norfolk counties.[22]

Voters in several towns redrew political boundaries to reflect social and economic realities. By 1873 annexation had formally joined Brighton, Charlestown, Dorchester, and Roxbury to Boston. On the other hand, voters in some towns altered political boundaries to mitigate the influence of the Hub City. In 1846 residents of the still rural parts of Chelsea, fearing contamination from the industrial and immigrant-populated area, had separated to form the town of North Chelsea. Voters in West Roxbury separated from the rest of town in 1851 for similar reasons. Nevertheless, by 1873 enough Boston-oriented people had settled in West Roxbury to reverse the earlier decision (map 1). Annexations ended abruptly in that year. Calls for political union continued, but, with the exception of Hyde Park (annexed in 1912), a majority of voters in the remaining suburbs chose political independence.[23]

The idea of one great city in which social, economic, and cultural activities were consolidated by political unification was destroyed by suburbanites' fears of the impoverished immigrants who swarmed into Boston. They saw their suburban towns as sanctuaries from the crime, vice, disease, and political corruption that flourished in the inner city and threatened communities that had opted for annexation. A degree of unification was achieved nevertheless through the creation of several commissions in the 1880s and 1890s to deal with problems that could be solved only by cooperation on a regional scale. Boston and its suburbs combined resources to obtain adequate water, sewerage, and park systems. Each community surrendered some control over these matters to a metropolitan commission but retained its sovereignty over taxation, schools, and other matters of local concern. During the nineteenth century Boston thus became not only a great manufacturing and distribution center but also the social, economic, and cultural focal point of a loose federation of some fifty towns and cities.[24]

To meet demands that the national and Atlantic economies and the metropolitan communities imposed on the Hub, Bostonians had to reorganize the internal life of their city. The 8,000 voters of the early 1820s simply could not meet together in one place; consequently, people stayed away from town meetings, and a quorum conducted municipal business. The city charter of 1822 addressed itself to that specific problem by legally transforming Boston into a city and replacing the direct democracy of the colonial era with a representative system. But the charter did little more than divide the city into several small towns (wards), wherein voter gatherings of the traditional sort resumed and from which representatives to a central administration were dispatched. The powers of that central authority were no greater than those formerly exercised by the townsmen assembled. Government was still conducted largely by committees of gentlemen volunteers.[25]

This form of administration was sufficient for the Boston of the 1820s, which still resembled the corporate commercial communities of medieval England. The city then was a tightly packed seaport whose leading citizens were well known to one another and to the inhabitants at large. In ethnic antecedents and religion it was homogeneous, and though it numbered the very rich and the very poor among its citizens, it was not polarized by wealth.[26]

The Boston of the 1880s was a decidedly different place. Six decades saw the population grow from 40,000 to 360,000. Great waves of immigration from Ireland and smaller ones from Germany, Scandinavia, and, after 1880, Italy and Russia overwhelmed Yankee inhabitants. Growth forced the municipal administration to assume responsibility for supplying water, combating crime, fighting fire, preserving public health, providing adequate streets, and educating children. The government-by-committee of the 1820s was too slow and cumbersome to meet these respon-

sibilities on a daily basis in the 1880s. Municipal management was no longer the proper task of part-time volunteers
but of full-time professionals. In 1885 citizens of Boston
persuaded the Massachusetts legislature to revise their
city's charter. Amendments transferred executive power
from boards, committees, and the city council to the mayor
and his embryonic civil service.[27]

The reconstruction of the municipal charter was only the
most conscious, visible, and formal of the means by which
Bostonians reorganized their society to respond to and encourage the development of their city as a great entrepôt
and manufacturing center of the Northeast. In addition, a
drastic adjustment provided facilities for new and expanding industrial and commercial activities as well as accommodations for thousands of additional participants in these
operations. Once undifferentiated spaces were divided for
commercial, industrial, and residential purposes; new
spaces were added; and a growing mass transit network
bound these specialized areas together. New discipline imposed on the burgeoning citizenry conditioned tens of
thousands to move between home and work place with
regularity and to perform reliably in both environments.
Morals, safety, and sanitation called for regulation of those
who did not conform to exacting standards of behavior.
Most difficult were the psychological adjustments demanded by the pace, promiscuity, and anonymity of life in
a growing city. Spatial manipulation, discipline, psychological accommodation—all left their marks in the form of
commercial and residential building, of transportation, of
nativism, of churches and schools, of police, of political reform, and of geographical and occupational mobility.[28]

Lower-court civil litigation, too, was affected. Not only
did the number of cases filed annually shoot up in the
1890s, but the combination of issues before the bench also
changed dramatically. As the issues changed, so did the collective character of plaintiffs and defendants.

TWO

PERSONAE

In the 1880s and early 1890s the municipal and superior courts sat in a gray, gloomy, Bastille-like structure with iron railings and stone stairways that had been built in 1832 on a site located between the North End and the central business district. By the mid-eighties the old fortress strained to accommodate a mounting collection of legal records. A new building, begun in 1887, was occupied in 1894. As the trial courts moved into new quarters they also moved into a new era of litigation, characterized by the growing importance of personal injury suits and the growing prominence of immigrants, women, and corporations among litigants.[1]

Plaintiffs and Defendants

Eighty-five to 95 percent of the suits filed in the superior and municipal courts in the late nineteenth century dealt with one of two broad topics: debt or injury. These, generally speaking, were the issues. But whose issues were they?[2]

As the total number of plaintiffs and defendants rose in the 1890s, the proportion of flesh-and-blood litigants decreased because appearances by corporations and other soulless organizations grew at a somewhat faster rate than did appearances by individuals. Significantly, almost all of the change took place among defendants. In 1880 about 75 percent of the plaintiffs were living, breathing individuals, and the same was true in 1900. But whereas 85 percent of the defendants of 1880 were mortal, the same was true of only 69 percent at the turn of the century. In both absolute and relative terms corporations were increasingly on the

FIG. 1. FORMER SUPREME COURT ROOM OF THE SUFFOLK
COUNTY COURTHOUSE

defensive in Boston's courtrooms as the century drew to a
close.[3]

As the litigants became less characteristically flesh and
blood, they also became less typically male (table 2). In absolute terms the number of female plaintiffs increased almost fivefold, and the number of female defendants nearly
tripled during the last two decades of the nineteenth century.[4]

In 1880 women who filed suit in Boston's trial courts
were chiefly concerned with debt. Two decades later actions for debt were hardly more important than those for
injury. This increasing attention to injury, however, was
not restricted primarily to suits involving women; a similar,
though less dramatic, change occurred in suits brought by
men (table 3). Injuries, moreover, had a leveling effect on
the balance of male and female litigants.

TABLE 2. DISTRIBUTION OF MALE AND FEMALE
LITIGANTS, 1880, 1900

Litigant type	Male (%)	Female (%)	N
1880			
Plaintiffs	86	14	*505*
Defendants	90	10	*544*
1900			
Plaintiffs	76	24	*563*
Defendants	87	13	*463*

NOTE: A chi-square test indicated the relationship between the year of litigation and the sex of the plaintiff was significant at the .001 level. The relationship was not significant for defendants but was suggestive in light of the plaintiff's results.

Most debt actions were related to capital accumulation, property ownership, and involvement in business affairs —areas of activity dominated by males in late-nineteenth-century Boston. The absolute increase of the number of debt actions brought by women between 1880 and 1900 suggests the increasing involvement of females in commercial activities and in real-property ownership. Indeed, most of the increase in female defendants was in the debt area. With new economic opportunities came new liabilities.[5]

The city streets, where most injuries later adjudicated were first inflicted, showed less favoritism to males than did the world of business. Trolleys and wagons injured men and women without prejudice; leaking gas asphyxiated both sexes; gentlemen and ladies slipped on ice or fell into unmarked holes and excavations. Of course, certain occupation-related accidents continued to plague more men than women, for example, those occurring at construction sites. Nevertheless, at the century's end, when actions for debt brought by men outnumbered those brought

TABLE 3. DISTRIBUTION OF MALE AND FEMALE PLAINTIFFS
BY SUBJECT OF LITIGATION, 1880, 1900

| Sex | Type of Litigation | | | |
	Debt (%)	Injury (%)	Miscellaneous and unknown (%)	N
		1880		
F	71	15	15	*68*
M	77	8	15	*431*
		1900		
F	56	41	3	*138*
M	67	29	4	*427*

by women by four to one, the ratio of male to female plaintiffs in actions for accidental injury was only two to one.
Both ratios indicate how far from equilibrium the sexual
balance among litigants was at the turn of the century. One
of Boston's few female attorneys explained that the city's
women were reluctant to sue because they did not stand
equally with men before the law. "There are," she said,
"certain needs and feelings relevant to the administration
of justice to women which only other women can understand." So long as the bench, bar, and juries remained
male, that understanding was unattainable.[6]

In the 1880s and 1890s four out of five plaintiffs and
defendants were professionals, proprietors, managers,
corporation or government officials, clerical workers,
salespeople, or dependents of individuals in these occupations. The rest were blue-collar workers in skilled and
semiskilled manual trades, service occupations, and unskilled or menial service jobs.[7]

Most of the disagreement about the meaning and usefulness of the terms *white collar* and *blue collar* has centered
on the nature of work in the twentieth century. In late-

nineteenth-century Boston white-collar jobs could be distinguished from blue-collar ones by such criteria as level and regularity of wages earned and by education and training required. Evidence justifies the further division of these classes into five strata. Thus, a high white-collar group consisting of professionals and major proprietors, managers, and officials can be distinguished from a low white-collar group consisting of clerks, salespeople, semiprofessionals, and petty proprietors, managers, and officials. Among blue-collar workers, distinctions appear between skilled, semiskilled, and unskilled individuals. The arrangement of litigants into these two classes, five strata, and their subgroups facilitates the identification of certain legal problems with specific occupational groups.[8]

The mixture of legal problems that brought white-collar workers to court at the turn of the century had changed over the preceding twenty years. In 1880 the typical white-collar action was for debt; for that matter, so was the typical blue-collar one (table 4). At the turn of the century white-collar plaintiffs continued to be most concerned with debt collection, but there was a growing emphasis on injury litigation (table 5). All occupational groups in both classes were suing more in tort, both in absolute terms and in relation to debt. The greatest increases came among blue-collar wage earners, those most likely to be injured on the job. Nevertheless, white-collar individuals brought about 52 percent of the accident cases in 1900, blue-collar workers the remaining 48 percent. Accident litigation, in short, was most important to blue-collar workers, but blue-collar workers were not primarily responsible for the total volume of accident litigation.

Because the sweeping changes of the eighties and nineties came in injury litigation, and because the defendants in this swelling body of cases were mostly corporations, there was little change during the period in the concerns of white- and blue-collar defendants. Debt, more than any other issue, continued to plague all groups.

TABLE 4. RELATIVE IMPORTANCE OF DEBT AND INJURY TO WHITE- AND BLUE-COLLAR LITIGANTS, 1880

Type of Litigation	Professionals	Major proprietors, managers, officials	Clerks and salespeople	Semi-professionals	Petty proprietors, managers, officials	Skilled blue-collar	Semi-skilled blue-collar	Unskilled blue-collar
Plaintiffs								
Debt (%)	88	85	84	92	83	83	81	75
Injury (%)	2	1	5	0	3	2	13	13
Miscellaneous and unknown (%)	10	14	11	8	14	15	6	13
N	*51*	*73*	*19*	*12*	*142*	*41*	*16*	*8*
Defendants								
Debt (%)	71	80	92	100	86	76	72	82
Injury (%)	4	7	0	0	3	2	7	0
Miscellaneous and unknown (%)	25	13	8	0	11	21	21	18
N	*28*	*46*	*36*	*9*	*161*	*42*	*29*	*11*

NOTE: Here and elsewhere percentages do not always add up to 100, owing to rounding.

TABLE 5. RELATIVE IMPORTANCE OF DEBT AND INJURY TO WHITE- AND BLUE-COLLAR LITIGANTS, 1900

Type of Litigation	Professionals	Major proprietors, managers, officials	Clerks and salespeople	Semi-professionals	Petty proprietors, managers, officials	Skilled blue-collar	Semi-skilled blue-collar	Unskilled blue-collar
Plaintiffs								
Debt (%)	77	90	40	86	72	45	31	20
Injury (%)	10	5	47	14	16	42	49	80
Miscellaneous and unknown (%)	14	5	13	0	12	13	21	0
N	51	58	30	7	135	31	39	10
Defendants								
Debt (%)	70	74	77	67	80	87	64	100
Injury (%)	7	19	3	17	9	8	20	0
Miscellaneous and unknown (%)	23	7	19	27	11	5	16	0
N	30	42	31	6	126	39	25	5

Although the superior and municipal courts were mainly white-collar forums in the late nineteenth century, the concerns of the different white-collar occupational groups that patronized them were not fixed over time. The same is true of the issues that touched the blue-collar minority. The growing dangers of everyday life gave importance to injury litigation, regardless of occupation. At the same time, increasing numbers of Bostonians from every occupational group were involved in actions for debt.

Black litigants were unusual. Indeed, the number of sample cases involving blacks is so small that it permits only one generalization: blacks did not sue, nor were they sued, more than a few dozen times a year. They were virtually excluded from the civil trial courts.[9]

At the turn of the century the number of plaintiffs and defendants whose parents were foreign-born or who were themselves foreign-born was much larger than it had been in 1880. Among first-generation immigrants (those born outside the United States), the number of suits brought increased six- or sevenfold over the twenty-year period. Among second-generation immigrants (those who were born in America of foreign-born parents), the increase was seven- or eightfold. Litigants who were born in the United States of native parents (hereafter referred to as "Yankees") brought fewer suits, not even doubling their number during the same period. Thus, the Yankees, who had represented a clear majority of the plaintiffs and defendants in 1880, no longer mustered even a plurality at the turn of the century (table 6).

Of course, immigrants were not a homogeneous group in 1880 or in 1900. In the earlier year Boston's recent foreign stock came principally from Ireland, Britain, English-speaking Canada, Germany, and Scandinavia. By the century's end sizable contingents had arrived from Italy and Russia, those from Russia being mostly Jews. The number of sample litigants from certain ethnic groups is too small to allow meaningful generalization about each

TABLE 6. DISTRIBUTION OF FIRST- AND SECOND-
GENERATION IMMIGRANTS AND YANKEES AMONG LITIGANTS,
1880, 1900

Litigant type	First-generation immigrants (%)	Second-generation immigrants (%)	Yankees (%)	N
1880				
Plaintiffs	31	8	61	218
Defendants	30	8	62	245
1900				
Plaintiffs	40	23	38	293
Defendants	38	26	36	231

national element. However, when the plaintiffs and defendants are placed in one of three broad categories—those
from English-speaking, common-law countries other than
Ireland; those from Ireland; and those from non-English-
speaking, non-common-law countries—some interesting
comparisons are possible. The categories were chosen
under the assumption that even the vaguest familiarity
with the language and procedures of the courts could have
affected the experience of the various ethnic types in adjudication. The Irish were singled out for special observa-
tion because they were the largest of the city's immigrant
groups and because they differed markedly from Boston's
other foreigners, English- and non-English-speaking, in
their inability to achieve "security, prestige and financial
rewards." Indeed, Irish litigants did not register the same
large increases in suits brought that other groups of
foreign-born did. The Irish pattern followed the Yankee
one, showing only slight growth between 1880 and 1900
(table 7). Yankees and the Irish clustered at opposite ends
of the socioeconomic ladder in late-nineteenth-century

TABLE 7. NATIONALITY OF LITIGANTS, 1880, 1900[a]

Litigant type/year	First-generation immigrants			Second-generation immigrants	Yankees
	English	Irish	Non-English		
Plaintiffs of 1880	253	316	174	194	1,456
Plaintiffs of 1900	1,070	611	1,199	1,653	2,733
Growth factor	4.2	1.9	6.9	8.5	1.9
Defendants of 1880	267	389	128	220	1,640
Defendants of 1900	1,119	379	769	1,571	2,177
Growth factor	4.2	0[b]	6.0	7.1	1.3

[a] The figures given are the actual numbers estimated from the sample.
[b] Actually a decrease of .03.

Boston. Both the most- and the least-favored groups, therefore, increased their court appearances at a far slower rate than the first- and second-generation immigrants who occupied the rungs between them. In absolute terms, the Irish in 1880 comprised the second-largest group of litigants after the Yankees but had become the smallest group by the century's end.[10]

In 1880 the primary concern of Yankee and immigrant plaintiffs and defendants alike was debt; injury was not an important legal matter for natives or newcomers (table 8). By the turn of the century the preoccupation of all nationality groups with disagreements over debt had been replaced by a growing concern with injury. Most of the change can be observed only among plaintiffs (table 9) because defendants in the growing body of torts were usually

TABLE 8. RELATIVE IMPORTANCE OF DEBT AND INJURY TO FIRST- AND SECOND-GENERATION IMMIGRANT AND YANKEE LITIGANTS, 1880

Type of Litigation	First-generation immigrants			Second-generation immigrants	Yankees
	English	Irish	Non-English		
Plaintiffs					
Debt (%)	71	89	86	85	82
Injury (%)	4	4	7	5	3
Miscellaneous and unknown (%)	25	7	7	10	15
N	24	27	14	20	133
Defendants					
Debt (%)	83	76	82	75	84
Injury (%)	0	3	9	0	1
Miscellaneous and unknown (%)	17	21	9	25	15
N	24	34	11	20	156

TABLE 9. RELATIVE IMPORTANCE OF DEBT AND INJURY TO
FIRST- AND SECOND-GENERATION IMMIGRANT AND YANKEE
LITIGANTS, 1900

Type of Litigation	First-generation immigrants			Second-generation immigrants	Yankees
	English	Irish	Non-English		
Plaintiffs					
Debt (%)	48	50	57	50	72
Injury (%)	28	23	26	29	20
Miscellaneous and unknown (%)	26	27	17	21	8
N	*40*	*26*	*46*	*70*	*111*
Defendants					
Debt (%)	73	94	72	70	78
Injury (%)	2	0	17	7	10
Miscellaneous and unknown (%)	24	6	10	23	12
N	*41*	*17*	*29*	*57*	*87*

public or private corporations. The increasing need for
such actions was relatively less strong among Yankees than
among first- and second-generation immigrants, but it is
incorrect to ascribe most of the burgeoning tort litigation
to greedy newcomers, which some contemporaries did. Responsibility can be divided roughly equally among Yankees, the foreign-born, and children of the foreign-born.[11]

Between 1880 and 1900 debt litigation became less exclusively the concern of Boston's Yankees as they were
joined by growing numbers of immigrants in these actions.
At the same time, both Yankees and immigrants made injury litigation a major portion of trial-court work.

Plaintiffs and defendants were a mature group of citizens. In both 1880 and 1900 few of them were in their
early twenties; three out of four were at least in their late

thirties, the largest group being over forty-five. In both 1880 and 1900 debt was the single most important category of litigation for plaintiffs and defendants of all ages; however, injury had become an important cause for action among all age groups by 1900. At the turn of the century a sharp difference existed between age patterns in debt actions and those in tort. Four out of five creditors and debtors were more than thirty-five years old, but only about half of the injury litigants had reached that age. No change in the overall age pattern appears between 1880 and 1900 because debt actions still outnumbered injury cases by three to one at the century's end. The preponderance of older people, then, reflects an involvement in business activities that increased with age, that is, with the acquisition of skills, property, and reputation. The dangers of everyday life, however, provided roughly equal opportunities for injury, and therefore litigation, to people of all ages.[12]

In summary, not only were many more people appearing in court at the century's end, but new types of litigants were commonly turning up. The courts remained the arena in which mostly older, white-collar creditors and debtors adjusted their disagreements. However, the proportions of women and immigrants among them grew substantially. Declining proportions of Yankees and Irish—those groups longest installed in Boston and, respectively, the most and least favored economically—suggest that recent immigrants on the middle rungs of the economic ladder, probably the city's emerging entrepreneurs, found the courts to be particularly useful devices for regulating financial relations.

Although debts of all kinds continued to be the most common subject of litigation, injury became an important legal issue. Men and women, Yankees and immigrants, white-collar and blue-collar people, regardless of age, brought torts in growing numbers.[13]

Someone had to represent these new plaintiffs and

defendants—the women and the immigrants—as well as the still growing absolute number of Yankees. Lawyers had to live with these changes. The city's bar, too, was in transition.

THE BOSTON BAR

Neither plaintiff nor defendant was required to have an attorney. There was no provision for assigned counsel in civil cases, and although a number of defendants tried to represent themselves, plaintiffs rarely did.[14]

Membership in the Boston bar nearly doubled between 1880 and 1900. Many, probably most, of the new lawyers rarely, if ever, argued a case before a judge and jury. Trial work required certain theatrical skills and a talent for extemporaneous discourse that many lawyers lacked. An informal division of labor along English lines between trial lawyers (barristers) and office lawyers (solicitors) existed in Boston and other major American cities. Trial lawyers were briefed, that is, asked to try cases by office lawyers, who were often their partners. The number of trial lawyers grew between 1880 and 1900, somewhat faster than the volume of litigation. Of course, certain lawyers had more briefs than others, but, on the average, the shares were smaller in 1900 than in 1880.[15]

Outwardly, the turn-of-the-century litigating bar was similar to that of 1880. Its ranks were almost exclusively male. Women lawyers were "lost in a sea of men," and the prejudice against female attorneys ran deep. For a short period in the 1880s unmarried women were ineligible for admission to the bar in Massachusetts. Harvard Law School would not accept them, nor would the Boston Bar Association. In court, the male image of what a lady should be handicapped them. They were expected to be polite, but politeness could cost the case in the give-and-take of a trial. If they acted as aggressively as male attorneys, they appeared "shrewish" or "strident" to male judges and jurors, to the prejudice of their clients. Boston's small group of women lawyers, therefore, confined its practice to office work, especially probate matters.[16]

The city's trial bar continued to be overwhelmingly white and Yankee. Only a handful of black attorneys practiced in Boston's courts in the late nineteenth century. In 1880 about 80 percent of the trial lawyers were of native stock, as were 70 to 75 percent of those practicing in 1900. Most of them were either solo practitioners or had one, at most two, partners with whom they shared one of the hundreds of little one- and two-room offices tucked away in several streets clustered near the courthouse. The day of the large, departmentalized law firm had not yet dawned. One of Boston's largest firm, Ropes, Gray, and Loring, with its five attorneys and eight staff members, occupied seven rooms on State Street, but it was the exception.[17]

Despite these outward similarities the turn-of-the-century litigating bar was much changed from what it had been in 1880. On the whole, its members were younger and less seasoned. In 1880 a majority of the men who appeared in court had practiced more than ten years, and only one out of four had spent five years or less at the bar. By 1900 the majority possessed less than ten years of experience, and one out of three could claim no more than five years in practice. Older lawyers frowned upon the growing number of young, impetuous, ill-trained, and ill-bred attorneys who swarmed into courtrooms before they had learned how to conduct themselves properly under the tutelage of a preceptor. Many trial lawyers of 1880 had served lengthy apprenticeships with master attorneys. About 40 percent had received no other training, another 40 percent had attended Harvard as well as clerked, and the rest had enrolled at some other law school, usually the new one at Boston University (founded in 1872). At the century's end long apprenticeships were far less common. Only about 15 percent of trial lawyers were trained entirely in that fashion. About 25 percent combined shorter clerkships with attendance at Boston University Law School; 50 percent attended Harvard Law School. These law-school lawyers were known among the veterans for their "lack of technical knowledge regarding the proper conduct of a lawsuit."[18]

The preponderance of Harvard students was particularly significant. Harvard had acquired a fine national reputation as a law school, but its recent graduates were notoriously unfamiliar with the subtleties of Massachusetts practice, in which the Boston University and office-trained students generally excelled. This was the result of a revolution in Harvard's curriculum in the late nineteenth century, a revolution that many of its older graduates and those trained elsewhere found disturbing. In 1870 Christopher Columbus Langdell became Dean of the Law School and for the next twenty-five years established, practiced, and perfected the case method of instruction. The law was not, said Langdell, a "handicraft" to be "learned by serving an apprenticeship to one who practices it." The dean and his disciples taught by legal abstraction, largely ignoring local law, and replaced lectures with the dialectic of the Socratic method. The emphasis was on how to study law, not how to use its content. Lawyers' tricks had no place in Langdell's classroom. He did not believe that law teachers had to be, or should be, practicing lawyers; he was not, and he recruited others like himself. Not every member of the faculty taught by the case method, but its influence was far-reaching.[19]

To many Boston lawyers Langdell's ideas were impractical. In protest, a group of them founded the law school at Boston University, stressed traditional lectures on local law and practice methods, and maintained close contacts with the city's law offices.[20]

The differences between those attorneys who had attended Harvard before Langdell's arrival and those who were graduated later were evident in more than their unfamiliarity or familiarity with the case method and its accompanying Socratic discourse. When Langdell came to Harvard, the Law School admitted any man of good moral character, and many of the students took a rather light-hearted attitude toward their studies. Desiring to encourage only the serious, Langdell persuaded the law faculty and the Harvard Corporation to bar from degree candidacy any student who had not previously manifested energy and ability by obtaining a bachelor's degree or by passing a difficult entrance examination. Requirements were stiffened in other ways. In 1871 the course of study was lengthened from eighteen months to two years. Examinations at the end of the first year to qualify for continued study were initiated in 1872. A third year in residence was recommended and in 1899 became mandatory for receiving the LL.B. degree. Despite stiffer requirements, enrollments went up from 136 in 1870-1871 to 400 by 1895. The small, slow-paced institution of the early nineteenth century was transformed into a large, vigorous school. In 1880 the typical trial lawyer with a Harvard education had been graduated before Langdell's arrival in 1870. At the turn of the century such men were rare. Indeed, the typical Harvard lawyer was a product of the late 1880s and 1890s, by which time Langdell's methods were firmly established.[21]

Those alumni who had not been exposed to Harvard's revolutionary curriculum and those lawyers who had received other preparation saw in the growing popularity of Langdell's approach the implication that their own training was somehow deficient. They countered by stressing that their form of legal education was superior for its applicability. One learned how law was practiced in the place where one intended to practice. In reality both the case and the textbook methods were utilitarian. Neither approach had a greater claim to practicality; their respective adherents simply disagreed about how a practical legal education was best achieved.[22]

Another revolution affected all attorneys, regardless of

training. Beginning in the 1880s, a flood of publications
rapidly engulfed the profession. Textbooks, casebooks, reports, digests, encyclopedias, and journals began to litter
law offices. It was easier than ever before to find out what
had been decided and what the present law was, but it took
more reading in order to be fully informed. In the 1890s
some 25,000 to 35,000 new cases were reported each year.
With so much new law to learn and so many new law books
and periodicals to read, lawyers found it difficult to choose
the right literature. Too many compendious treatises appeared on minor legal subjects. Several efforts were made
to incorporate in a single reference work all of the decisions that the average lawyer might wish to consult. The
record-breaking 3,563 pages of the *American Annual Digest*
for 1898 led one exasperated Boston reviewer to lament,
"Oh, what a pitiable book-burdened profession we are, to
be sure." He admitted that he rarely "read any law book
through for the purpose [of reviewing it], and it is not expected that he should do so." In the old days, he reminisced, "when we had fewer books we had more certain
law and better lawyers." At the century's end there was "too
much to read, not enough time to think." He offered to
burn the more than 200 law books on which he had col-
laborated, if others would burn theirs. Such observations
were less important for their accuracy than for the frustra-
tion they conveyed.[23]

Stacks of journals and books were not the only new ac-
cessories appearing in Boston's law offices at the century's
end. The well-equipped attorney also needed a typewriter
and perhaps a telephone. Stenographers were available to
type on a piece-work basis, and messengers were still a
common way of communicating quickly, but the office with
a typewriter and telephone had an air of prosperity and
modern efficiency that impressed clients. Unfortunately,
gains in efficiency were often achieved at the expense of
the personal touch. "Delicious bits of philosophy, or sparks
of temper, revealing the character of the writer" of a

handwritten letter disapppeared in the dry, formal corre-
spondence that the typewriter mysteriously inspired. The
telephone was less formal, but to older attorneys it was
even more foreign than the typing machine.[24]

The flood of law books and the new means of communication gradually affected how lawyers chose to practice.
Earlier in the century the decision to operate alone or in
partnership with others was guided largely by personal
temperament. Some men preferred to hold all direction
and responsibility to themselves and disliked having to take
advice; others enjoyed sharing the responsibility and the
work. But the expense and time involved in keeping up
with legal literature at the century's end and, to a lesser
extent, the increased costs of communication encouraged
more lawyers to associate themselves with one or two
partners.[25]

Most lawyers, especially those just starting out, did not
earn much money in 1880 or 1900. A joke claimed that
young physicians had to marry in order to make their
female patients comfortable but that marriage was a luxury
the young attorney could ill afford. In 1880 the three
partners in the prominent Ropes-Gray firm divided less
than $12,000 in profits, a comfortable but not munificent
sum. In 1882 the firm's first salaried junior associate was
paid $800 for a year's work. The following year a public
report estimated that a typical working-class family of five
needed at least $725 annually to subsist in Boston. At the
century's end the average lawyer in the city was lucky to
make $500 during his first year in practice, $1,000 in his
second, and $1,500 in his third. A bookkeeper could ex-
pect to earn over $1,000 per year and a traveling salesman
nearly $1,500.[26]

Although twenty years brought little change at the bot-
tom of the professional pay scale, considerable change occurred at the top. In 1900 the five partners of Ropes-Gray
split nearly $68,000 in profits, three and a half times their
individual 1880 earnings. The following year Louis Bran-

deis earned over $70,000. In 1903 Samuel J. Elder con-
cluded a long-fought case for which he was paid $100,000;
in the 1880s Elder's most important action had netted him
a mere $3,000. Young lawyers, although they had trouble
making ends meet, could at least dream of earning such
enormous amounts, of achieving wealth virtually unheard
of among lawyers earlier in the century.[27] Even as they
dreamed, however, some of the traditional functions that
afforded the attorney at least a decent income—debt collection, trust administration, and title searching—were
being taken over by "unauthorized practitioners." Ironically, as the practice of law held out the promise of greater
financial success to a few top attorneys, the average lawyer
had to strain harder than ever to make a living.[28]

The profession's obsession with money alarmed members of the established bar. The spirit of commercialization, the willingness to peddle one's legal skills to the
highest bidder, was part of a pattern that, they believed,
differed sharply from the one they had known as young
men. They looked back to the heroes of their youth, who appeared to embody all that was great in the practice of law
and all that had gone out of it by the century's end. Rufus
Choate was their favorite, admired for his hard work, his
dedication to the law and to the legal profession, his courtesy, wit, clarity, and modesty. They reminisced about lei-
surely hours spent in political debate before blazing fires in
law-office parlors; they recalled the dignified environment
of the 1870s courtroom, when the chief justice of the
superior court always sat in full evening dress. In those
days, they remembered, a trial was a real battle. "The judge
lashed the trial lawyer, who in turn criticized the judge,"
but they respected each other for their ability, learning,
and self-reliance. Briefs were short, no more than a page;
every case rested on the oral arguments presented. Somehow, the art of pleading had been lost by the century's end,
replaced by the dull formalism of longer briefs.[29]

In 1876 a number of well-known attorneys, already uncomfortable with the changes they perceived, resurrected the old Bar Association of the City of Boston, which had been inactive since the 1830s. The association was "to promote social intercourse" among lawyers, "to elevate the tone of the bar and to look after cases of malfeasance." The organization also lobbied fruitlessly to raise standards for bar admission, that is, to bring standards into conformity with its own image of proper character and training. That image was so diffuse, however, that no strong campaign could be mounted. Many of Boston's attorneys, including "reputable and able" men, refused to join the association, or, having joined, resigned. Younger and middle-aged lawyers, in particular, questioned the usefulness of such an organization, and as time went by, its membership, which had always included only a minority of Boston's lawyers, came to represent an even smaller portion of the city's practitioners.[30]

In 1880 Boston's legal community was feeling the winds of change; by the turn of the century they had struck with gale force, leaving the bar battered and cracked. Gone was the feeling of fraternity, the sense of homogeneity, the notion of a community of interests. Like the cracks in a wall, the fissures in the bar did not follow a straight line but moved crookedly along a series of faults and gaps. It was not simply a difference of generations, though age was a factor. Nor were the differences mainly ethnic, though the addition of Jews and Italians to the growing number of Irish lawyers might have had its effect. Langdell's methodology, a flood of complex legal literature, increasing financial opportunities, growing competition, typewriters, telephones—all had quickened the pace of legal practice. It was for many attorneys an uncomfortable change and seemed to irritate most those who remembered, or thought they remembered, a more congenial legal world with far fewer bothersome choices about what to learn and how much to earn. At the turn of the century about one out of every five Boston trial lawyers could remember what it was like to practice in 1880 or earlier. Among them was a particularly important group of men: the judges of the city's trial courts.

THE BOSTON BENCH

Massachusetts was one of the few states where judges were appointed, not elected, and its judiciary enjoyed a reputation for honesty and legal competence. Rarely was a lawyer appointed to the bench in Massachusetts before he had practiced at least twenty years; thirty years was typical. The modest salary of a judge was itself enough to keep younger men with thriving practices and growing families from accepting an appointment. The 1880 bench was occupied by men who had trained for the law between 1830 and 1860. Their legal education and practice experiences were roughly similar to those of younger men who had trained in the 1860s at Harvard, at Boston University in the 1870s, or in law offices at any time. Of the fourteen judges who sat on the municipal and superior courts, six were Harvard alumni, two had attended another law school, and the remaining six were office trained, a distribution similar to that of the 1880 trial lawyers. They resembled the litigating bar in other respects as well. The all-male bench was Yankee, each man and his parents having been born and raised in New England. Each had practiced law for many years in Massachusetts, mostly in larger cities, and so the Boston environment was not unfamiliar. Half of them had dabbled in politics, several were legal scholars, but most owed their success to court and office work. In short, the judges of the city's trial courts, though older than most of the lawyers who pleaded before them, shared a common background, a common tradition.[31]

At the turn of the century twenty-seven men sat on the municipal and superior benches, almost twice as many as in 1880. One of their number had been born in England, another in Ireland, but both had been raised in Massachusetts; a third was the son of Irish immigrants. Otherwise, native stock prevailed. Practicing lawyers, rather than noted legal scholars or politicans, were still the typical appointees. All of the municipal court and more than two-thirds of the superior court judges had practiced in Boston or in one of the other cities of Massachusetts. They were, in the main, products of the older tradition of legal training. Only two from each tribunal had been schooled at Harvard in the Langdell era. The rest were older Harvard alumni, Boston University graduates, or former office apprentices. All of them had begun, and only five had not finished, their legal training by 1880. In contrast, four out of five of the lawyers appearing before these justices had begun to practice after 1880, and over 40 percent of them were Langdell-era Harvard graduates.[32]

Most of the justices remained silent about the new styles of legal training and practice. At the turn of the century, however, one superior court judge, who had begun to practice on the eve of the Civil War, publicly decried the commercialization of the law, the "insatiable desires for something new," the denunciation of tradition, and the sophomoric behavior of recent law-school graduates. A fellow justice who had also read law and been admitted to the bar in the 1850s saw further evidence of the alienation of bench and bar in a spate of judicial impeachment petitions that disgruntled attorneys filed with the legislature in the 1890s. What had developed between and within the bar and bench was not so much a feeling of hostility as a loss of affection. The removal of familiar surroundings and of usual associates, of a fraternal life, troubled bar and bench at the century's end.[33]

This estrangement almost certainly made the litigation process more cold-blooded. Judges and lawyers of different generations lost interest in pursuing the intimate aspects of a case in a familiar way. For litigants, this change

most likely meant that their cases were reduced to specific
points of law or fact, abstractions to be decided more
legally, less socially than before.[34]

TWELVE GOOD MEN AND TRUE

The social distance that many in the profession felt was developing between lawyers and judges was not unlike that
which existed between the practitioners and the jurors they
faced in the superior court. Judges and lawyers, after all,
were presumed to be people of superior character and
education, whereas juries included average members of
the community. The rules and methods of jury selection in
late-nineteenth-century Boston ensured that juries would
not include many people of high social or economic standing or represent a cross section of the community. In addition to judges, attorneys, other court officers, police personnel, and state legislators, statutes exempted from jury
duty federal officers, clergymen, physicians, and adminis-
trators and faculty members of colleges and of incorporated academies and public schools, as well as others in essential occupations and those over sixty-five years of age.
Women were excluded indirectly. Jurors were selected
from lists of people registered to vote for state representatives, and women did not yet have the franchise.
Employers could ask a judge to excuse them or their key
employees from jury duty on the grounds that others
would suffer by their absence. If the judge refused, they
faced a mere forty-dollar fine for failure to appear. But
judges were often sympathetic; the best men rarely served
on juries.[35]

Jurymen were a popular subject in law journals and
magazines. Writers objected to the important powers
granted to what they considered to be little clans of little
men. There was probably some truth in the charge of clan-
nishness, at least in 1880. Juries then were chosen and sat
for an entire court term, about ninety days. The same jury

might hear several dozen civil cases, with insults or disagreements originating in one trial carrying over into another. From 1881 jury duty was limited to thirty days of service. The same legislation also changed the selection of jurors' names from an alphabetical to a lottery system. This eliminated the possibility of advance identification of jurors, decreasing the opportunity for bribery or intimidation. Antijury lawyers were not satisfied. They pointed out that one or two jurors could still be influenced to tie up deliberations. One remedy suggested was to allow less than unanimous verdicts; others advocated abolishing altogether the right of jury trial in civil cases. Jurymen, they claimed, were uniformly an obstinate, prejudiced, and puzzled lot, whose incompetence resulted in too many verdicts being appealed and overturned. Jurors were too easily swayed by emotion, rhetoric, and what they had read in the newspapers. The antijury lawyers were further angered by the limits on a judge's power over the jury. A judge could only instruct juries about the law and testimony in a case; he could say nothing about his opinions regarding the facts.[36]

Other lawyers, though they accepted the misgivings of critics, believed that juries had a place in civil trials. They reminded critics that the success of popular government in America depended on participation of the whole citizenry. The justice system was part of the government, and in a state where judges were not elected, the only chance for popular participation in the judicial process was through the jury.[37]

Evidence about the actual makeup of juries in late-nineteenth-century Boston is sketchy. Nevertheless, some conclusions can be drawn cautiously from a list of several hundred people known to have served on juries at the turn of the century. Although these jurors do not represent a cross section of the community, their aggregate profile does not differ greatly from that of the people they were impaneled to judge. They were, roughly speaking, juries of peers. The foreign-born Irish were more noticeable among jurors than among litigants at the century's end, comprising about 20 percent of those who sat in judgment and less than 10 percent of those judged. Otherwise, the ethnic differences between jurors and litigants were insignificant (table 10). The white-collar–blue-collar ratio was somewhat

TABLE 10. DISTRIBUTION OF JURORS AND LITIGANTS BY
NATIONALITY, 1900

Nationality	Jurors	Plaintiffs	Defendants
First-generation immigrants			
English (%)	10	15	19
Irish (%)	21	8	6
Non-English (%)	13	17	13
Total (%)	44	40	38
Second-generation immigrants (%)	27	23	26
Yankees (%)	29	38	36
N	203	293	231

TABLE 11. DISTRIBUTION OF WHITE- AND BLUE-COLLAR
WORKERS AMONG JURORS AND LITIGANTS, 1900

Occupation	Jurors	Plaintiffs	Defendants
White-Collar Workers			
Professionals (%)	1	16	10
Major proprietors, managers, officials (%)	2	17	13
Clerks, and Salespeople (%)	27	8	11
Semiprofessionals (%)	4	2	2
Petty proprietors, managers, officials (%)	25	37	41
Total (%)	59	80	77
Blue-Collar Workers			
Skilled (%)	30	8	14
Semiskilled (%)	10	10	8
Unskilled (%)	1	2	2
Total (%)	41	20	24
N	263	359	304

different; among plaintiffs at the turn of the century it was four to one, among defendants, three to one. However, the ratio for jurors was three to two (table 11). Furthermore, the largest blocks of jurors came from the clerical and sales and the skilled blue-collar occupational groups, while the majority of the litigants were businessmen and professionals. Jurors and litigants were not polarized socially, but they were occupationally misaligned. That is, the typical daily docket saw white-collar entrepreneurs, including independent professionals, being judged by a jury of white-collar and blue-collar wage earners.[38]

LEGAL FUNCTIONARIES

The actions of jurors, as well as those of litigants, lawyers, and judges, were informed, enforced, and recorded by an array of legal functionaries. Most influential were the masters, referees, assessors, and auditors who in complex cases were appointed by the presiding judge to investigate and report on a list of particulars about which there was insufficient information or disagreement. Judges normally accepted the findings and recommendations of these officials and ruled for the litigant favored in their reports. The clerks of each court were also influential people. Their job was to safeguard and make available all of the documents filed in each case and to receive and keep account of all moneys offered as bonds or in settlement. Their real power, however, stemmed from their responsibility for scheduling trials. Statutes and court rules established guidelines for listing cases but left room for clerical discretion. The lawyer with connections in the clerk's office could buy precious time for his client or deny it to the opposition. Less influential functionaries were the deputy sheriffs, who maintained order in the courtroom, summoned witnesses and jurors, and served writs on litigants. The diligence with which they served processes certainly affected the pace, if not the outcome, of litigation. One other group of officials deserves mention: stenographers, who recorded

the give-and-take of a trial. The manner in which they did
their jobs probably did not influence the course of justice
significantly, but it certainly has had an effect on our understanding of civil litigation.[39]

Legal functionaries formed a tight little circle of people
who resented change and feared interlopers. For example,
the appointment of the first women stenographers at the
turn of the century caused an uproar. Opponents argued
that females would embarrass judges and lawyers in indeli-
cate situations. "The evidence as to the past and present
health of suitors," argued one, "is almost invariably of such
character that no women should be asked or expected to
take it down and read it aloud in open court." He also
maintained that "There is, too, a deepening conviction
among lawyers and judges that for rapid work, the taking
of technical medical testimony and matters involving machinery and all sorts of trade terms and commercial usage,
a man's report is uniformly better than a woman's." The
prejudice against female capabilities was genuine, but
more important was the fear that women stenographers
would displace men because statute set female compensation lower than that for males.[40]

Trials ranged from five-minute vignettes involving a
single judge, a plaintiff, and a stenographer to sprawling
sagas that engaged a succession of judges, lawyers, jurors,
masters, referees, assessors, auditors, and deputy sheriffs,
as well as dozens of litigants and witnesses. If it were possible simply to identify all of the people who participated in
the actions considered here, it still would be impossible to
evaluate such important personal traits as the skills of op-
posing counsel or the biases of witnesses. Even if such assessments could be made, there would still be the danger of
placing too much emphasis on the personalities and not
enough on the issues that brought them together.

That danger is indicated by the fact that the variable
most closely associated with a favorable judgment was not a
litigant's age, sex, occupational, or ethnic characteristics or

the social background of counsel, but the litigant's status as plaintiff or defendant. Plaintiffs usually won regardless of their or their counsel's background. A strong case, in other words, was the most important factor once suit was filed. It is possible, however, that meritorious cases were not filed owing to litigants', lawyers', or judges' social prejudices, real or perceived. Recorded cases, unfortunately, do not confirm or deny this. They do show that the minority of young, female, or blue-collar plaintiffs won favorable judgments with about the same frequency as the mature, male, white-collar majority (table 12).

The remainder of this inquiry, therefore, does not concentrate on the relationship between variables of social

TABLE 12. JUDGMENTS FOR THE PLAINTIFF BY PERSONAL CHARACTERISTICS OF PLAINTIFFS AND THEIR LAWYERS, 1880, 1900

Characteristics	1880		1900	
	Judgments for plaintiffs		Judgments for plaintiffs	
	(%)	N	(%)	N
All plaintiffs	72	*631*	73	*684*
Age				
35 or younger	77	*43*	57	*75*
Over 35	79	*155*	68	*184*
Sex				
Male	70	*399*	65	*381*
Female	71	*62*	66	*127*
Occupation				
High white-collar	69	*115*	68	*101*
Low white-collar	70	*161*	71	*153*
Blue-collar	68	*60*	65	*71*
Ethnic origins				
First-generation immigrant	78	*55*	66	*101*
English	71	*17*	74	*38*
Irish	78	*27*	81	*21*
Non-English[a]	91	*11*	52	*42*
Second-generation immigrant	67	*12*	61	*66*
Yankee	79	*125*	62	*99*

TABLE 12 *(cont.)*

	1880 Judgments for plaintiffs		1900 Judgments for plaintiffs	
Characteristics	(%)	N	(%)	N
Lawyer listed by Hubbell				
Yes	62	98	65	49
No	70	507	70	622
Lawyer's ethnic origins				
First-generation	73	22	74	31
English	67	3	77	13
Irish	71	17	57	7
Non-English[a]	100	2	82	11
Second-generation	73	26	77	52
Yankee	70	293	65	207

[a] Note that in 1880 first-generation immigrants from non-English-speaking countries (usually Germany) were more often successful plaintiffs than those from English-speaking lands, including Ireland; but in 1900, when most newcomers were from Italy or the Jewish ghettos of Eastern Europe, the opposite was true. The samples for both years are small, but they do suggest, if only crudely, that ethnic antecedents were a factor in successful litigation. Contradicting that evidence, however, is the fact that in 1900 plaintiffs' lawyers who were born in non-English-speaking countries (usually Italy or Russia) won cases for their clients more often than attorneys born in Ireland or other English-speaking lands.

background and the outcome of cases; that is, it does not seek chiefly to sharpen further the image of discrimination. The broad outlines of bias have been presented. Subsequent chapters focus on legal problems common to majority and minority litigants. The main concerns are the nature and cause of disputes, how the trial courts treated them, and the effect of that treatment on urban development.

PART II

The Anonymous Marketplace

THREE

COMMERCIAL CREDIT

Boston's growing population became a source of profit, a great internal market for a variety of goods and services. In order to make money in this anonymous marketplace one had to trust a stranger's financial integrity and his ability to meet payments when due. Trust was necessary for most wholesale and many retail exchanges, for providing professional, clerical, and manual services, and for transactions in real property. When confidence proved misplaced and the parties could not otherwise reach a settlement, court was the forum in which to put the matter in order.

THE URBAN MARKET

Since ancient times the city has served as a place for the exchange of goods and services. City governments or merchants' associations have traditionally provided conveniences to facilitate this process. In addition to such physical amenities as stalls, squares, wharves, and warehouses, buyers and sellers were furnished with peace keepers and tribunals to resolve those conflicts that inevitably arise from the conduct of business. Boston's trial courts functioned in that tradition.[1]

Exchange in the urban market took place in two spheres, one local, the other encompassing numerous marketplaces. Boston courts were primarily concerned with transactions of the city's local market, which in the late nineteenth century included the city and its suburbs. The area and population of "that central and suburban territory" that was "commercially and socially Boston" defies precise measurement; it comprised from 500 to 1,000 square miles and contained a population of one to two million. The city's

larger market was the rest of the world. During the first
half of the nineteenth century the horizons of this larger
market had expanded, but the local one had remained unchanged. The local market before the Civil War was really
a cluster of small neighborhood markets. Although producers, wholesalers, and some retailers attracted customers
from all parts of the city and suburbs, most retail merchants measured their territory in blocks and its population in the dozens or hundreds at most. In the second half
of the nineteenth century the scope and operation of the
local market were transformed.[2]

Between 1850 and 1875 Boston's population expanded
rapidly. Growth continued after 1880 but was slower than
before, hovering below the national urban average. Migra-
tion, more than any natural increase through a rising birth
rate or declining death rate, contributed to the growth of
the city's population. In-migration exceeded out-migration
to yield a net increase, but the amount of movement in
both directions was high. Nearly 400,000 new names were
added to city directories between 1880 and 1890; at the
same time more than 350,000 were dropped![3] A population growing largely by immigration meant not simply new
additions to established families and households but a host
of new families, households, and individuals. The accompanying high mobility rate brought a quick succession of
new faces.

To the merchant this swelling and shifting citizenry presented a local market of unprecedented size. At the same
time, technological innovations made available a greater
variety of wearing apparel, food, furniture, and dozens of
other personal and household items. Increased supply and
demand combined harmoniously to lower prices steadily
on most of these items between the Civil War and the turn
of the century, further encouraging consumption. The
combination of buyers, merchandise, and price structure
offered local traders a singular opportunity for profit.[4]

In some trades the response was primarily expansion of

the average selling network of established merchants. For example, the number of retail furniture dealers did not increase as much as did the number of customers per dealer. Furniture retailers were reaching into each other's markets, competing for the business of several neighborhoods or perhaps the entire city. The development of more sophisticated, wide-reaching advertising techniques, along with the evolution of an extensive, fast, and inexpensive street-railway system, assisted in expanding the circle of customers. In other trades—for example, the retail grocery business—the primary reaction was a proliferation of small dealers in new or newly crowded neighborhoods.[5]

An established merchant who was building a larger clientele drawn from greater distances or coping with a more transient population in his traditional territory, as well as a newcomer who was attempting to establish himself as a tradesman, faced an increasingly anonymous group of customers. Before, a local trader had known nearly all of his patrons personally. A following was carefully constructed through mutual recommendations, merchant and customer gradually testing each other's tastes and integrity. But in the local marketplace of the 1880s successful merchants were tempted and struggling traders forced to deal more and more with customers they did not know or who were not known by any regular patrons. This presented few problems in cash-and-carry transactions but posed difficulties in credit sales. How was one to judge the reliability of a stranger?[6]

Traditionally, merchants selling on account to people they did not know relied on the recommendations of trustworthy customers, other merchants, bankers, and correspondents acquainted with a new client. Producers and wholesalers continued to do so in the late nineteenth century. They were assisted by the development after 1840 of mercantile agencies that published credit reference books purporting to evaluate most of the businesses in a given town or city. The rapid acceptance of these books, despite their cursory and often questionable descriptions, was a manifestation of the urgent demand for credit information of any kind. Personal recommendations, reference books, and, where possible, individual investigations helped producers and wholesalers to grant credit in appropriate amounts to reliable jobbers and retailers. Retailers, however, could not check many, probably most, of their new credit customers by these means. There were simply too many of them for personal recommendations or investigations, and only certain categories of businessmen appeared in the reference books. The merchant had three choices: deal strictly on a cash basis, losing all credit sales; give credit only to well-known or recommended customers, losing some sales to trustworthy but unknown buyers; or allow credit to anyone who appeared to be a good risk, that is, anyone who had a steady job or business or owned some property in town or nearby. Those who chose the third policy took the greatest chance, but they were gambling that the profits from increased sales would outweigh the losses from unpaid accounts.[7]

A trader's desire for profit, his experience, his clientele, and his intuition influenced his choice of credit policy, but not exclusively. The structure and nature of specific businesses also affected one's posture on credit. Most producers and wholesalers were forced to extend a great deal of credit, as were certain retail merchants. Other retail sellers did not have to be and, indeed, could not afford to be so liberal. Similarly, the structure and nature of specific credit-granting businesses helped to determine the utility of trial courts in debt collection. In certain trades litigation was more useful and necessary than in others. The most competitive, credit-dependent enterprises were also the most litigious.

PATTERNS OF COMMERCIAL LITIGATION

Retail liquor was a largely cash-and-carry business because the unit price was low and the product was a habit-forming

FIG. 2. NEWSPAPER ROW, WASHINGTON STREET, BOSTON, JULY 8, 1889

luxury, often demanded most by those least capable of paying. It was a neighborhood business. Credit was extended for short periods, probably until payday, and only to well-known customers. Unsettled debts were likely to be small, owed by a regular patron who had fallen on hard times. Litigation against such a person was profitless and in any case might have generated ill will in the neighborhood, which would have been bad for business. Moreover, a liquor retailer sold at about a 35 percent margin in the 1880s and 1890s, among the highest of any retail trade. His actual loss per sale was probably lower than average and more easily compensated for by other sales. Not surprisingly, retail liquor dealers did not sue often (table 13).[8]

The retail grocery business resembled the liquor trade in several respects. It was a neighborhood operation; expansion occurred more through the proliferation of small, in-

TABLE 13. CASES BROUGHT PER 100 DEALERS IN CERTAIN
COMMODITIES, 1880, 1900[a]

	1880	1900
Retail		
Liquor	3	11
Groceries	21	30
Furniture	2	3
Clothing	48	61
Producers and Wholesalers		
Liquor	63	115
Wool	25	[b]
Cigars	61	[b]
Drugs	[b]	149
Paper	[b]	535
Bankers and Brokers		
All	70	108

[a] The number of dealers in a specific commodity was determined from the business section of the Boston city directory; it is only an approximation.

[b] Sample insignificantly small.

dependent stores than through the growth of established grocers. Here, too, credit was granted piecemeal for short periods, a week or a month; therefore, most unpaid balances were small. However, the similarities end there; the differences are significant.[9]

A grocer granted a great deal of credit, more than any other retailer, although the increasingly transient nature of the trade in the late nineteenth century might have curtailed this practice somewhat. Pressures on a grocer to sell on account were considerable. Competition was keener than in most other lines, certainly more so than in the liquor business, where licensing automatically restricted the number of rivals. The margin on groceries was among the lowest and the turnover demand among the highest, which forced a grocer to make as many sales as possible, relying on high volume for profits. Furthermore, his products were necessities; credit was often difficult to deny for moral reasons.[10]

It took little money to get started in the grocery business. A man rented a small store, "put in a few barrels of flour and of sugar, a few boxes of crackers, a few gallons of kerosene," and "an assortment of soap of the 'save the coupon' brands." Several barrels of potatoes, a stack of kindling wood, and "an alluring display of penny candy" completed the beginner's inventory. The new merchant put out a sign that read "Strictly Cash," then proceeded to grant credit to all "good" customers. The grocer knew "from the gossip of his customers around his herring barrel" the financial situation of those who traded with him. Despite his own precarious financial circumstances, he could be benevolent to those who had fallen on hard times, accepting partial payment each week or month and letting the balance stand by the year. Those well-off, however, were expected to pay promptly. Driven to liberal credit policies, Boston's retail grocers resorted to court to clean up their overdue accounts. They were far more litigious than liquor merchants (table 13).[11]

Furniture dealers were also liberal grantors of credit. By the turn of the century half of the stores in Boston made about 60 percent of their sales that way. However, they did not require the assistance of the courts as frequently as grocers did (table 13). The explanation for this lies in the early and extensive use of installment buying in the furniture trade. The system was adopted because of the high unit price of merchandise and the stiff competition from department stores, which also sold furniture on time.[12]

The installment plan enabled furniture dealers to avoid much of the risk encountered in simple, open-account credit systems employed by grocers. The required down payment secured a portion of the purchase price in advance, and a merchant had the opportunity to assess a customer's financial situation while arranging a repayment schedule. He could give each sale careful consideration because his turnover requirement was among the lowest of any retail trade. A dealer usually insisted on a conditional sales contract, which meant that he retained title to the goods until the last installment was paid. If the customer failed to pay, a dealer could repossess the furniture, generally without litigation. A merchant who required 20 percent down and sold at the customary 30 percent margin could sell repossessed items at half price and still break even.[13]

Retail clothing, like the grocery and furniture businesses, was a credit-dependent trade and became increasingly so in the late nineteenth century. Clothiers followed furniture dealers in attempting to rationalize their credit sales by means of the installment plan. They were not as successful and were forced to rely on the courts far more often, even more often than grocers (table 13).[14]

Retail clothing dealers simply could not afford to be as cautious as furniture traders. Always highly competitive, the apparel business became even more so under the influence of a rising fashion consciousness, which was catered to by a booming ready-made industry that provided ever more choices of kind and quality. Both the retail margin and the turnover rate in clothing stood roughly midway between those figures for groceries and furniture. The clothier, in other words, needed to make fewer individual sales than the grocer but more than the furniture dealer. The unit price of clothing also lay somewhere in the middle, making the credit risk of each sale seem unimportant. This, coupled perhaps with the knowledge that they were selling a necessity, induced clothiers to grant credit liberally.[15]

For the apparel retailer, repossession was impractical. Even if he went to the trouble of using a conditional sales contract and then somehow managed to reclaim the highly portable merchandise, its resale value was low. The availability of inexpensive ready-to-wear garments had severely reduced demand for secondhand items, associating that part of the trade with the poorest class of customers, and to combine used with new stock was bad for business. It was preferable to insist on payment or forget a debt entirely.[16]

Of course, not all exchange in the urban market took place at the retail-consumer level. Items moved from the producer to the retailer and, in so doing, often passed through the hands of one or more wholesalers. Credit was extremely important in sales made at the production and wholesale levels. Indeed, nineteenth-century wholesalers customarily financed retailers. It was less customary for producers to finance wholesalers, who usually financed themselves or persuaded a bank to do so. Nevertheless, those producers who acted as their own jobbers had to extend credit like any other wholesaler. Credit terms were stabilized somewhat after the Civil War. There was usually a 2 percent discount for full payment in ten days, net cash in thirty days. Longer terms were normally secured by a promissory note. One source rated thirty-day customers as "gilt-edged," sixty-day "good," ninety-day "fair," and four-to six-month debtors "doubtful." These, however, were generalizations. As in retail lines, the various credit structures of Boston's manufactures forced certain businesses into litigation. The more competitive a trade, the more litigious its tradesmen were likely to be.[17]

Liquor manufacturers, especially malt brewers, were the most litigious of Boston's producers and wholesalers in 1880 and 1900 (table 13). This was a highly competitive business during the last quarter of the nineteenth century. In the 1870s most breweries were small, local operations, delivering by horse-drawn wagon. Each brewer knew the limits of his market and was able to maintain them with little competition. After 1880, however, technological changes in brewing enabled those with sufficient capital to produce enough beer for regional or national markets. At the same time, refinement of regional and national railroad networks made delivery to wider markets easier. Big brewers, assisted by sophisticated advertising, began to give local merchants stiff competition. Rivalry in Boston and in other major cities was further accelerated by the speculation of British syndicates in the American beer market during the 1890s. Several price wars erupted as offshoots of the battle for customers. The profit margin on malt liquor was low, and dealers relied on a high volume of sales for profit. Hoping to hold or to win customers, Boston brewers granted as much credit as possible.[18]

Although no other Boston industry relied as heavily on litigation as did the malt brewers, other industries made considerable, if only temporary, use of the city's courts. Like the malt brewers, dealers in these other industries were experiencing competition in their systems of distribution, which led to liberal extensions of credit. For example, the chaotic state of Boston's wool trade in 1880 is reflected in the high visibility of wool merchants in court (table 13). In the early nineteenth century wool cloth was customarily sold by a producer through commission agents. After the Civil War most producers distributed through a single agent. The rise of the wholesale clothing industry completely wrecked this stable system. New, large-scale manufacturers and retailers began to buy directly from cloth producers, bypassing wholesalers. Producers developed sales forces in the 1880s to build their network of direct contacts with wholesale clothing manufacturers and large department stores. By 1900 the wholesale cloth merchants of Boston had been virtually eliminated. With peace restored to the wool industry, litigation declined (table 13).[19]

Tobacco men, especially cigar makers, appeared often in court in 1880 (table 13). At that time the tobacco industry, especially cigar making, was dominated by local producers. Boston had several large factories but was not one of America's leading production centers. The local market was divided among many small producers who competed fiercely for the patronage of tobacco, candy, and grocery stores, newsstands, barber shops, and restaurants. The wholesale margin on cigars was low. Concentration and consolidation began in the 1880s and continued into the following decade. By the turn of the century one company, American Tobacco, bought 70 to 80 percent of all leaf produced in the United States. Cigar making, however, did not lend itself as readily to mechanization as did other forms of tobacco processing, and it resisted the forces of consolidation. Nevertheless, Boston's small independent cigar makers were probably producing no more than 25 percent of the local product by 1900, perhaps as little as 5 percent. They had also virtually disappeared from the trial-court dockets (table 13).[20]

Boston's wholesale druggists were prominent in court in 1900 (table 13), even though there had not been much of a wholesale drug industry in Boston in 1880. Drug manufacturing and jobbing had been conducted from a few large centers, the nearest of which was Pittsburgh. If Boston was a selling battle zone, the combatants were not Bostonians; legal battles raged elsewhere. In the late 1880s and 1890s, however, out-of-town wholesalers met increasing competition from local, short-line specialty houses. Local, independent manufacturers and wholesalers fought the monopolization schemes of large, national firms in a series of federal lawsuits between 1894 and 1907. They also struggled to maintain credit discipline in a competitive, disorderly market by resorting to Boston's trial courts.[21]

In the second half of the nineteenth century paper making was among the fastest growing businesses in Boston and throughout the Northeast. Massachusetts became the second-largest producer of paper in the United States after New York. In the 1890s the industry began to suffer from overproduction and falling prices. A brief upturn in prices occurred in 1898-1899, as the Spanish-American and Boer wars drove up newspaper circulation dramatically. But prices fell off sharply early in 1900, and competition accelerated. Consolidation had only just begun in 1899, as independents disregarded the gentlemen's agreements that had been made in order to limit production, maintain prices, and control distribution. Once again a battle for customers produced too much credit and a subsequent increase in litigation (table 13).[22]

Producers and wholesalers shared credit opportunities and risks with bankers and note brokers. The mechanism was simple. A customer would confirm his debt to a producer or wholesaler by a promissory note. The note was then sold at a discount for cash or credit to a broker, who in turn sold it to a bank at a discount slightly less than his own. In some cases the note was discounted directly to a bank.[23]

In the late nineteenth century note discounting was an appropriate, profitable investment for a portion of a bank's surplus funds, but there were dangers. In 1880 neither brokers nor bankers knew much about the reliability of promisors. Notes were purchased with only a superficial investigation or none at all. Bankers sometimes bought commercial paper (notes) "by the inch" from brokers who could say nothing about its quality. Prompted by heavy losses in the 1880s and by increased profits to be found in high-grade paper, some larger banks in the 1890s began to investigate the businesses whose obligations they acquired, and brokers also became more cautious. Nevertheless, note discounting remained a chancy business. Although Boston's banking and brokerage circle contracted between 1880 and 1900 through mergers, the amount of commercial-paper litigation did not decline (table 13). In other words, consolidation into fewer, larger institutions did not completely offset the litigious effects of increased note speculation.[24]

Although commercial litigation was dominated by certain lines of enterprise, the courthouse was not a preserve of Boston's business elite. The retail and wholesale merchants, the manufacturers, bankers, and brokers who brought suit presided over businesses of varying magnitudes. In the 1880s and 1890s established businessmen—those with $1,000 or more in assets and a "good" or "high" credit rating—had recourse to the courts in numbers roughly equal to marginal operators—those with less than $1,000 in assets and only a "'fair" credit rating or none at all.[25]

Marginal operators also accounted for about half of the debtors. Another quarter were professionals, clerical workers, and salespeople. The rest were mostly established businessmen or skilled blue-collar workers. Fewer than one out of ten defendants pursued a low manual (semi- or unskilled) trade. Those who occupied the middle rungs of Boston's socioeconomic ladder were most frequently called to account for commercial debts.[26]

In 1890 a New York businessman published *Whom to Trust*. The title of this little book on mercantile credit stated a pressing urban problem most succinctly. In late-nineteenth-century Boston a combination of population growth and high mobility created a local market of unprecedented size. Never before were the city's merchants presented with so many potential customers just a short distance away. Indeed, the boundaries of that "short distance away" continued to expand with the outstretching street-railway network.[27]

If the opportunities for profit were novel, so were the accompanying dangers. In order to exploit the new market, merchants were forced to sell on credit to strangers. The problem was as old as trade itself. Boston's national and overseas traders had faced it for centuries. The difference lay in the number of buyers and sellers, the volume of transactions, and the seller's resources for investigating a potential credit buyer. Some businessmen avoided the credit dilemma altogether by operating a largely cash-and-carry store. This was sensible when unit prices were low, margins high, and competition limited, as in the retail liquor trade.

A variety of retailers could not conduct a strictly cash business, but liberal credit terms did not automatically mean chaos. Furniture dealers were able to rationalize their credit system by use of the installment plan, but only because their low turnover demands, high margins, and high unit prices dictated and permitted caution in every sale. The opportunity for repossession and resale further reduced the risk, allowing a certain amount of self-policing. Clothiers, faced with higher turnover requirements and lower margin and unit prices, could not afford to be as cautious. Grocers faced similar, even more compelling economic problems. Producers and wholesalers caught in the throes of accelerated competition were also forced to grant credit freely, and their obligations were often purchased by brokers and bankers without regard for quality. All of these businessmen carried a number of uncollected debts on their books.

Experts on collections advised them to litigate only as a last resort. Better to write letters, they argued, be understanding, renegotiate terms, even take a complete loss in some cases. This last alternative was especially wise when a lawsuit was likely to seem harsh and alienate other customers. If one practiced prudent credit policies in the first place, such losses would be small. Internal discipline was a far better policy than reliance on litigation. Unfortunately, internal discipline was not always enough, and creditors turned with greater frequency to the trial courts. Those who did often learned that the credit experts' warnings were well founded.[28]

The Efficacy of Litigation

In nine out of ten commercial lawsuits plaintiffs demanded that defendants make good on an unpaid open-book account or promissory note. The remaining actions were of three kinds: replevin, conversion, and breach of contract involving the nondelivery of goods purchased.[29]

Whatever the form of action, the plaintiffs' first consideration was the likelihood of winning, which they usually did. In the 1880s and 1890s retailers, wholesalers, and manufacturers received favorable judgments in three out of four lawsuits. Brokers and bankers did not enjoy the same rate of success—they won about three out of five cases—primarily because most of the notes in question were double-name obligations. The plaintiffs, in other words, probably did not know the original promisors. They had a right of action against the party from whom they purchased the note, the endorser, but usually acted against the original maker only. Apparently, the endorsers could not be found or were not able to pay.[30]

The ability of defendants to pay was an important part of the plaintiffs' second consideration: how much were they likely to recover? The preponderance of small businessmen, professionals, clerical workers, salespeople, and skilled blue-collar workers among defendants, to the virtual exclusion of low-manual workers, indicates that suit was brought only against those formerly good risks from whom something might still be recovered. The same qualities that made someone a good credit risk in the first place—property ownership, regular employment, a marketable skill—also made him a prime defendant. Creditors who paid their filing and lawyer's fees wanted more than a moral victory.[31] Indeed, these basic fees made a suit for small amounts unprofitable. Rarely did retailers initiate an action to recover less than $25. Most wholesalers, manufacturers, brokers, and bankers did not sue unless the debt was over $100.[32] Creditors were also careful not to let their unpaid accounts go too high before taking legal action. Retailers usually sued before debts exceeded $150; wholesalers, manufacturers, brokers, and bankers filed suit before debts topped $500.[33]

A few lucky plaintiffs recovered all of what they were owed. Yet it was unusual to recover less than 20 percent. The mean recovery rate in the 1880s and 1890s was about two-thirds of the actual debt, plus court costs amounting to $25 or less.[34] A merchant suing for $150 was likely to receive in judgment about $100 and court costs. From this his attorney took at least $10, which left the creditor with $90. The merchant's margin ranged from 8 to 52 percent, depending on his line. Subtracting that percentage range from the original debt of $150 yields $72 to $138, the price the merchant paid for the goods. A creditor who sold on high margin could still make a profit after litigation (recover $90 on items that had cost him as little as $72), but a creditor who sold on low margin reclaimed less than two-thirds of what he had paid for the goods ($90 on items that had cost up to $138). A merchant had to sell at a 40 percent margin just to break even in a typical lawsuit. None of the businesses that patronized the courts heavily sold at margins above 35 percent. Most creditors, in other words, did not recoup even the original purchase price of the merchandise in question.[35]

The third important factor for plaintiffs was time: how long would it take to recover a claim? Delay meant different lengths of time to different creditors. If the plaintiff's business were seasonal, his tolerance varied throughout the year. One prominent Boston lawyer suggested that three months was ample time for the preparation and settlement of "a large majority" of cases. Measuring Boston's commercial litigation against that three-month standard, the process was often slow. One-fourth to one-third of the cases remained on the docket for more than three months.[36]

Litigation proceeded much faster in the municipal court than in the superior court. In 1880, 91 percent of the actions brought in the lower tribunal were finished in three months or less; twenty years later the figure was 73 percent. In superior court only one-third of the cases were adjudicated that quickly in both years. Commercial creditors found the swiftness of the lower bench attractive, and so they brought 70 to 80 percent of their lawsuits there.[37]

In the 1880s and 1890s, then, creditors typically brought and won suits without undue delay, but the sums recovered were substantially less than those claimed. Nevertheless, partial compensation was preferable to none at all. Moreover, an occasional lawsuit was a useful disciplinary tool for an entrepreneur who granted credit routinely. It served notice that he was to be taken seriously by customers who wished to avoid the expense and embarrassment of litigation.

At the turn of the century the credit "industry" was developing in Boston. About thirty mercantile agencies were operating in the city, and more than sixty individuals or firms were in the collections business. Yet, the National Association of Credit Men, founded in 1896, had only just begun to formulate the principles upon which a vast, extrajudicial collections network would be built in the twentieth century. Litigation was still a tool frequently employed even by professional debt collectors. The Boston Chamber of Commerce, though it professed to adjust controversies and misunderstandings, was mainly concerned with promoting harbor and railroad improvements and the construction of an Isthmian canal.[38] Thus, despite the advice of collection experts to avoid court whenever possible and the often disappointing results of litigation, creditors turned increasingly to bar and bench. The number of commercial actions filed annually more than doubled between 1880 and 1900, from 2,600 to 5,800.[39]

The changing character of the bar may have contributed somewhat to the greater inclination to litigate. Older, established lawyers who complained that young, avaricious attorneys brought unnecessary lawsuits in order to make a living correctly sensed that the proportion of young lawyers—those in practice five years or less—did rise among the ranks of counsel in commercial litigation. The increase, however, was modest.[40]

Also important was the slowly growing proportion of women and immigrants among plaintiffs. This suggests that the courts were particularly useful institutions for the city's emerging entrepreneurs, those whose inexperience or lack of sufficient capital made them most vulnerable to the pressures of the new local market. Although growth of the bar did not guarantee that demand for commercial litigation would increase significantly, the problems of granting commercial credit in the anonymous marketplace ensured that it would.[41]

FOUR

EMOLUMENTS

WAGE EARNERS

In 1916, as he was about to join the U.S. Supreme Court after thirty-five years of law practice in Boston, Louis Brandeis reflected on how sharply the conditions of employment had changed in his lifetime. Many once independent people worked for someone else, he observed; most men and women could no longer reasonably expect to be self-employed. As a result, a large measure of the responsibility for their welfare had shifted from them to their employers and to the state. The change was all the more significant because society had hardly yet perceived it, let alone adjusted to it. The law, in particular, had not yet been altered to fit new conditions.[1]

The realm of Brandeis's immediate experience was Boston, and he correctly understood the changes in employment patterns that had occurred there in the 1880s and 1890s. In 1880 there were approximately 14,500 salaried clerks, copyists, salespeople, bookkeepers, and accountants working in Boston; in 1900 there were nearly 40,000 such people in the city. During the same period the number of wage earners in manufacturing and mechanical firms rose from 53,900 to 82,000. Moreover, the number of individuals working for large firms appears to have increased. In such work places the employer-employee relationship was necessarily impersonal. The worker could not precisely identify the boss: one person hired, several supervised, another paid.[2]

Whether in large or small establishments, Boston employers and employees often had little opportunity or incentive to get to know each other well. The city's labor market had a casual, random air. Regular, long-term employment was not uncommon, but occasions for changing jobs arose frequently. Several factors were responsible for this fluid situation: the fluctuating level of prosperity in Boston, the comparative prosperity elsewhere, and the appearance of new trades and the demise of old ones. In addition, the development of an extensive, reliable, and cheap public transit network stretched the boundaries of the area within which an individual could conveniently accept new employment. Transfer to a new work place did not necessitate uprooting a household. Between 1880 and 1890 more than 55 percent of Boston's skilled blue-collar workers changed jobs at least once, as did more than 60 percent of low-salaried white-collar employees.[3]

Where the number of employees was large or their turnover rate high, an employer's attitude toward them as individuals was unavoidably indifferent. Growing labor unrest in the late nineteenth century drew increasing attention to the indifference characteristic of employer-employee relationships in the factory towns and cities of Massachusetts and elsewhere. Managerial callousness toward wages and toward other problems of workingmen and workingwomen was copiously documented by organized labor, reform groups, and public agencies.[4]

Owners and managers recognized the importance of maintaining employee purchasing power but would not tolerate a serious reduction in their own returns or profits. Several payment schemes invented by employers linked a worker's earnings directly to personal productivity. Inside contracting, profit sharing, and the piecework system emphasized the individualism of a worker, rewarding him with higher pay for good work, lower pay for poor. The entrepreneur who paid a fixed wage could view his workers as voiceless junior partners who shared his risks and rewards. Owners and managers with such attitudes did not hesitate to withhold pay for allegedly inferior workmanship or for routine breakage. Faced with a cash shortage, they postponed payday and used the payroll to cover operating expenses. In such instances employers viewed workers simply as additional creditors.[5]

Each year several hundred workers who encountered refusals to pay brought suit in one of Boston's trial courts. Most were blue-collar wage workers, skilled and unskilled, and they were joined by a variety of low-salaried white-collar workers—clerks, salespeople, and petty functionaries (table 14). Observers of wage earners' problems in the late nineteenth century, then and since, have focused on blue-collar workers, especially those toiling in factories or on farms. But low-salaried white-collar wage earners, though somewhat better paid, did not own the means of production. Like factory workers and day laborers, they worked for those who did.[6] Despite the growing number of blue-collar and low-salaried white-collar workers in Boston in the late nineteenth century (table 14) and considerable agonizing over wage problems, the number of claims brought in the trial courts was small. An examination of the experiences of those who did file actions explains why so many others stayed away from court.[7]

A claimant weighing the option of litigation would ask

TABLE 14. INCIDENCE OF WAGE CLAIMS, 1880, 1900

Year	Number of blue- and white-collar workers[a]	Number of cases[b]	Number of cases per 1,000 workers
1880	84,600	413	4.9
1900	151,600	218	1.4

[a] Precise figures are not available. The figures given represent the number of clerks, copyists, salespeople, bookkeepers, and the like employed in Boston's offices and stores, the total number of those working in manufacturing and mechanical lines, and the number of those in service. Sources: Department of the Interior, U.S. Census Office, *Tenth Census of the United States, 1880*, Vol. 1, *Population*, p. 864; *Twelfth Census of the United States, 1900: Occupations*, pp. 494-498.
[b] The approximate number of actual cases estimated from the sample.

himself the same questions as the businessman contemplating a lawsuit. Can I win? How much will I recover? How long will it take? Is there a better way?

Wage claims were often difficult to prove because of the absence of written agreements or of customary payments for a particular kind of labor. Only one-third of the plaintiffs recovered all of what they claimed was due them. Another one-third realized less than fifty cents on the dollar. The rest left court empty-handed.[8]

A client might have to wait a year or more for judgment or for settlement. If he lived on little or no margin, a difference of weeks was crucial. In any suit, moreover, time was usually on the defendant's side. He retained use of unpaid wages while witnesses became harder to find and memories dimmed. Therefore, most attorneys for the plaintiff filed actions in the Boston Municipal Court, where adjudication came quickest. The claimant who sued in municipal court could expect to finish in three months at most. Those few cases filed in superior court or taken there on appeal from the lower court dragged on for a year or longer. The long-running cases usually involved larger wage claims, for fifty dollars or more, although smaller amounts were contested on appeal. Cases involving larger sums were likely not only to take longer but also to result in no recovery or in only a partial recovery for the plaintiff (tables 15 and 16). When the stakes were higher, defendants were more contentious.[9]

Although plaintiffs with small claims sued more successfully than those with large demands, few very small claims were filed. Workers with petty demands had difficulty finding counsel to represent them. Virtually all of those who brought petty suits had a lawyer, but these were probably charity cases. A five- or ten-dollar wage claim was hardly worth an attorney's time. Litigation might have consumed several days, for which the lawyer could reasonably have expected to receive no more than two or three dollars—as much as he could have charged for one office counseling

TABLE 15. INFLUENCE OF SIZE OF CLAIM ON LENGTH OF
LITIGATION, 1880 AND 1900 COMBINED

Size of claim	Cases completed in three months or less (%)	Cases requiring more than three months (%)	N
Under $50	80	20	30
$50 or more	50	50	10

NOTE: A chi-square test indicated significance at the .10 level.

TABLE 16. INFLUENCE OF SIZE OF CLAIM ON RECOVERY,
1880 AND 1900 COMBINED

Size of claim	Cases in which full recovery was awarded (%)	Cases in which partial or no recovery was awarded (%)	N
Under $50	79	21	24
$50 or more	15	85	20

session or for writing a letter or two. A new attorney trying
to gain courtroom experience and build a practice while
existing on a slender budget might have taken such a case,
but the sample actions show that plaintiff's counsel in petty
wage suits was usually a man who had been in practice in
Boston for at least ten years. Such charity work had always
been part of law practice, but there were simply not
enough willing veteran lawyers to handle the growing
number of petty wage claims in the 1880s.[10]

For those workers lucky enough to receive free counsel
or those with claims large enough to attract paid counsel,
further factors militated against litigation. Even if a lawyer
provided his services free of charge, a plaintiff still had to
advance court costs for filing, often five to ten dollars or
more. A worker financially pressed enough to bring suit

for five or ten dollars in pay could ill afford to lose that amount or more in an unsuccessful action, assuming that he could assemble that much cash in the first place. Five dollars amounted to roughly one-third of a working family's weekly budget and was an entire week's wages for the average single workingwoman. If the amount at issue were larger, fifty dollars or more, investment in a court case was a more sensible risk.[11]

Delay was probably the greatest obstacle to litigation. A plaintiff forced to sue for five or ten dollars perhaps earned little more than that in a week and needed a quick recovery. A day or two was lost finding and talking to a lawyer; another day or two was spent in court. In other words, a plaintiff probably had to forgo nearly a week's wages to recover a week's wages. A plaintiff with a larger claim might have had no greater resources than one with a smaller demand, and the larger the claim, the longer the litigation was likely to last.[12]

In sum, litigation was the last resort of a worker with a wage claim; for most it never merited serious consideration. A claimant pressed enough to sue for five or ten dollars was often too poor to pay a lawyer. When he was lucky enough to be offered free counsel, he could not afford the investment of time and money that a lawsuit required. A worker with a claim of twenty dollars or more had less trouble finding a lawyer but still had to advance costs, which might have been no less a hardship for him than it was for the person with a small claim. When the sum was larger, the case might well have taken months to settle, and the odds of making a full recovery were less than even.

This cumbersome and inequitable judicial machinery was one of the factors that encouraged champions of the wage earner to seek improvements through legislative processes. Organized labor, the Democratic party, and reform-minded Republicans and political independents supported a variety of measures designed to eliminate the worst abuses of the wage system. Beginning in 1879, a series of weekly-wage laws was enacted in Massachusetts. By 1900 they required the weekly payment of wages to employees of all corporations, to workers in the construction industry and in manufacturing, and to all public employees. The laws probably benefited other workers indirectly by inducing unaffected employers to match the wage security offered by regulated employers. Police officers and inspectors of factories and public buildings were authorized to make criminal complaints against violators, who could then be fined ten to fifty dollars. Now it was the boss, not the worker, who was at a financial disadvantage before the law. It cost the wage earner nothing to swear out a complaint against the employer who would not pay. If the complaint were verified, the fine probably exceeded the amount withheld, so the employer had nothing to gain by unlawfully denying wages.[13]

The founding of the Boston Legal Aid Society in 1900 was also a boon to wage claimants, for it regularly handled a number of petty wage disagreements. Faced with the same problems that frustrated private lawyers who took charity cases—a client's inability to advance court costs or to wait very long for recovery—the society's lawyers preferred out-of-court settlements and became skilled at arranging them. They were particularly adept at designing manageable repayment schedules for defendant employers in a weak financial position.[14]

The passage of weekly-wage legislation and the efforts of the Boston Legal Aid Society effected a sharp decrease in wage claims filed in the city's trial courts. In 1900 there were 60 percent fewer cases in the superior court than there had been in 1880. The municipal court experienced a 40 percent decrease during the same twenty-year period.[15]

A third factor also helped to reduce the number of wage claims. The courts—not Boston's trial courts specifically but courts in general—had developed a distinct antilabor image in the 1880s and 1890s. Much of the bench's reputation was earned in areas that did not directly concern wage claims—workman's compensation and the right to strike—but judicial conservatism in all matters regarding the workingman was often assumed.[16]

Whereas the number of wage claims filed in 1880 might have been larger if more attorneys had been willing to prosecute small cases, the number in 1900 might well have been smaller if fewer inexperienced attorneys had been willing to forgo prosecution. There is no clear relationship between an attorney's inexperience and his propensity to litigate, but plaintiffs' lawyers at the turn of the century were distinctly less seasoned than their 1880 counterparts. Of this earlier group, over half had been in practice more than ten years, and only one-fifth had practiced five years or less; over one-third were prominent members of the Boston legal fraternity. Prominent attorneys were rarely involved in wage lawsuits at the turn of the century. Moreover, half of the lawyers had practiced five years or less, and only one-fourth possessed more than ten years of experience.[17]

Few of the cases in 1900 concerned very small sums. Most lay in the twenty- to thirty-dollar range and earned a lawyer five or ten dollars for his efforts, a worthwhile fee for the struggling young attorney. The competition for clients was stiff, especially among new men. They might have been willing to take marginal cases and to pursue them further than prudence dictated, as is suggested by the discouraging rate of decisions favorable to the plaintiff.[18]

Nevertheless, it would be unfair to blame green or avaricious lawyers for all of the wage litigation at the turn of the century. A number of workers, especially those in service in homes, restaurants, hotels, and the like, were not covered by weekly-wage laws. For them, Boston's trial courts remained a genuinely useful, albeit always expensive, sometimes slow, and often risky means of collecting unpaid wages from an employer who did not respond to friendly persuasion.[19] Yet these wage earners were not the only Bostonians who sometimes met difficulty in collecting their pay. A growing class of independent professionals, especially physicians and lawyers, faced the same problem.

DOCTORS AND LAWYERS

The 1880 U.S. Census recorded over 7,000 professionals residing in Boston; in 1900 the number was nearly 15,500. Several categories had been added by the Census Office (for example, literary and scientific persons and artists), which makes exact comparison impossible, but the additions themselves suggest the growth and diversification of the professions. Like blue-collar or low-salaried white-collar workers, these professionals sold their services in the urban market to a variety of people whom they did not know well, and they trusted these clients to pay for services rendered. Both the ethics and economics of medicine and law compelled doctors and lawyers to perform immediately and be paid later. When these professionals felt that their compensation was being unjustly withheld, they could not rely on weekly-wage laws to assist in recovery. If repeated demands for payment were ignored, they could forget a debt or sue. But whereas Boston's physicians turned increasingly to litigation, attorneys did not (table 17).[20]

TABLE 17. INCIDENCE OF FEE CLAIMS BY DOCTORS AND LAWYERS, 1880, 1900

Year	Number of practitioners[a]		Number of cases[b]		Number of cases per 100 practitioners	
	doctors	lawyers	doctors	lawyers	doctors	lawyers
1880	925	1,150	102	244	11	21
1900	1,725	2,130	523	285	30	13

[a] The number listed in the city directory.
[b] The approximate number of actual cases estimated from the sample.

Physicians practiced under a special obligation to treat without setting terms in advance. Indeed, they did not expect to be paid if a patient or a patient's family was financially hard pressed. However, some patients who could pay nevertheless delayed, sometimes indefinitely.[21] The doctor's bill was, proverbially, the last to be settled. This sort of delinquency was practiced in the towns and in cities, but it was a particular problem in the metropolis. In rural areas and in small towns there was little, if any, choice of physician. In Boston a patient could choose from among hundreds of doctors. New physicians eager to build practices were willing to overlook completely a new patient's financial situation. These struggling doctors even treated known "deadbeats" in the hope of earning good reputations as medical men and as creditors. By 1880 there had developed in Boston a group of habitual debtor-patients who simply switched physicians when a bill grew too large or when the current doctor refused further treatment on account. Litigating doctors commonly sought repayment for five to ten visits made over a period of six months to a year.[22]

Delinquent patients capitalized on a physician's fear of pressing his claim too hard. They knew that he worried about offending reliable patients and fellow physicians with seeming insensitivity. In the 1870s and 1880s doctors rarely sued patients living near their offices. Most of those who did bring suit practiced in the central business district or the South End, where there was more transient, walk-in business.[23]

The physician's collection problems worsened after 1880, as the medical profession began to deal more competently with a growing number of ailments. Progress inspired greater confidence in doctors, raising the demand for their services. But the improved training, equipment, and medicines that were responsible for this progress inflated the costs of treatment substantially in the late nineteenth century. The more that people believed in medicine, the more expensive it became.[24]

As his overhead rose and his collection problem grew, a physician's tolerance for financial sacrifice diminished. As early as 1871 an enraged Dorchester doctor, noting that one-fourth to one-third of his annual work went uncompensated, demanded of his colleagues that they be more businesslike. The following year a medical blacklist of bad credit risks was published in Boston for the first time. In the 1880s and 1890s doctors became more aggressive creditors. Advice books on the financial side of medical practice appeared in the 1890s and in the first few years of the new century. In the 1870s a physician had to apologize for even raising the question of collections; by the turn of the century debt collection was openly discussed in respectable medical journals, and the AMA was recommending a course in business principles for every medical student.[25]

Boston trial dockets clearly reflect this change in attitude. The number of lawsuits brought by physicians increased fivefold between 1880 and 1900. Although the growth of the city's medical community during those two decades accounts for some increase, the number of suits per doctor nearly tripled during those twenty years (table 17).

In 1880 most suits were for amounts between twenty and twenty-five dollars. Doctors won about 80 percent of their actions and almost always recovered exactly what they demanded, probably because their customary charges were well established. In 1900, however, cases involving sums under twenty dollars were not uncommon. Although victorious physicians still recovered 100 percent of their claims, they won less often—about 60 percent of the time—and had to fight more appeals. Doctors were apparently bringing pettier and more easily contested suits at the turn of the century.[26]

Similarities between the actions of 1880 and of 1900 are as important as the differences. Doctors continued throughout the period to avoid lawsuits against those who lived near their offices, and they preferred the quick judi-

cial process of the Boston Municipal Court to the weari-
some justice of the Suffolk County Superior Court. Furthermore, doctors new to Boston rarely appeared in the
dockets. Most plaintiffs had been in practice in the city for
five years or more. A new man simply could not risk the
damage to his fragile reputation that an irate defendant
might have caused. Ironically, those physicians who were
probably most often victimized by bad debtors were least
responsible for the growing litigiousness among medical
men. A singular combination of competition and ethical
standards, less self-imposed than demanded by the public,
kept the rising number of doctors' lawsuits from multiply-
ing even faster.[27] Patients, on the other hand, did not often
use the courts as a disciplinary tool against doctors. Not a
single malpractice suit appeared in the sample cases.[28]

The legal community, like the medical one, grew faster
than the city's population, yet attorneys sued less frequently in 1900 than they had in 1880. Among lawyers,
ethical and economic considerations suppressed litigation.[29]

During the last quarter of the nineteenth century Boston
attorneys, especially older, established members of the bar,
observed that the lawyer's image had become tarnished
since the 1830s, when Tocqueville identified him as the
American aristocrat. A majority of citizens, they felt, had
come to see him as something of a confidence man, who
was more concerned with his pocketbook than with his
clients' welfare. As a result, they believed, lawyers influenced the public conscience less than they had earlier in
the century.[30]

Boston's self-conscious lawyers blamed their fall from
public favor on a variety of influences, chief among them,
the increasing commercialization of the law. They accepted
some responsibility for this but placed much of the blame
with the host of "undesirables" admitted to practice each
year. In the eyes of many established lawyers the family
background and breeding of these men made it impossible

for them to have "the same high ideals of legal conduct as
actuated the old-school lawyer with generations of professional ancestors." "Half-educated young men" swarmed
into the profession. They talked too loudly and too long,
chased after cases, and preyed upon the misfortunes of
their clients. In court they were excessively theatrical, play-
ing to the gallery. They simply were not gentlemen.[31]

Acting through the Boston Bar Association, established
lawyers exercised some direct influence over the discipline
of practicing attorneys. By arrangement with the supreme
judicial court, the association was responsible for the identification and prosecution of Boston lawyers deserving sus-
pension or disbarment, a responsibility its members began
to take seriously. From 1806 to 1876 only a single attorney
had been disbarred in Suffolk County. Between 1876 and
1900 seventeen lawyers were disbarred and one sus-
pended.[32]

The anxiety of the established bar over certification of so
many allegedly unqualified lawyers had economic as well as
ethical origins. Too many new attorneys were appearing
each year, and there simply was not enough legitimate
work for all of them. They depressed the value of legal
services directly by their offers to perform at competitive
prices and indirectly by subsequent displays of greed and
incompetence, which discouraged those with genuine legal
problems from seeking an attorney. Needless litigation was
said to be the stock in trade of these shysters.[33]

To limit the volume of unnecessary litigation, the Bar
Association began a campaign to sell the business community on the idea of preventive law. Merchants and bankers
with legal problems were urged to see a lawyer before a
lawsuit became their only choice. The association was certainly not trying to reduce the income of the bar. Indeed,
its members believed that a reduction in the number of
needless, expensive lawsuits would build public confidence
in the legal profession, attract more clients, and result in a
net increase of earnings for all but the pettifoggers. Litiga-

tion was becoming increasingly costly for clients in the late nineteenth century; to encourage it was self-destructive.[34]

Lawyers' lawsuits for unpaid fees embodied both the ethical and economic problems of the profession. They created an impression that the attorney's charges were unjust, "for, even though the amount of the charge be known, the public, being unacquainted with the facts," could "never judge the matter fairly." The lawyer was certain to be blamed and the reputation of all lawyers thereby stained. Moreover, legal action was inefficient. Compensation derived from a compromise out of court was likely to equal the net recovery from a lawsuit. Only when a client "willfully and in a spirit of meanness" withheld a "hardearned fee" was a suit justified. Indeed, court action in such cases was advisable, for if a client had "the hardihood to attempt to overreach one so amply able to defend himself" and was "not rebuked," he would "hesitate at no degree of importunity."[35]

The influence of these ethical and economic forces was manifested in the dockets. In 1880 the lawyers who sued for unpaid fees were usually men of long experience in their profession. Over half had practiced for more than ten years, most for more than twenty. Among them were charter members of the Boston Bar Association, including several of the city's more prominent barristers. By 1900 a typical plaintiff had been at the bar less than ten years, and prominent lawyers were absent among them.[36]

REMUNERATION THROUGH LITIGATION

At the turn of the century Boston's blue-collar and low-salaried white-collar workers appeared less often before the city's trial courts than they had twenty years earlier to plead for pay they believed was unjustly denied them. Weekly-wage laws had eliminated many of the shady withholding practices of employers. When a wage disagreement arose, the Boston Legal Aid Society was there to help, and its lawyers preferred out-of-court settlements. Counsel for the society understood that the low-paid worker who lived on little margin usually could not afford the investment of time and money demanded by the judicial process.

An uncompensated attorney was restrained from suing by growing ethical and economic concerns. Lawyers' lawsuits made the entire bar seem avaricious, frightening away more fees than they collected. High ethical standards coupled with restraint were good not only for the lawyers' image but also for business.

Medical ethics, however, were moving in the opposite direction. Uncompensated physicians sued more often at the turn of the century than they had in 1880. Litigation could be just as inefficient for them as it was for lawyers, but doctors derived a long-run economic benefit not enjoyed by attorneys. The typical physician experienced a rapidly increasing demand for his services as advances in medicine and surgery created greater public confidence in his skills; by the turn of the century medical progress not only had made the physician's art more reliable but had also placed its working beyond the comprehension of the untrained. Still, the young doctor trying to build a practice did not risk the ill will that legal action might have caused. But the established doctor who provided competent treatment could venture an occasional lawsuit. Not only was he likely to recover his fee, but, more important, he demonstrated to his patients that he was a creditor to be taken as seriously as any businessman.[37]

Lawsuits for emoluments remained expensive, time-consuming, often disappointing for low-salaried white-collar people and for blue-collar workers. On the other hand, lawyers, with growing reservations, and doctors, with shrinking inhibitions, found them useful for disciplining clients and patients.

FIVE

A PLACE TO LIVE

THE PROBLEM OF SHELTER

Writing on "The Housing Conditions in Boston" at the turn of the century, a prominent Brahmin lawyer and reformer explained that "dilapidated and unsanitary buildings" not only endangered health but also engendered pauperism and criminality. Similar environmental arguments about the pernicious effects of slum dwellings appeared in the writings of other improvers in Boston and elsewhere.[1]

In the Hub City there was enough concern to prompt a variety of public agencies and private watchdog groups to produce nearly a dozen housing surveys and reports between 1888 and 1908. Each described how thousands of newcomers annually jammed into already overcrowded tenement and lodging-house districts. Each decried dark halls, airless rooms, bone-chilling dampness, and sickening smells. These studies expressed or implied a belief that properly constructed living quarters could be the keystone of a model urban social structure: good homes would make good citizens.[2]

Public officials and self-appointed overseers found it easier to identify shelter as a critical urban problem than to offer practical solutions. City and state government acted on other municipal problems, for example, using public funds and management to guarantee adequate water and mass-transit systems. In these areas, as in housing, an important issue was the appropriate mixture of public and private initiative. There was general agreement that private capital should provide shelter but that its quality should be regulated by public authorities.[3]

A building code adopted after the great fire of 1872 was actually a series of new statutes and ordinances, which were modified occasionally over the next twenty-five years. By the 1890s the code was a hodgepodge of regulations, and responsibility for enforcement was divided among several city departments, which did not coordinate their activities very well.[4] Most regulations defined health and safety violations that prevailed in the worst slums, and limited resources for enforcement were concentrated in these sections. The majority of Bostonians, however, did not reside in slums. Since the housing laws aimed to achieve a standard of accommodation at or above which most of them already lived, their shelter arrangements were largely unregulated. Builders, owners, buyers, and tenants traded in a free market.[5]

Although single-family dwellings, tenements, and lodging houses were fabricated and occupied with little direction from statutes and ordinances, the law was not without influence. Much of this influence, however, was not to be found in the clear wording of new legislation or of recently delivered high-court opinions. It lay rather in the daily application of well-established, common-law principles and older statutes to cases brought before the trial courts as these tribunals attempted to settle a variety of disputes involving the rights of owners and occupiers of real property.[6]

LANDLORDS AND TENANTS

In the late nineteenth century most Bostonians rented homes, and the conflicts that came to court usually arose from tenancy (table 18). There were three main rental districts in the city (map 3). Within the boundaries of the old eighteenth-century town lay the compact North and West ends, which were well established as low-rent neighborhoods by 1845. Between the southern fringes of the central business district and Roxbury sat the South End, a wide

TABLE 18. RELATIVE IMPORTANCE OF CERTAIN
REAL-ESTATE ACTIONS, 1880, 1900

Type of action	(%) of all real-estate actions	
	1880	1900
Ejectment from rented dwelling	39	10
Landlords' rent claims	39	52
Tenants' complaints	1	2
Builders' claims	14	12
Petitions for assessment of damage and betterment	7	24
N	*102*	*97*

corridor of streets filled with tenements and lodging
houses during the three decades that followed the Civil
War. In that same period Boston continued to experience
rapid population growth. From overseas and from the
city's hinterland newcomers of modest means poured into
these three districts in search of low-priced shelter near
principal places of employment. As the demand for housing grew, a host of petty entrepreneurs divided larger
spaces in older buildings to create more living units. Where
land was available, new structures went up.[7]

By 1880, with pressure on the rental housing supply still
considerable, landlords and their agents did not have to tolerate tenants who were late with the rent or who offended
them in some other way. Fourteen days' notice in writing
was sufficient to terminate the tenancy of one who did not
pay rent when due. Tenants without a lease, probably the
majority, could be asked to leave without explanation, provided they were notified in writing. The minimum notifica-
tion period equaled the interval between the days of payment; for example, monthly renters were entitled to one
month's notice. Tenants who knew the difficulties of
finding accommodation elsewhere sometimes clung tena-
ciously to a room or flat, despite repeated demands to leave.

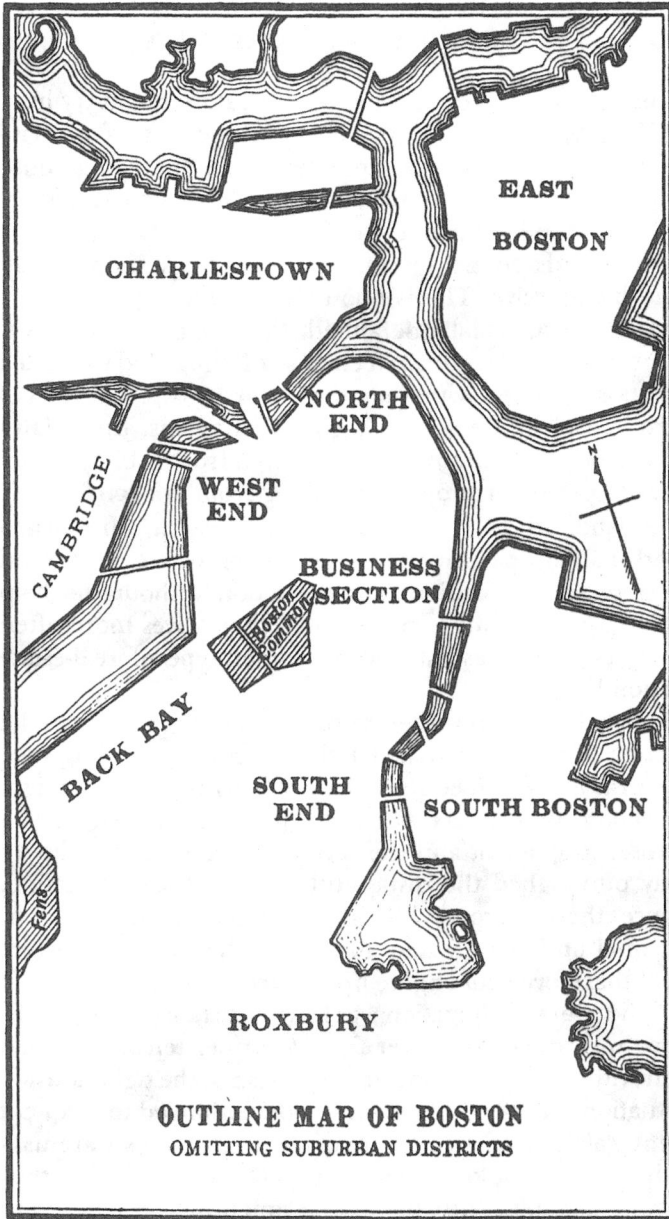

MAP 3. OUTLINE MAP OF BOSTON (from Robert A. Woods,
The City Wilderness [Boston, 1899])

Confronted with this, a frustrated landlord might try himself to expel the tenant, which sometimes resulted in violence. The prudent owner of a tenement or lodging house avoided such problems by turning to the Boston Municipal Court for an ejectment order.[8]

Landlords found ejectment proceedings simple, fast, and inexpensive. The petition had an uncomplicated format. Tenants usually defaulted, the ejectment order was normally issued within a week or so of filing, and the actual eviction followed within another week or two. Court costs and constables' fees were then levied against the tenant. The landlord, moreover, was absolved from liability for injury to person or property resulting from eviction.[9]

A landlord, motivated by thrift or passion, who wished personally to participate in the ejection of a tenant could best do so by petitioning for eviction without the help of a lawyer. Plaintiffs represented themselves more often in ejectment cases than in any other type of real-estate action.[10]

A landlord who wished to place the entire matter in the hands of an attorney had little difficulty in finding one. Several lawyers specialized in evictions in specific neighborhoods or districts. For these practitioners the ease of prosecuting a suit and the certainty of a client's ability to pay outweighed the distasteful nature of such litigation. Since there were few surprises in ejectment hearings, counsel and client could anticipate what would transpire and therefore could agree upon a fee in advance.[11]

The course of litigation was less predictable when a landlord was trying to recover from a former tenant who had left without paying overdue rent. Despite the tight housing situation, the rapid turnover in population led to frequent rent claims. Like ejectment actions, rent claims were usually won by landlords, who normally recovered what they demanded, plus costs. Unlike ejectment proceedings, rent cases were frequently contentious and drawn out.[12]

There was often genuine disagreement over the amount

actually owed, usually a sum ranging from $20 to $100, which represented from one week's to five months' rent, depending on the premises. Landlords must have been careful not to allow overdue rent to accumulate much above $100. They probably found a lawsuit for amounts below $20 not worth the necessary investment of time and money. Few landlords attempted to prosecute their own rent claims, because the action was subject to the complexities of common-law proceedings, unlike ejectment, which was a more clearly defined statutory procedure.[13]

The greater legal complexity of claims for rent and the stronger resistance encountered in these actions became increasingly important as Boston's housing market changed during the last two decades of the nineteenth century. In those years the city's population continued to grow at about the pace of the 1870s. At the same time, large new residential districts sprang up in the suburbs. Proliferating streetcar lines connected new suburbs, older residential areas, and commercial and industrial districts by a speedy, reliable, and inexpensive mass-transit system. For thousands of Bostonians, place of employment no longer dictated residence in a specific neighborhood. Those who were willing to invest ten cents and half an hour daily in a trolley ride could search for a home in an area measured by miles, not blocks.[14]

The steady rate of population growth and the creation of new and accessible residential districts relieved some pressure on the housing market but did not affect all sections of the city equally. The North and West ends remained overcrowded because most post-1880 immigrants, East European Jews and Italians, settled there. Both groups displayed a cohesion that kept them, even some of the well-to-do among them, in those crowded neighborhoods. Yet many did move to streetcar suburbs. The pressure on the housing supply in these two ghettos was also relieved somewhat by new laws that eliminated many tenement sweatshops in the late 1880s. Not only was some commer-

cial space freed for residential use, but residential rents became less influenced by the higher rents that landlords
could exact from commercial tenants. Even these two most
populous of Boston's neighborhoods experienced tenement vacancy rates of 5 or 6 percent in the early 1890s.[15]

In the South End the influences of the new housing
market were greater. All three districts were filled with
shoddy tenements and lodging houses, but the South End
contained no cohesive ethnic ghettos and was not separated physically from other residential areas. Its population consisted of a mixture of Yankees and British-Ca-
nadians, liberally sprinkled with Italians, Jews, Irish, and
Portuguese. It adjoined the business district to the north
and Roxbury to the south (map 3) and was crossed by all of
the major thoroughfares that connected center city with
the southern suburbs. Much of the shelter in the South
End was to be found in dreary lodging houses that catered
to the needs of the single young people who came to Boston each year by the thousands from rural New England
and Canada to work in shops, banks, and offices, in factories, and in the homes of the well-to-do. The South End
belonged to transients and so to no one in particular. Social
worker Robert A. Woods knew the district well, describing
it as a place "made up of people who have no local attach-
ments and are separated from one another by distinctions
of race and religion." There was "no concerted action for a
better social life, no watchfulness over common interests."
Offering little more than a variety of inexpensive accommodations, the South End could not compete with the
idylls of suburban life. In the early 1890s the vacancy rate
of South End tenements stood at 8 or 9 percent. The district's population continued to grow, but not as quickly as
the number of tenements for rent.[16]

As the housing supply expanded, landlords in all three
districts found themselves less bothered by tenants who refused to vacate and more aggravated by those who left
without paying overdue rent. Thus, they began to use the

trial courts more as collection agencies, less as ejectment
services (table 18). At the turn of the century they won
their rent claims as often as they had in 1880, but several
important case characteristics had changed. Although tenants defended themselves as frequently as they had in
1880, a larger portion of actions was finished quickly. At
the same time, partial recoveries became more common.
Landlords, it seems, were willing to settle for less in return
for a speedier conclusion. Unpaid rent was a grievance less
easy to redress through litigation than was refusal to vacate, so landlords adjusted their expectations accordingly.[17]

At the turn of the century landlords were still making far
greater use of the trial courts than were their tenants (table
18). Of course, the high proportion of rent claims that
were resisted represented one form of tenants' participation in the litigation process, but few lawsuits were initiated
by them. The odd suit brought by a tenant was usually one
of two kinds: a demand for the unused portion of rent paid
in advance or a claim for injuries sustained in a fall that was
caused by poor lighting, faulty stairs, or the like. Recovery
for property damaged by a ruptured pipe or leaking roof
was also sometimes at issue.

It is difficult to generalize about tenants' lawsuits from
only a handful of actions. The most significant point is that
there were so few of them. Some problems, notably those
involving violations against the building codes, were probably brought to the attention of city inspectors and handled
as criminal matters. Moreover, the fact that most tenants
did put up a defense indicates that they were not destitute
individuals running away from a large debt. Indeed, most
of them pursued white-collar occupations. Apparently, a
number of rent disputes began as tenants' informal attempts to adjust some disagreement with a landlord; that
is, tenants who believed they had been overcharged or injured in some way sought informal justice simply by withholding rent.[18]

BUILDERS AND THEIR CLIENTS

In landlord-tenant disputes tenants usually enjoyed the advantage of having no permanent stake in the premises. The property was the landlord's investment; it was up to him to protect it. In conflicts that arose between builders and their clients both parties had an investment to protect. When a builder sought to secure through litigation what he considered just compensation for his labor and materials, his claim was usually disputed by the defendant. Defendants were especially anxious to contest petitions for mechanic's liens, under which the court could sell the structures in question to compensate builders with the proceeds. Many defendants were protected by a statutory provision that exempted from mechanic's liens property owned by a third party, for example, a bank or trust company that held a mortgage on the premises. But there was no protection from a simple action for debt, and this was the form of litigation usually resorted to by builders. Defendants were scarcely less contentious in these cases than when threatened with a lien, because the disagreements between builders and their clients over the amount due were seemingly genuine, with neither party completely right in most cases. Setoffs and counterclaims were often established. Most actions were withdrawn or discontinued, which suggests that out-of-court settlements were common. When judgment was rendered or a written agreement concluded, the plaintiff's recovery was normally a partial one. Liens, too, were rarely enforced. In short, the outcome was usually a compromise agreed to by the parties or, occasionally, imposed by the court.[19]

Mechanic's liens and debt actions substituted for mortgage foreclosures in some cases. Many builders provided their clients with a mortgage or simply extended credit in lieu of one. Foreclosure was not only a harsh measure, it also left a builder-mortgagee with a property to dispose of. Some preferred to use litigation to pressure a mortgagor into accepting a modified repayment schedule.[20]

The court's intervention was important in encouraging the expansion of the housing supply. In 1880 cases usually involved new construction, most of it taking place in developing residential districts, such as the Back Bay (map 3), Dorchester, Roxbury, and West Roxbury (map 1). At the turn of the century litigation focused more often on repairs and renovations, especially plumbing installations, in homes in those sections. In 1880 and 1900 cases typically involved several hundred dollars, substantial amounts for the normally small-time builders and businessmen who faced each other across the courtrooms. These petty entrepreneurs operated in a disorganized building market. Cost accounting was virtually unheard of, and estimates were notoriously unreliable. A structure was erected; then builder and client tried to agree on a final price. Some could not. By acting as a sounding board in these troubled transactions and applying pressure when needed, the trial courts reduced friction and helped petty entrepreneurs to work together to provide new housing and to keep older dwellings fit for use.[21]

GROWING PAINS

The vigorous home construction industry of the late nineteenth century fashioned residential areas in Roxbury, West Roxbury, and Dorchester (map 1). These new neighborhoods were connected to employment districts by a street-railway network that was the product of private capital and decision making. Street-railway companies determined where service was needed, or soon would be, and laid their tracks accordingly. The very streets were also creations of private entrepreneurship. Developers laid them out as they saw fit. Gas mains, electric lines, and telephone cables were installed in a similar manner. Coordination was the exception, not the rule. From 1891 to 1897 a

Board of Survey offered some guidance, but it was difficult to impose a rational system of expansion on the parties involved in suburban development. While one city agency struggled to control the chaos, others blithely participated in it. The grading and paving of streets and installation of water mains and sewers beneath them were municipal responsibilities. It was not uncommon for the municipality to put in water mains and sewers and pave a roadway, only to have a gas company or a street railway subsequently tear up everything in order to install pipes or lay rails. Similar incidents occurred in older neighborhoods as real-estate speculators, builders, utilities, and government officials struggled to meet the needs of growing populations in those districts.[22]

The burden of keeping up with the demand for new or improved roadways, water mains, and sewers was relieved somewhat by the power of eminent domain, a statutory right that permitted the city to take or to authorize the taking of private property for public use. Municipal authorities had little power to control private development, but the extraordinary power of eminent domain helped them to keep pace with it.

When the city exercised its right to seize real estate—for example, to extend or to widen a street—it was required to compensate the owner. An owner who thought the city's offer too low had the right to petition the superior court for greater compensation. As Boston grew, the number of petitions presented annually grew as well. By 1900 the volume of such actions was fifteen times what it had been in 1880.[23]

The property in question was usually a small plot of land, less than an acre, and the petitioners were mostly small businessmen or businesses. The disagreement usually focused on the relative values of damage and betterment. If part of a lot were taken for street improvement, was the remainder worth less because it was smaller and changed in shape or worth more because it now abutted an improved street? In some cases there was no trade to negotiate. When the city put in a new street without damaging an abutter's property, assessors had the right to raise taxes on the improved real estate. There was, however, considerable undervaluation in developing neighborhoods in the 1890s, much of it the product of bribery. The number of petitions for the assessment of betterment (that is, for higher evaluation) at the century's end was thus smaller than it had been twenty years earlier.[24]

The final disposition of petitions for damage and for betterment was usually not made by the court. Although the city solicitor and petitioners commonly haggled for two or three years over values, they rarely failed to find a compromise figure. The court's role was to help the parties to reach a settlement.[25]

REGULATION THROUGH LITIGATION

Except for the worst slums, there was little public regulation of housing in late-nineteenth-century Boston. In the search for shelter the financial resources of builders, buyers, and tenants, as well as fashion, governed. The housing market was largely self-regulating, but the potential for chaos was always present in thousands of disagreements over rent, construction costs, and damage to property, real and personal.[26]

Many of these disputes were settled informally, but this required some personal relationship between the parties. Rent was "payable on strong demand," recalled one Bostonian who had grown up in the South End of the 1880s and 1890s. The landlady climbed the stairs weekly but "seldom succeeded in collecting the full amount of the rents from her tenants." She was, nevertheless, insistent. "Her knock on the door was clear, sharp, unfaltering; it was impossible to pretend not to hear it. Her 'Good-evening' announced business; her manner of taking a chair suggested the throwing-down of the gauntlet." She lectured her tenants on their laziness and dishonesty, "enumerated her losses through nonpayment of her rents," and threatened to evict them within the week. This went on for months, sometimes years, the tenants "living in fear of her, she in distrust" of them. The alternative was a settlement in the formal environment of a courtroom.[27]

Indeed, the real-estate business of the courts in the late nineteenth century suggests that litigation was the resort of plaintiffs who did not know the defendants well, if at all. Most plaintiffs in ejectment and rent cases were absentee landlords, men and women who lived not only in other buildings but in other neighborhoods. Similarly, builders rarely sued clients who lived near them. Most impersonal of all was the relationship between victims of eminent domain and the city government.[28]

The important function of physical and social distance in generating litigation was further demonstrated by the fact that at the turn of the century the landlords and tenants of the cohesive neighborhoods of the North and West ends used the courts less frequently to settle disputes than did their counterparts in the disorganized South End (table 19). Furthermore, much of the increase in the number of landlord-tenant disputes between 1880 and 1900 was the result of rent claims involving a defendant who lived in Boston proper and a plaintiff who resided in the suburbs

TABLE 19. DISTRIBUTION OF LANDLORD-TENANT
LITIGATION BY NEIGHBORHOOD,[a] 1880, 1900

Year	North End (%)	West End (%)	South End (%)	N
1880	23	11	66	64
1900	19	19	63	32

[a] Landlord-tenant litigation includes the total number of sample cases involving ejectment from rented property, landlords' rent claims, and tenants' claims against landlords.

or in one of the satellite towns. The only other important growth area in litigation was the volume of petitions arising out of unsatisfactory eminent domain negotiations (table 18). It was for the solution of such impersonal conflicts that the trial courts became an increasingly popular forum.[29]

The courts thus injected some order into the housing market. The host of petty entrepreneurs who provided most dwellings in Boston felt more secure about their investments because these tribunals stood ready to settle disagreements. The overwhelming majority of plaintiffs in real-property litigation pursued low-income white-collar or skilled blue-collar occupations. Moreover, between 1880 and the century's end the proportion of immigrants and women among them more than doubled. Such newcomers to real-property entrepreneurship probably found litigation particularly useful for rectifying errors in judgment and protecting their investments. In the long run the ability of trial courts to satisfy the needs of petty property owners made it easier for all Bostonians to find a place to live.[30]

PART III

The Dangers of Everyday Life

SIX

ACCIDENTS

BOSTONIANS lived in the midst of thousands of machines, which, when carelessly operated, maimed and killed. The crowded conditions of urban life likewise increased the chances of injury in older and more familiar forms: gaping holes in the pedestrian-packed thoroughfares, leaking gas, falling shingles and chunks of ice. In addition, malicious injury to person, property, or feelings generated a small but growing number of lawsuits.

As the motorman wrenched the rheostat sharply to zero and pulled back hard on the brake, passengers were suddenly thrown forward, several of them falling to the muddy floorboards. Screeching wheels drowned out the shrill scream of the schoolboy whose foot was trapped below. Another inch and it would have been amputated. An inch less and he would have disappeared down one of the nearby alleys.

I was on my way to school—six years old. A friend was with me. He was six months older. We crossed when the traffic seemed slow. There were no traffic lights or policemen on the streets in those days. A wagon appeared suddenly, and to keep from being hit, my friend and I spun around and stepped back. A trolley came out of nowhere, and the next thing I knew my right foot was caught under one of its wheels. It was crushed. I lost some toes.

We had no insurance, but my father was offered a settlement by the company. He wanted more and hired a lawyer, Mr. K _____. We lost the case. I don't remember why—some technicality. Shortly after that Mr. K _____ became a lawyer for the trolley line. Eventually, he became a judge, and I lost the leg up to my knee.[1]

SOUNDS OF THE CITY

The sounds in the streets of Boston at the century's end were noticeably different from those of twenty years earlier. The staccato pounding of horses' hoofs and the tinkle of harness bells were drowned out by the grinding wheels and whirring gears of electric trolleys. Silent snowfalls were no longer followed by the almost equally noiseless rush of runners through fresh powder but by the abrasive scraping of iron plows and shovels. At building sites the tapping of the carpenter's hammer and the rhythmic shuffle of the mason's trowel could not be heard over the buzz of power tools. In the streets, homes, and commercial establishments of Boston the hiss of gas lamps was being replaced by the crackle and hum of arc lights and the silence of incandescent bulbs. Blasts of locomotive steam were louder and the shrieks of factory whistles more frequent.[2]

To some ears these were the sounds of progress, heralding the arrival of inventions that created jobs, raised the standard of living, and contributed to general prosperity. To others the new sounds were menacing, signaling the passing of a familiar, gentler, and safer way of life. A balance had to be struck. The benefits of new machines had to be reconciled with the damage they did. It was not easy to locate the point at which new technologies and the accompanying systems of organization for production, deployment, and consumption began to lower rather than raise the quality of life. The average person could speculate, but immediate practical action was demanded of lawmakers. Although some groundwork had been laid earlier in the century, the suddenness and intensity with which certain technologies developed required considerable refinement of older, more general policies and a complete rethinking of others.

Statutes and judicial opinions dealing with personal injury multiplied quickly in the 1880s and 1890s but left much undone. The state legislature found it difficult to write general laws that could deal fairly with the injured and with wrongdoers in all cases. The supreme judicial court provided the formal, but individualized, resolution of exceptional cases that simultaneously expanded the rules. The law of torts, especially relating to negligence, grew monstrously large and perplexing. The supreme judicial court found it difficult to determine precisely what constituted contributory negligence or to fix the monetary value of culpability and damage. Such decisions were left largely to the judges and juries of the trial courts. In those tribunals the outlines of policy blurred, and the system that developed can best be described as a *modus vivendi*.[3]

PROXIMATE CAUSES

Traffic Accidents

No new sound echoed louder through the courtrooms of Boston than the roar of electric streetcars. The first broomstick trolley sprinted between Boston and Brookline on New Year's Day 1889; the last horsecar crawled down Marlboro Street, in the Back Bay, on Christmas Eve of 1900. In those eleven years the number of reported trolley accidents on lines serving Boston rose from barely 200 to more than 1,700.[4]

The accident rate had been increasing before the introduction of electric cars, rising eightfold during the last eight years of the horsecar era (1880-1888). The streetcar system grew tremendously in that period. Lines serving Boston carried 43 million passengers over 7.5 million miles in 1880; by 1888 the ridership had jumped to nearly 100 million and the mileage to over 16.5 million. Most responsible for this growth was Henry M. Whitney's West End Street Railway Company, which handled more than 85 percent of the city's trolley traffic in the late 1880s. New lines radiated from the central business district to the outer limits of the city and into the suburbs. At the center, street-car blockades became a diurnal ritual. Inevitably, such heavy traffic meant an increased number of accidents.[5]

Electric trolleys plunged into this worsening traffic prob-lem, exacerbating it. The speed and power of the new cars made them attractive because they could carry more people more quickly and at a lower cost than horsecars. They easily negotiated hills too steep for horses and so were able to serve formerly inaccessible areas. As a result, the limits of the streetcar city widened; the riding public swelled two and a half times in a single decade, to over 250 million in 1900. But the speed and power of the new trams also made them more dangerous, dovetailing with conges-tion to send accident rates soaring. Horses had a difficult time adjusting to these mechanical monsters and were fre-quently frightened by them with injurious consequences. Streetcar motormen had an equally difficult time adjusting to the pace of horse traffic in the crowded streets of old Boston. In the horse age five miles per hour was consid-ered fast. In the suburbs electric trolleys cruised at ten to fifteen miles per hour, but downtown they inched along at one-fourth that speed, while drivers and passengers grew impatient. Long processions of powerful trolleys filled with impatient people, crawling through streets clogged with horses, carts, and pedestrians, created unprecedented op-portunities for carelessness and injury.[6]

The mounting number of injuries elicited little response from the state legislature or the city council. Both bodies were satisfied with existing regulations regarding the oper-ations of street railways, most of which were enacted before 1880. These regulations became hopelessly outdated dur-ing the last two decades of the century. In 1871 the legisla-ture passed a bill that permitted local governments to con-trol certain aspects of street-railway traffic, if they wished. Boston's Board of Aldermen did not take advantage of the

FIG. 3. TROLLEY ACCIDENT ON THE BROADWAY BRIDGE,
SOUTH BOSTON, JUNE 12, 1912

enabling statute until 1879, when it adopted a set of "rules
and regulations as to the rate of speed of street cars, the
mode and use of street railway tracks, the removal of snow
and ice from the same, and the giving notice of warning
of the approach of street cars by drivers or conductors
thereof." The new law established licensing for drivers and
conductors, set a maximum speed limit of seven miles per
hour, required drivers to keep at least ten feet away from
other cars, and forbade the blocking of intersections. Conductors were to prevent women and children from enter-
ing or leaving the cars while in motion, though it was per-
missible for adult males to do so. Specific prohibition of
driving a car "against or foul of any person or vehicle, or
anything whatever in the streets of the city" revealed the
novelty of writing traffic laws in the late 1870s and early
1880s. Then, trolley traffic was still light enough to be suf-

ficiently controlled by only five policemen working full time. Twenty years later, when street-railway accidents had increased seventyfold, the laws remained unchanged. The maximum penalty for violating streetcar regulations was still only twenty dollars.[7]

Blockades and accidents had become enough of a problem by 1885 to prompt a special investigation by the Board of Aldermen. Recommendations to limit the number of cars a company could run over its lines each hour were twice considered by the board, then finally dropped with a vague reference to their unfairness. The public demanded frequent service. Limitations of the carrying capacity of street railways, moreover, would have reduced their profits. The traction industry, under the leadership of Henry M. Whitney, lobbied powerfully against any bills that would have curbed earnings and growth. Whitney's street railways were a primary area of local investment in late-nineteenth-century Boston, and his interests found sympathy among the well-to-do.[8]

The inadequacy of preventive legislation placed a strain on common-law remedies for the injuries that resulted. The supreme judicial court was forced to spend more and more time on questions generated by burgeoning street-railway litigation in lower courts. At least two important decisions favored street railways. The court held in one case that the fact that a car was driven faster than the legal speed limit was not conclusive proof of negligence. In another opinion a child injured while trespassing on a trolley or on other street-railway property was denied the right to recovery. The latter was a particularly important decision in a city where the streets were the principal playgrounds of children. "I learned to cut across the tracks in front of an oncoming car," recalled one child, "and it was great fun to see the motorman's angry face turn scared, when he thought I was going to be shaved this time sure."[9]

Legal questions concerning contributory negligence were numerous. Under the common law a plaintiff whose negligence in any way contributed to the injuries sustained could not recover damages. What constituted contributory negligence was unclear, however. The supreme judicial court considered a number of specific situations, but these served only as examples; the variety of accidents defied the creation of any uniform standards. The court could be extremely lenient on a plaintiff. It found, for example, that a seventy-nine-year-old man who was blind in one eye and partially deaf did not contribute to his own injury when he failed to look and listen at a crossing, driving his team into the path of an oncoming trolley. On the other hand, a man who spent eight seconds adjusting his pants cuffs in the street at a point on a curve where one needed seven seconds to move out of the way if a tram suddenly appeared was held partially responsible for his injuries. The ambiguity of high-court opinions, as well as the demand for individualized justice in negligence suits, placed on the trial courts most of the burden for adjusting to the rising tide of trolley injuries.[10]

The rise in the number of streetcar torts during the last two decades of the nineteenth century was as dramatic as the rise in the number of reported streetcar accidents. In 1880 a dozen or so suits were filed in superior court alleging damage caused by negligent operation of a horsecar. At the turn of the century over 800 actions were filed in superior court and nearly another 600 in municipal court.[11]

At the turn of the century most of the negligence suits involving vehicles stemmed from streetcar accidents; yet a smaller, but still significant, number of lawsuits arose out of traffic accidents that involved other forms of transportation. Trams shared the streets with a growing number of carts, carriages, wagons, and, beginning in the 1890s, bicycles and automobiles. More than 500 people were injured and more than a dozen killed by these vehicles in 1900. In 1880, when horsecar torts barely exceeded a dozen, these other conveyances were responsible for nearly 50 actions (table 20). As streetcars battered their way to preeminence in negligence dockets, torts involving other vehicles multiplied six times, nearly reaching 300 per year at the turn of the century.[12]

The fact that cart-and-carriage actions were outnumbered nearly five to one by streetcar lawsuits in the dockets at the century's end helps to explain why cart-and-carriage accidents stimulated little legislative interest. The argument prevailed that it would have been unfair and senseless to regulate the use of streets by other vehicles so long as the main cause of traffic problems, streetcars, operated without proper regulations. In 1894 the Boston Transit Commission was created and charged with developing a comprehensive plan for traffic regulation; by 1900 its work was far from completed. Even though cart-and-carriage accidents made no specific demands on the supreme judicial court, the growing body of negligence law applied in a general way in such cases.[13]

In the transportation field the specific attention lavished by the high court on street-railway accidents was matched only by its concern with steam-railroad mishaps. Indeed, in the 1880s steam and street railroads were frequently considered as two halves of the same industry in case law and

TABLE 20. DISTRIBUTION BY CAUSATION OF LAWSUITS FOR ACCIDENTAL INJURY, 1880, 1900

| | (%) of all accidental-injury actions | |
Cause of injury	1800	1900
Streetcars	14	42
Carts, carriages, etc.	43	9
Trains	0	5
Gas	0	13
Industrial mishaps	0	12
Miscellaneous	43	19
N	14	151

statutes. The first locomotive ran in Massachusetts more than fifty years before the first electric trolley. Beginning in the 1840s and continuing to the end of the century, a stream of opinions poured forth in response to the appalling personal and property damage done by these iron monsters. During the 1870s an average of 300 people were reported injured each year in railroad accidents in Massachusetts. By the 1890s the average annual number of reported casualties exceeded 1,000.[14]

In the 1870s most of the injured could not sue the railroads. The law did give passengers and innocent bystanders a right to damages, but only for nonfatal injury. A dead victim's survivors could only seek retribution through a criminal indictment, because the common law provided no civil remedy for wrongful death. A grim joke explained that it was cheaper for railroads to kill people than merely to maim them. Moreover, most of the injured were not passengers or bystanders but employees or trespassers, who had virtually no civil remedies under the common law for injury of any degree.[15]

Major changes in the law occurred in the 1880s. A statute enacted in 1881 permitted survivors of fatally injured passengers and bystanders to bring a civil action for wrongful death. Two years later the state legislature granted employees or their survivors the right to sue for work-related injury or death that was the result of a railroad's negligence. The supreme judicial court sustained the change through a dozen challenges made in the 1880s and 1890s.[16]

Though a dynamic doctrinal subject, the steam railroads generated relatively little business for the Boston trial courts. Probably fewer than a dozen actions were brought against them for negligence in 1880, and there were under 200 at the turn of the century (table 20). Unlike street-railway accidents, steam-railroad mishaps were not a pressing internal problem in Boston. Although the city was a major railroad center, most of the highly dangerous switching operations took place at four locations in nearby counties. Furthermore, a number of hazardous grade crossings within the city limits were eliminated in the 1890s. Finally, injured employees, passengers, or bystanders usually could bring suit in one of several state courts or in federal court. Boston litigation was less related to the railroad accident rate in or near the city than it was to the number of victims who found it most convenient to file suits in the city's trial courts. In 1900 about 40 percent of the plaintiffs bringing such suits in Boston lived in nearby suburbs.[17]

Nonvehicular Accidents

An almost equally large number of negligence suits was prompted by accidents that had nothing to do with vehicles (table 20). Illuminating gas was not a new utility, having come to the city in the 1830s, but during the 1880s and 1890s a rapid extension of the gas system was accompanied by an equally dramatic growth in the number of consumers. During the last fifteen years of the century gas pipe mileage jumped from 400 to 800, and the average number of customers per mile rose from 77 to 124. Expansion was not uniform throughout the city, being greatest in the sprouting southern suburbs.[18]

The brighter light and cleaner heat of gas was appearing in new spaces and was enjoyed regularly by a growing segment of the population, but with the benefits came the dangers of asphyxiation and explosion. Gas killed twenty-five Bostonians during 1900, although some of the "accidents" were apparent suicides. On the whole, gas was more dangerous than electric current, which reportedly injured only three people that year.[19]

There was already enough concern in 1885 to prompt creation of a permanent state Board of Gas Commissioners, which was charged with gathering statistics on the industry and making recommendations to the legislature. In 1897 the Boston Common Council ordered the building commissioner to report "whether or not there is any system of inspection of gas-piping and fixtures in force." None existed, save for the supervision of gas companies themselves. In that same year an ordinance passed that required the licensing of gas fitters by examination, a permit for every installation or major repair job, and an inspection of all work done. Violators would have their licenses revoked and be fined up to $100. This law, however, had no influence on the major cause of gas accidents: consumer carelessness.[20]

As the gas system expanded and grew older, leaks and explosions became a greater threat. The dockets reflect the problem. No more than a handful of negligence cases was brought against gas utilities in 1880; twenty years later there were 400 such lawsuits.[21] A consumer who carelessly left on an unlighted gas jet had no right of legal action for any injuries that resulted, but an individual who was injured by a leaking main did. The supreme judicial court first considered the liability of utilities for damage done by escaping gas in 1857. Over the next twenty years that liability was firmly established, but only where the victim did not contribute to his own injury by failing to notify the company as soon as a leak was discovered, by failing to move away from the contaminated area, or by using a flame where a leak was suspected.[22]

The volume of litigation in late-nineteenth-century Boston concerning accidents in the work place displays a pattern similar to gas litigation. Only a handful of cases was brought in 1880, but in 1900 some 400 actions were initiated. However, no comparison between the two bodies of lawsuits is possible when one considers the great attention accorded the subject of industrial accidents by the state legislature and the supreme judicial court. Indeed, their growing concern with the doctrines regarding industrial accidents contributed to the growth of lower-court litigation in that area.[23]

In the early 1880s the common law regarding an injured employee's right to compensation from an employer re-

mained, as it had for forty years, severely limited. The doctrine of assumption of risk barred recovery if the plaintiff
willingly put himself in a position of danger, and the courts
declared that a worker assumed ordinary risks simply by
taking a job. The fellow-servant rule barred recovery for
injuries caused by the negligence of a fellow worker. Only
when the employer personally caused an injury by his own
negligence was the employee entitled to damages. The rule
of wrongful death, which protected railroads from numerous damage claims by the survivors of fatally injured
employees, also covered other employers.[24]

In 1887, four years after the legislature had negated the
wrongful death rule in the railroad industry by giving a
statutory right of action to next of kin, the legislature extended that right to the survivors of all employees killed on
the job. Motivated by the pitiable situation of disabled
workers and their dependents, as well as by the growing
burden that such people placed on public charity, legislators also passed an Employers' Liability Act. Under its
provisions an injured employee, or his legal representative,
was granted a right of action if the injury were caused by a
defect in equipment or in the work place resulting from
the employer's negligence or the negligence "of a person
acting as superintendent with the authority or consent of
such employer." The maximum that could be awarded in
any case was $4,000 for injury or $5,000 for injury and
death. An employer was absolved of liability if the worker
"knew of the defect or negligence which caused the injury,
and failed within a reasonable time to give, or cause to be
given, information thereof to the employer, or to some
person . . . entrusted with general superintendence."
Domestic servants and agricultural laborers were expressly
barred from recovery under the statute.[25]

The Employers' Liability Act left the supreme judicial
court with a number of fuzzy phrases to bring into focus.
Most important, "defects" had to be defined, as well as the
"negligence of a superintendent." In nearly three dozen

FIG. 4. IMMIGRANT YOUTH MAIMED IN AN INDUSTRIAL
ACCIDENT

cases brought in the late 1880s and 1890s the high court
tried to define these terms by specific examples. Each case
had to be judged by its own set of circumstances. The right
of action granted by the Employers' Liability Act, plus the
supreme judicial court's inability to do more than define by

example, burdened the trial courts with difficult decisions.[26]

The growth of litigation in the categories discussed thus
far could be explained by the rapid deployment of hazardous inventions or by a liberalization of circumstances under
which their victims were entitled to compensation. But
there was also growth in the number of lawsuits that were
not directly connected to technological change or to major
alterations of legal doctrine. In the late nineteenth century
hundreds of Bostonians were seriously injured annually in
commonplace mishaps involving a fall or a falling object.
Such accidents were responsible for perhaps 50 lawsuits in
1880. By 1900 the figure exceeded 600.[27]

The proliferation of these timeless lawsuits suggests that,
even as the changing conditions of urban life increased the
incidence of injury and thus the need for court action, litigation itself became an increasingly popular response to injury. Bostonians became more litigious by choice as well as
out of necessity.

A Note on Property Damage

Some 250 personal-injury suits filed at the turn of the century (less than 10 percent of the total) also included claims
for property damage. Another 200 actions were initiated in
which the only claim was for property damage, not personal injury. The characteristics of the small sample of
cases filed suggest why there were not more of them.[28]

A variety of damage was represented. One man sued a
mover for breaking furniture, another made claim against
the city of Boston when sewer construction flooded his cel-
lar, an electric power company filed suit against a builder
who had cut its lines while excavating. Nevertheless, most
property-damage cases resulted from the collision of a
powerful trolley and a comparatively fragile carriage or
wagon. Encounters between carriages and wagons apparently did not result in damage severe enough to warrant

litigation. The wealthy streetcar corporations, too, may have been more enticing defendants than an individual wagon or carriage owner.

Streetcar-carriage accidents normally gave rise to only a single property-damage claim by the owner of the horse-drawn vehicle; at the same time, they often resulted in the personal injury of, and subsequent suit by, several passengers in both vehicles. Moreover, streetcars, not carriages, were the principal conveyers of Bostonians at the turn of the century. Only the well-to-do owned their own rigs. It was the proliferation of the privately owned automobile in the twentieth century that began to involve the common man in costly property-damage suits.[29]

ACCIDENT LITIGATION

The salient feature of accident litigation in the late nineteenth century was the rapid growth in the number of such suits filed annually. In 1880 approximately 120 negligence actions were entered in the dockets of the municipal and superior courts. By 1900 the figure had climbed to 3,300. To process that many new cases each year, lawyers and judges adopted certain routines.[30]

The municipal court was an important forum for hearing accident cases at the turn of the century, although twenty years earlier a personal-injury suit was customarily heard only in the jury sessions of the superior court. By 1900 the volume of negligence business in the municipal court roughly equaled that of the higher tribunal, but the pattern of litigation was dissimilar. Compared with superior court actions, municipal court suits were for small sums, were short-lived, were less likely to be settled by agreement, and were more likely to be appealed.[31]

A statute that placed a $2,000 ceiling on claims brought before the municipal court ensured that most of the cases filed there would be pettier than most of those brought in superior court, where there was no maximum limit. Litigation took less time in the lower tribunal for two reasons. First, there were no jury trials before the lower bench. Time-consuming selection and deliberation processes were eliminated, as were the lengthy and often vacuous examinations, cross-examinations, and summations that lawyers employed in order to impress juries, to the great annoyance of judges. Second, lengthy out-of-court negotiations leading to settlements probably occurred less frequently in municipal court proceedings, since plaintiffs and defendants were automatically entitled to appeal unfavorable judgments to the superior court.[32]

Thus, the municipal court, in addition to being the forum in which a plaintiff with a strong case and a claim of $2,000 or less could count on a fast recovery, was also an excellent proving ground for questionable cases. Plaintiff's counsel experimented with his own argument while probing defense counsel's. Costs usually did not exceed $10, so plaintiffs and their attorneys tested the wind for a modest investment of time and money. Nearly 30 percent of the unsuccessful claimants then appealed to the superior court. It was there that most negligence actions were resolved.[33]

The superior bench was, in practice, normally the court of last resort. Once a case arrived there, either directly or on appeal, there was considerable pressure on both parties to finish it in that tribunal. A last appeal to the supreme judicial court could have taken several additional years to conclude and would have required the special services of a small group of high-priced attorneys. Because of the further delay and expense involved, less than 4 percent of Boston's accidental-injury actions went up to the supreme judicial court at the turn of the century.[34]

The unpredictable behavior of judges and jurors placed further pressure on superior court litigants to settle before the case went to the jury or the judge. The ambiguous nature of negligence law often made negligence lawsuits arbitrary, emotional matters, where the prejudices of judges and jurors weighed heavily. Of those cases that demanded a finding, about as many were decided in the plaintiff's favor as in the defendant's. The capricious nature of accident adjudication and the difficulty of further appeal led to the settlement of 70 percent of superior court accidental-injury suits at the turn of the century.[35]

Anticipating negotiations, plaintiffs and their attorneys filed extravagant claims in superior court, typically demanding between $5,000 and $25,000. A large *ad damnum* (damage claim) not only was intended to start the bargaining at a higher price but was also supposed to impress the jury, if not the judge, with the gravity of the case.[36] Plaintiffs and their lawyers could not have expected to recover the *ad damnum*, however, for that rarely happened. If they expected to bring a higher settlement by making greater demands, they were usually disappointed. Greater demands did not consistently result in larger settlements. The same was true of those cases terminated by a decision of a judge or a jury.[37] What did develop, however, was an informal ceiling on recoveries. Nearly 85 percent of the recoveries made by an agreement or a finding in the superior and municipal courts were for $500 or less. In contrast, nearly 90 percent of the initial claims were for $2,000 or more. Indeed, the sum recovered rarely equaled more than 10 percent of the *ad damnum*.[38]

An award of $500 or less was probably intended to compensate the plaintiff for some or all of his legal and immediate medical expenses. It may have also included some payment for lost income; however, the awards appear to have provided only minimal compensation. Moreover, the recovery of a few hundred dollars, after suing for several thousand for some months or even years, was certainly a psychological, if not a financial, defeat.[39]

Attorneys for the defense were obviously skilled at scaling down drastically the claims of plaintiffs. Indeed, most of them were experts in the defense of negligence cases of a particular type. At the turn of the century the Boston

Elevated Railway (successor to the West End Street Railway) was the defendant in nearly 30 percent of all personal-injury suits and in 70 percent of those actions directed against street railways. The Boston "El" was usually represented by the firm of Hyde and Baxter, although some cases were turned over to at least three other lawyers. The firm of Hurlburt, Jones, and Cabot represented four smaller lines in the remaining streetcar lawsuits. Similarly, the office of Matthews and Thompson specialized in defending express companies in vehicular torts. During his four terms as mayor of Boston (1891-1895), Nathan Matthews, had taken a special interest in the city's traffic problems, promoting, among other things, the new subway. He was willing, apparently, to apply his considerable expertise to negligence practice. The firm also specialized in the defense of employers in workmen's compensation actions, a specialty shared with the office of Dickson and Knowles. The Dickson firm also represented gas companies, a business divided with solo practitioner Robert Harbison. The New York, New Haven, and Hartford Railroad, defendant in most of the actions brought against steam lines, was regularly represented by Frank A. Farnham. Even the class of miscellaneous lawsuits resulting from falls or falling objects produced at least one expert defense firm: the office of the city solicitor, which participated in about one-third of these actions at the century's end.[40]

Defense attorneys were a homogeneous group. Most were Yankees who had attended Harvard, clerked with a prominent lawyer, joined the Boston Bar Association, and practiced for ten years or more. This circle of specialists handled more than three-fourths of all negligence defenses presented in 1900.[41]

Specialization enabled defense counselors to concentrate their professional reading on new developments in their particular area of the law of torts. Moreover, after participating in dozens or hundreds of similar lawsuits, they became most skilled in examining victims and their witnesses, as well as in guiding defense witnesses into favorable testimony. Finally, in addition to knowing what their clients could afford, defense specialists developed notions of what the opposition was willing to accept in settlement at certain points in a trial, and they acquired a feeling for the sort of settlement that satisfied the judge's sense of justice.

Delay was the defense's best weapon, and mounting caseloads guaranteed a certain amount of it in any lawsuit. As time went by, witnesses became harder to find, while the memories of those who testified grew dim. Time also healed many wounds, reducing the sympathy of judge and jury for the victim. Victims themselves became frustrated and anxious to settle the case. Defense attorneys extended proceedings by filing a variety of motions, requesting continuances, and proceeding as slowly as possible in the courtroom. Seven out of ten suits remained on the dockets for more than three months, four out of ten for more than a year. One lawyer estimated that personal-injury suits consumed 75 percent of the superior court's time, although they represented only 40 percent of the actions filed there.[42]

In addition to the benefits of their own expertise and delay, defense lawyers usually had the advantage of facing plaintiffs' attorneys who did not specialize in negligence cases. Contrary to common belief, only a handful of lawyers concentrated on the filing of accident suits at the turn of the century, and they represented no more than one-fourth of the plaintiffs.[43]

The expertise of defense counsel, the benefits of delays that occurred naturally or were manufactured, the relative inexperience of plaintiffs' attorneys, the vagaries of negligence law, and the difficulties that plagued judges and jurors in trying to set damages allowed a coterie of defense lawyers to shape the process of accident litigation. Initial moves lay, of course, with plaintiffs and their lawyers, and the potential power to decide issues rested with judges and jurors. But in the tedious confusion of negligence litigation, the experience of defense attorneys was of paramount importance. As the high proportion of cases terminated by agreements suggests, all concerned normally preferred to have the parties and counsel work out a settlement. The seasoned defense lawyer knew that he could usually end a suit with a reasonable offer, and he knew best what offer was likely to seem reasonable to the opposition, to his client, and to the court.

As court dockets became congested with accident cases, the established bar grew concerned. Criticism, however, was not directed at the tactics of delay employed by defense counsel but at the eagerness with which plaintiffs' attorneys filed new actions.[44] One member summarized the Boston Bar Association's attitude in a little poem:

Who are those greedy objects who swarm the city street?
Oh those, sirs, are the lawyers who in accidents delight,
The chasers of the ambulance—the modern *trolleybite*.[45]

The elite bar suspected that many negligence suits were the trumped-up speculations of dishonest attorneys and clients. At the heart of this alleged pettifoggery was the contingent fee, "that is, the practice of accepting a percentage share in the recovery as compensation for legal services that might not otherwise be obtainable by the litigant." If the case were won, the lawyer took a large portion of the winnings; if the case were lost, he charged nothing. Only court costs had to be advanced by the plaintiff; if a case were strong, a lawyer might even advance them himself. Some believed that contingent fees opened the door to a host of unmeritorious negligence suits by poor people, especially poor immigrants, who conspired with young shysters to swindle wealthy corporations.[46]

Dishonest attorneys undoubtedly filed false claims, while others kept weak cases alive in hope of making a settlement that would provide a generous contingent fee. In negligence suits involving streetcars, which accounted for more than 40 percent of all accident cases, the annual volume of new actions increased by a factor of 93 between 1880 and 1900, while the annual number of reported accidents rose by a factor of 68. Plaintiffs' counselors, however, were not distinguished by any particular characteristics; they were evenly distributed by experience at the bar, and no nationality group was prominent.[47]

The plaintiffs themselves included a variety of Bostonians. Most were small businessmen, low-income white-collar workers, and skilled or semiskilled blue-collar wage earners, but among them were also professionals and major proprietors, as well as unskilled workers. About three-fourths of them were first- or second-generation immigrants, roughly the same proportion as in the city's population. About 30 percent of the plaintiffs were women.[48]

Late-nineteenth-century actuarial records are not specific enough to show which occupational, nationality, or sex groups were over- or underrepresented in court. The dockets, however, suggest that plaintiffs were diverse. The fact that only about 30 percent of the plaintiffs pursued low manual occupations means that negligence suits were not characteristically the speculative ventures of poor Bostonians. Moreover, the proportions of women and immigrant plaintiffs imply that accidental injury was a broad-based problem, drawing into litigation groups that previously had had little need for the trial courts.[49]

The plaintiffs had no single common characteristic; they were injured while walking in the streets, riding in vehicles, working, or just staying at home. It could have been almost anyone. If stereotypes were to be pointed out in personal injury suits, then one should have pointed to the defense table, which was normally occupied by a well-bred Yankee barrister on behalf of a large business or the city government.

SUPPLEMENTS TO NEGLIGENCE LITIGATION

As new technologies and crowded living conditions generated more injuries each year, the tort business of the trial courts grew in importance. The paucity of preventive legislation, as well as the inability of high-court judges to establish clear standards of care and culpability, placed primary responsiblity on the inferior courts for disciplining wrongdoers and indemnifying their victims.

In a typical case the plaintiff's several-hundred-dollar award was not a large penalty for a corporate defendant to pay. However, several dozen or several hundred such payments each year constituted a considerable financial burden. In the traction industry, for example, damage payments were second only to wages on the list of operating expenses, costing more than coal to fuel the generators.[50]

If the judicial process favored defendants in negligence suits, it did not favor them enough to prevent potential defendants of all sorts from seeking additional protection in the form of liability insurance, the popularity of which grew considerably during the 1890s. Similarly, the typically minimal indemnification of victims led growing numbers of individuals to protect themselves or their loved ones with accident and life insurance. Perhaps nine times as many Bostonians were covered by life policies in 1900 as were in 1890. The amount of accident insurance in force probably doubled in the same period.[51]

The purchase of life or accident insurance did not guarantee that the insured or beneficiaries would avoid litigation in all cases, but it did guarantee at least minimal compensation, regardless of what was attempted or achieved in court. In most instances insurance companies paid their policyholders or their beneficiaries with little fuss. There were few lawsuits over claims at the turn of the century. Insurance firms were more contentious for a time in the 1890s, but they were not usually successful and returned to favoring out-of-court settlements. Judicial "reverence for the letter of the law and the sanctity of private interest" was not as "strongly rooted" as judicial "belief in the overriding public worth of a responsibly constructed" insurance system. The judicial process, which made it difficult for accident victims to recover directly from wrongdoers, made it comparatively easy for them to recover from their own or the wrongdoers' insurance companies.[52]

The growth of the life, accident, and liability insurance enterprises, as well as the propensity of litigants to settle out of court, meant that even as trial courts entertained more negligence suits, they imposed a decreasing portion of the settlements that followed accidents. Victims and wrongdoers, their lawyers, and insurance companies assumed primary responsibility for achieving the precise dollar-and-cents adjustments that the dangers of everyday life increasingly demanded.

SEVEN

MALICE

THE swelling wave of negligence suits engulfed and obscured from view a small but rising tide of cases filed in response to a variety of malicious injuries. Fraud, assault, slander, breach of marriage promise, alienation of affection, bastardy, and divorce were civil actions normally founded on the willful infliction of harm. In 1880 there were about 300 lawsuits in these categories, twenty years later, more than 1,000. In both years these actions accounted for 5 or fewer out of every 100 suits initiated. They thus represented a regular, but small, portion of trial-court business.[1]

Lawsuits deriving from malicious injury were concerned with two broad topics: crime and matrimony. Fraud and assault were criminal acts, punishable by the state in its own name. However, when they caused special injury to individuals that was distinct from any suffered by the general public, they gave rise to a civil action. Breach of marriage promise, divorce, and bastardy were matrimonial matters. So, too, were most cases of slander and alienation of affection, because usually they were based on accusations of adultery. Though small in number, civil lawsuits arising from crime or marital misconduct were nevertheless important because they dealt with issues that were vital to the order and harmony of social life.[2]

CRIME

Fraud was a growing concern among Massachusetts legislators in the late nineteenth century. Doubting the capacity of the free market or of contract law to guarantee fair play without help, lawmakers enacted a series of criminal fraud statutes. This spate of legislation obscured continuing attempts to deal directly with fraud through civil litigation.[3]

Legislators' worries notwithstanding, arrest statistics indicate that fraud was a declining problem. Arrest records, however, are suspect because of the nature of the offense. *Fraud* was a vague term of convenience, intended to cover a variety of acts. Legal definitions were fabricated, but it was also asserted that the common law gave no definition. Sociologically speaking, most frauds did "contain the kernel of the 'confidence game' procedure—the creation . . . of a relation of confidence, through which a swindle is effected." Such a broad definition, however, only makes the crime more difficult to measure.[4]

Fraud was probably reported rarely, although it may have been "the most prevalent crime in America." Many victims never realized that they had been defrauded; others were ashamed to reveal their gullibility. Still others developed a close personal relationship with a swindler, which prevented them from making an official complaint. Furthermore, police and prosecutors were reluctant to act on complaints because fraud was difficult to prove if a swindler's misrepresentations related to future rather than to past or present fact. Official reluctance to arrest and to prosecute led victims who were intent on legal action into civil litigation.[5]

The handful of fraud actions filed in 1880 had increased to nearly 100 by the turn of the century. Most lawsuits in 1900 concerned investment swindles, which reflected an increase in speculation, especially in mining stocks, by Bostonians in the late 1890s. The rise in the number of actions for fraud was also the result of the superior court's improved capacity for dealing with swindles through its equity sessions, where half of the suits were filed. Equity did not follow strict common-law rules; its flexibility was ideal for handling the frequently complex circumstances surrounding fraud cases. A judge was empowered to order litigants to take a variety of actions not provided for in common law or statutes. The "unstructured and indefinable" nature of equity powers, however, made Massachusetts lawmakers reluctant to vest the lower courts with them. The superior court was not granted full equity jurisdiction until 1883. It was not conferred on the municipal court, and few, if any, civil cases of fraud were heard there in the 1880s and 1890s.[6]

Both courts were entertaining more torts for assault in 1900 than they had twenty years earlier. There were perhaps 50 such suits entered in 1880, 150 at the turn of the century. Like *fraud*, *assault* was a term used to describe a variety of offenses, but unlike fraud, assault was clearly defined in common law. Criminal statutes specified compound assaults—for example, assault with intent to murder—and prescribed punishment. Civil law, however, dealt with assault, as it did with fraud, not in terms of crime and punishment but in terms of injury and compensation.[7]

Although the civil dockets would seem to reflect a substantial increase in the incidence of assault, police records show only slight growth. The two sets of data may be complementary, however. The police, pressed by an increase in serious crime—murder, manslaughter, robbery, and rape—and increasingly occupied with new duties, such as traffic control, probably devoted less attention to assaults where no serious injury was sustained or where circumstances made indictment and conviction doubtful. Victims of assault, then, filed civil actions when criminal justice was insufficient.[8]

As Boston grew in size and complexity, "the private, direct response to criminal injury was no longer necessary or approved. . . . The victims of violence and theft were conditioned to seek official help." But during the last two decades of the nineteenth century the public may have found policemen less willing to investigate and arrest, prosecutors less inclined to seek indictments and convictions, and judges less prone to punish adequately in minor or hard-to-prove cases of assault and fraud. Moreover, the idea of punishment by fine or imprisonment left some victims dissatisfied, revenged but not materially compensated.[9]

A civil suit depended only on the initiative and persistence of the plaintiff, not on the priorities of the police or district attorney. If damages were awarded, they compensated the victim, not the state. Civil litigation, in short, served as an alternative to extralegal action—an eye for an eye—and as an alternative or a supplement to the abstract retaliation of the criminal justice system. It was the late-nineteenth-century version of the biblical principle of restitution by the criminal to the victim.

Individual initiative was both the strength and the weakness of a civil lawsuit for assault or fraud. It allowed a victim to act legally and independently of public enforcement agencies, but it also forced a victim to rely on his own resources. The plaintiff, not the state, bore the financial burden of prosecution. Plaintiffs' attorneys could have reduced initial costs by taking cases for a contingent fee, but it is unlikely that many of them did so. Those cases too marginal to interest the public prosecutor were, after all, probably too weak to attract the financial interests of an attorney in private practice. Even stronger cases were difficult to prove. Indeed, the results of those civil actions pursued indicate that the financial return was usually not worth the investment. Defendants normally contested suits to the end, rarely defaulting. Three out of every four or five plaintiffs recovered nothing, most of them agreeing to a judgment for neither party or simply dropping the case.[10]

Nine out of ten plaintiffs were skilled blue-collar or white-collar workers, that is, people who presumably had enough income to meet trial costs and to guarantee their lawyers at least a minimum fee. Civil redress for assault or fraud was probably beyond the financial means of low-income manual workers. Moreover, such lawsuits were not directed at them: the defendants, too, came from the white-collar and skilled blue-collar strata. Civil litigation concerning fraud or assault was a frequently vain endeavor in which only people of at least moderate means engaged.[11]

MATRIMONY

Middle-class Bostonians also demanded that the civil trial courts deal increasingly with matrimonial as well as with criminal problems. There was a great deal of argument in the late nineteenth century about the duty of the courts to protect the sanctity of marriage. At issue was the fundamental structure of society. The difficulties between husband and wife were "peculiarly intimate" and as "elusive as human nature itself." They involved "the security of the home, on which the existing state" was "founded, and the welfare of children, on whom the future state" depended.[12]

Controversy centered on divorce. Legislatures and courts were, in practice, at odds on the question of whether it was in the best interests of society to make permanent separation easy or difficult. Statutory grounds were reduced, or at least not expanded, in many states, but the nation's courts granted an increasing number of divorces. The superior court, which had jurisdiction in the matter, followed the national pattern.[13]

In Massachusetts there were eight grounds for divorce, six of which demanded that the libelee (defendant) had committed acts that were knowingly harmful to the libelant (plaintiff). Extreme cruelty as well as cruel and abusive treatment were grounds that clearly required malicious behavior. In addition, a degree of malice was usually a factor in divorces sought for adultery, nonsupport, desertion, and intoxication. The two remaining grounds—imprisonment and impotency—did not usually involve the willful infliction of harm on the libelant, but they accounted for only a few petitions each year. Adultery and desertion were the stated reasons for two out of three actions.[14]

Stated reasons for divorce were not necessarily the real sources of marital discord. Existing evidence indicates that the last third of the nineteenth century saw the rise of the collusive divorce action nationally. Indeed, nine out of ten suits filed in Suffolk County at the turn of the century were uncontested, which suggests that some degree of mutual consent was present in most of them. Moreover, desertion, probably the easiest case to prove, was the basis for more than 40 percent of the suits. Doubtless suspicious of collusion in many suits, the superior court nevertheless approved virtually any petition, if the libelant persisted. Of 415 petitions for divorce filed in Suffolk County in 1900, 351 were granted and 64 withdrawn—that is, not one was refused. Justices were probably swayed by the fact that four out of five plaintiffs had been married for five years or longer and understood their marriages well enough. The superior court apparently felt that when a marriage was dead neither the couple nor the state benefited by denying official recognition of its demise.[15]

Such recognition was not readily available to Bostonians of all classes, however. Plaintiffs were, for the most part, people of at least moderate means. The Boston Legal Aid Society, founded in 1900, willingly represented the poor in nonsupport actions, but it refused most requests to bring divorce libels. The society felt to make divorce easy and cheap would have discouraged reconciliation. Those who could not afford court and lawyer's fees but desired some formal acceptance of their marriage's dissolution filed for a legal separation, "the poor man's divorce," in probate court, where fees were lower and relaxed procedures made counsel unnecessary.[16]

The superior court also dealt with potential as well as existing marriages in actions for breach of marriage promise, of which there were several dozen at the turn of the century. The action was a hybrid, contractual in form, but sounding in tort for damages. That is, when damages were assessed, defendants were assumed to have injured plaintiffs.[17] The law favored a plaintiff in several respects. Although the contract had to be a "clearly apprehended agreement and mutual in character," it did not have to be "formal" or "expressed." To succeed, a defendant had to prove a plaintiff guilty of felonious conduct or of concealing unchastity, serious disease, or severe physical incapacity. Lack of affection was no defense in Massachusetts. Furthermore, the wealth of the defendant, the lost potential wealth of the plaintiff, and the plaintiff's chances for subsequent marriage were taken into consideration when damages were calculated. The law of marriage promise was intended to protect decent women from unscrupulous or irresponsible suitors. The plaintiff whose own moral character was in question, however, was at a disadvantage.[18]

The impulse behind these lawsuits is suggested by the fact that no pair of litigants lived in the same neighborhood. When, for example, a marriage contract between a teacher from Roxbury and a real-estate agent from Braintree was broken, there was little likelihood of effective mediation by their families or by a mutually trusted clergyman. Gone, too, was community pressure, neighborhood or congregational opinion, which encouraged settlement. In their place stood the courts, which acted in much the same propitiatory way as family, church, or neighbors did. That is, the courts usually did not impose a solution, as they did in divorce cases, but allowed the parties to spar with one another for several months, or even years, until they worked out an agreement, typically one that saw no money change hands, at least on the record.[19]

Similarly disappointing financial results were encountered by women who brought paternity suits. Bastardy was the only form of matrimonial action that did not become much more common between 1880 and 1900, although the law continued to favor the prosecutrix. The proceedings, though in substance civil, were still quasi-criminal in nature; that is, a putative father could be arrested under a warrant by the police or by a sheriff at no cost to the plaintiff and held under bond to appear for trial. Moreover, attempts by the defendant to discredit the plaintiff's character were normally rejected, unless they bore directly on the paternity in question. Furthermore, guilt did not have to be established beyond a reasonable doubt, as it did in purely criminal cases. Finally, the courts tended to ride roughshod over procedural matters—imperfect pleading or erroneous writs—raised by the defense.[20]

Nonetheless, the law in action did not favor the prosecutrix. Adjudication was slow. A preliminary hearing in a district court was required before trial could be had in superior court, and suits usually dragged on for four months at least, sometimes for several years. A prosecutrix's reward for her perseverance was disappointing. Only one in four won a favorable decision, and the awards were paltry, based largely on the ability of the father to pay, not on the financial needs of the mother and child. Furthermore, there was little the court could do when a father did not pay. If his whereabouts were known, he could be jailed, but that provided no funds to mother and child.[21]

Compared with the bleak prospects of a bastardy action, the resources of Boston's social agencies for handling the problems of an unwed mother and her child were more attractive. Beginning with the formation of the Associated Charities in 1879, the efforts of various welfare organizations were coordinated through a central index of aid recipients. Relief funds were budgeted to the needy over time, not in emergency lump sums. Important attitude changes were also taking place among charity officials, which may have made their assistance more inviting. Most important was a recognition that the problems of aid recipients had social causes and were not simply the result of personal inadequacy. There was also a growing reluctance to penalize children for the sins of their parents and less readiness to institutionalize illegitimate children.[22]

If unwed mothers were losing interest in legal action

against putative fathers, the charities to which they turned were not. Prior to 1900 a charity retained a lawyer only if prosecution seemed especially necessary or substantial recovery likely. This policy changed with the founding of the Boston Legal Aid Society in that year. It gave the charities a sort of legal department, and they made good use of it in several areas, including the prosecution of bastardy actions. But for the insistence of philanthropic groups, the number of paternity suits filed in 1900 probably would have been much smaller. Yet these actions rarely went to the judge or jury, a settlement being the norm. By 1911 the leadership of the Legal Aid Society, reflecting on the troublesome litigation process, recommended that charities would do better to attempt settlements before resorting to court.[23]

Strictly speaking, bastardy was not a matrimonial cause, but marriage was one possible result of filing suit or of simply threatening to do so. Similarly, slander and alienation of affection were torts that had no formal link to matrimony but in practice usually focused on alleged acts of adultery. Like bastardy and breach of marriage promise, these actions usually took a long time to finish and resulted in no recorded financial gain for plaintiffs, who normally agreed to judgments for defendants or for neither party or simply discontinued suit. From a financial viewpoint, these lawsuits were hardly worth a plaintiff's time and expense.[24]

LITIGATION AS A SAFETY VALVE

Disappointing rates of recovery suggest that most lawsuits for willful injury probably had no practical financial goal. They served instead as outlets for the release of strong emotion. There was an element of emotion in many lawsuits for debt and injury that did not derive from the willful infliction of harm, but the role of feelings is highlighted in this small collection of actions resulting from malicious injury. Often the courts did little more than provide a forum in which the parties aired their views until they settled the matter between them or the plaintiff simply lost interest. Divorce was the notable exception. Reconciliation was uncommon in those proceedings.

While divorce became a lucrative specialty for some lawyers, fraud, assault, breach of marriage promise, bastardy, slander, and alienation of affection did not. Charity workers arranged for the prosecution of some bastardy suits without charge, but lawyers probably took cases for malicious injury only when an alleged victim could guarantee a minimum fee, regardlesss of the outcome. Indeed, four out of five plaintiffs in actions other than divorce came from white-collar or skilled blue-collar backgrounds, that is, they were probably able to afford counsel. Divorce litigants, too, were typically people of moderate means.[25]

With the exception of assault and certain divorces that involved physical abuse, these litigants engaged in legal battles over willful harm to property, reputation, or feelings. It was such forms of loss issuing from crime or marital misconduct that drew an increasing number of Bostonians into civil litigation. In divorce cases the court normally served as a final arbiter, in other lawsuits as a patient listener. In matters of fraud, assault, bastardy, slander, and alienation of affection the process was at least as important as the end result.

CONCLUSION

AT THE THRESHOLD OF THE LAW

THE BUSINESS OF THE TRIAL COURTS

The municipal and superior courts of Boston were forums for the settlement of specific types of disagreements. Debt resulting from extensions of commercial credit, from employment, and from real-property transactions, together with personal injury and property damage, mostly accidental but sometimes willful, accounted for most of their business. In substance, there was nothing unusual about these cases; such actions had comprised the traditional business of the trial courts in Boston for more than two centuries. But the number of lawsuits and proportions of certain actions were unprecedented. The changing litigation pattern stemmed from alterations in the fabric of urban life, imposed by Boston's development from a provincial seaport into one of America's principal manufacturing and distribution centers.[1]

Expanding economic opportunities in commerce and industry attracted and supported thousands of newcomers each year. Boston's growing population itself became a source of profit, a great internal market for a variety of goods and services. In this anonymous marketplace money could be made by trusting a stranger's financial integrity and his ability to meet payments when due. Trust was necessary for conducting most wholesale and many retail sales, for providing professional, clerical, and manual services, and for concluding transactions in real property. When confidence was misplaced, the courtroom was the forum in which to put the matter in order, if the parties could not otherwise reach a settlement. The swelling volume of debt litigation placed a strain on the personnel and facilities of the trial courts. Judges were added to the municipal and superior benches, but dockets remained congested.

The blame for this excessive accumulation cannot be distributed evenly among all types of lawsuits. Individual commercial actions did not remain on the docket much longer in 1900 than they had in 1880. The same was true of eviction petitions, rent claims, and wage demands, which were terminated in three months at most. Mechanic's liens and petitions for assessment of damages or betterment, however, usually remained in court for a year or more. Yet these last two forms of action were few in number; if they had been the only time-consuming lawsuits, dockets would not have remained constantly clogged. The main source of congestion lay outside the area of debt, in the realm of personal injury. At the turn of the century torts amounted to less than half the number of new briefs filed each year in superior court. Nevertheless, it was estimated that they consumed three-fourths of the court's time.

Boston's role as a manufacturing and distribution center in the late nineteenth century meant that Bostonians lived and worked amid thousands of machines, which, when carelessly operated, maimed and killed. Industrial work places were filled with dangerous devices, but most injurious was the streetcar, especially the electric "broomstick" trolley, which came into general use during the 1890s and harmed thousands annually. Wagons, carts, carriages, and trains also contributed to the rising tide of vehicular accidents.

The crowded conditions of urban life likewise increased the chances of injury in older, more familiar ways. Holes in pedestrian-packed thoroughfares created hazards. Danger lay beneath heavily traveled and thickly inhabited streets in the form of leaking gas and hovered above them in the form of debris ready to fall. In addition, malicious injury to person, property, or reputation generated a small but growing number of lawsuits.

Torts took longer to resolve than matters of debt because they were usually surrounded by an air of uncertainty. The applicable substantive law was often vague, particularly about the important issue of contributory negligence. Moreover, the cash value of a specific loss was difficult to estimate. Much depended on the testimony of sometimes elusive or uncertain witnesses. Plaintiffs customarily demanded a jury trial, believing that it was easier to win sympathy from their peers than from an experienced, hardened judge. The impaneling of jurors, the lengthy examinations and summations that lawyers employed to impress them, and their deliberations at the end of a trial added days or weeks to the process. Furthermore, the contingent fee gave the plaintiff's attorney a personal as well as a professional interest in a case, encouraging him to hold out for a settlement that at least covered his fees.

By comparison, the law of debt based on negotiable instruments and other commercial documents was better defined than was tort law in the late nineteenth century. Plaintiffs normally presented documents to substantiate their claims. A properly executed promissory note or other instrument of indebtedness made the calling of many witnesses unnecessary and also made it easier to determine the amount owed. Most debt actions were open-and-shut affairs in which defendants did not contest plaintiffs' demands. But although they could be adjudicated in several minutes, such actions often waited on tort-clogged calendars for weeks or months before coming to trial. Troublesome lawsuits delayed completion of easily settled ones.[2]

The unprecedented quantity of litigation in the 1890s fundamentally affected the administration of justice in Boston. In addition to facts and law, delay became a major element of each case, a factor always considered and often used by the parties and their attorneys. In litigation, time was indeed money, and time was usually on the defendant's side. In an action for debt, the duration of the trial was a de facto extension of the repayment period. In an action for personal injury, time healed wounds, reducing or erasing the suffering of victims and with it the sympathy of judges and jurors. Litigants and lawyers of the 1890s had to ask themselves, more cautiously than ever before, whether litigation was worth the time and expense. In thousands of instances annually the answer was still yes. For those who decided to litigate, however, the question was not asked once but several times during the course of a trial. An early agreement could have been more satisfactory to both parties than a judgment coming months or years later.

An important part of the routine by which the bench and bar handled the voluminous business before them was the unofficial specialization of the municipal court in debt cases and of the superior court in personal-injury actions. The latter originated in the preference of victims for a jury trial, either initially or on appeal. As torts began to monopolize the resources of the superior court, creditors with demands below the municipal court's $2,000 claim limit developed a preference for its swifter, juryless sessions. Neither tribunal assumed exclusive jurisdiction over debt or injury matters, but an informal division of labor existed by 1900.[3]

In superior court, settlements also became routine. At the turn of the century nearly half of the actions ended with written agreements. Harried judges were content to let litigants find their own solutions. This was especially true in torts, where the determination of culpability and the assessment of damages were often nightmarish tasks for the bench.[4]

In both courts costs and delays in various common forms of action established figures below which it did not pay to sue. Similarly, costs and delays fashioned informal recovery schedules that the parties understood and employed in reaching out-of-court settlements. They also guided judges and jurors in rendering judgment.

These schedules influenced plaintiffs and their lawyers

when setting the amount of a claim, the *ad damnum*. If they expected to negotiate a settlement, the initial demand had to be the highest they could justify. The *ad damnum* was also adjusted to a figure above or below $2,000 to ensure an initial hearing in either municipal or superior court, whichever seemed most advantageous.

The specialization of the municipal court in debt and of the superior court in injury litigation, as well as the creation of routines in each tribunal for managing its caseload, was accompanied by the specialization of some attorneys in the prosecution or defense of particular kinds of lawsuits. At the turn of the century most trial lawyers were still generalists, but experts were appearing in the fields of accidental injury and eviction. In the tort area, a poorly defined, rapidly evolving body of law rewarded concentration and experience with an impressive rate of success. In eviction hearings, success came by scrupulously following statutory procedures.

Specialization and routinization could have lubricated judicial machinery, reducing delay and expense. A lawyer who concentrated on a specific area of practice acquired a working knowledge sufficient to permit him to manage ordinary cases without much research and to identify quickly problems that demanded special attention. An efficient specialist also spent fewer hours working on an ordinary case than did a generalist, saving money for his client and time for the court. However, experts in defense, especially those who represented street railways and other enterprises in negligence suits, used delay to save their clients money. They could keep cases alive for years, if necessary, until plaintiffs became discouraged enough to settle. If routine maneuvers expedited debt litigation, especially the petty actions filed in the municipal court, personal-injury litigation, especially in the superior court, was just as routinely delayed.[5]

The sequence of congestion, delay, expense, and routinization affected the quality of justice obtainable in

the Boston trial courts. Merchants and moneylenders recovered only portions of what was owed them. They might
have won their money in a few weeks, but it often took several months, sometimes years. Blue- and white-collar wage
claimants faced similar situations. Indeed, the wages in
question were often so small that no lawyer would take the
case, except as an act of charity. Lawyers and doctors
employed the credit practices of tradesmen, which included suing on a debt, if necessary. They usually recovered the full amount claimed but were subject to the
same delays as commercial people. Landlords who wished
to evict tenants had an easy time in court, but landlords
bringing money claims against tenants encountered the
same problems with expense and deferred action as did
commercial and professional plaintiffs. The same was also
true of builder-creditors and of property owners contest-
ing eminent-domain valuations.

The books on debt collection that appeared at the end of
the nineteenth and beginning of the twentieth centuries
were unanimous in recommending litigation only as a last
resort. Lawsuits, their authors advised, were too slow, too
costly, and too likely to stir up emotions that would harm
business. These credit manuals emphasized a preventive
course of action, involving financial investigation of pros-
pective debtors, substantial down payments, and clearly
stated, manageable repayment schedules. If debtors fell
behind, credit experts advised creditors to send carefully
worded letters and even to renegotiate terms. A lawsuit was
a final dunning device, proper only when the sum out-
standing was substantial or when an uncooperative customer needed to be disciplined. Many who tried to collect a
debt through the Boston trial courts would have called this
sound advice.

Unfortunately, credit ratings, the backbone of the preventive approach, were compiled only on some of those
who owned businesses. Local associations of merchants
and professionals sporadically published lists of habitual

debtors, but the typical customer, client, employer, patient, or tenant did not appear in any credit reference at the turn of the century. Creditors relied on intuition, cajolery, and, ultimately, on the trial courts to avoid serious financial losses.

Creditors could at least minimize the need for litigation because they could estimate the extent of their risks in advance, but victims of personal injury usually faced a loss that was, at best, only vaguely anticipated. Everyone who worked around machinery, rode trolleys, or simply walked the city streets knowingly chanced injury, but they had no idea when or to what extent they would be harmed. The odds were that nothing would happen to them. Every year, however, a few thousand unlucky people were hurt or killed in falls, collisions, explosions, and assaults. A few hundred more were swindled or had their reputations sullied. In the late nineteenth century prudent Bostonians protected loved ones with life insurance policies. Some companies were selling casualty insurance, but the enterprise was new. There was no insurance against losses from fraud or insult.

Losses from death not covered by insurance and from most nonfatal injuries could be indemnified through litigation. Indemnification, however, was hardly the word to describe the actual process of accidental-injury adjudication in the Boston trial courts, at least not if the plaintiffs' claims bore any resemblance to the real value of the injuries sustained. Rarely did the victim recover more than 10 percent of the *ad damnum*. Claims were inflated, of course, as part of a plaintiff's bargaining strategy. It was difficult for judges and jurors to assess actual damage, and the passage of time has not made it easier for the historian to say whether or not the compensation received was just. Certainly the recovery of $100 from a $5,000 claim after a year or more of litigation was a psychological, if not a financial, defeat.

The system was apparently one of minimal compensation. A typical award of $500 or less resembled a penalty against an erring defendant more than an actual valuation of culpability and loss. The victim received enough to meet some or all of his legal and immediate medical expenses, while the defendant was fined for carelessness. The precise sum in each case was usually reached in out-of-court negotiations. Compensation was a commodity to be bought and sold. Delay and the costs of litigation were the decisive market factors.

When awards were insufficient to cover the financial needs of injured parties or their dependents, who as a result required charitable assistance, the effect was to shift the burden of negligence from the individual defendant to the community. For Boston's street railways, the defendants in nearly half of the negligence suits at the turn of the century, this resulted in a considerable subsidy.

On a much smaller scale, individual plaintiffs subsidized public welfare by bringing suits for malicious injury. Using their own resources, they prosecuted putative delinquents for alleged acts of assault, fraud, bastardy, and slander, which were injurious to public order. Culprits were usually not treated severely; little money changed hands. In these actions, too, awards resembled fines more than recompense. Such lawsuits were useful as safety valves for relieving emotional pressures. They punished a little as they compensated a little. The process was at least as important as the result.

The Constituency of the Trial Courts

The direct costs of litigation, that is, court and lawyers' fees, plus the indirect costs of delay—loss of time from work, diminished evidence of injury—meant that few of the poor in Boston could afford to sue. White-collar Bostonians—professionals, businessmen, clerical employees, salespeople, and members of their households—accounted for about 80 percent of the plaintiffs in the 1880s and 1890s. The rest were predominantly skilled blue-collar workers.

On the defense side, a similar white-collar pattern prevailed. If blue-collar workers, especially the semi- and unskilled, did not sue frequently, they were at least not sued often. The same lack of means that prevented many of them from litigating also protected them from lawsuits, because there was little to gain by pursuing a penniless defendant. They were judgment-proof. There was potential gain, however, in filing suit against a wealthy corporation, and Bostonians did this increasingly between 1880 and 1900. Damage actions against street railways, steam railroads, express companies, gas utilities, and the city government multiplied at a greater rate than other types of lawsuits during those twenty years.

Profitability was as much a concern of plaintiff's counsel as it was of his client, particularly when all or part of his fees were contingent on the outcome of a case. Members of the bar complained that some trial lawyers were more concerned with profitability than with a client's best interests. They noted, and evidence assembled here confirms, that considerable increases in litigation at the century's end were accompanied by increases in the number of lawyers practicing in Boston's trial courts.

It is difficult to say whether the trial bar met or exceeded the need for litigation. Damage actions against street railways, most often suspected of being shysters' speculations, multiplied somewhat faster than the number of streetcar accidents. Increased litigation concerning commercial credit, emoluments, and real property, however, is attributable to real changes in the marketplace. There is, finally, no sure way of determining which lawsuits were unnecessary. In any case, the critics' argument that a lawyer's quest for income led him to draw clients into unnecessary litigation assumes that such a policy was always most profitable. Lawyers, however, prosper in the long run not by deceiving their clients but by satisfying them. The

attorney who wished to build a practice was not likely to
expose his clients to the frustrations of the judicial process
unless all other measures had failed. Critics of trial lawyers
pointed to the crowded dockets, but they did not know how
many legal problems were settled without litigation. Had
they known, the number of disagreements adjudicated
might have seemed small indeed.

The Function of the Trial Courts

Since thousands of legal conflicts were settled without litigation, the function of trial courts was to enter those disputes arising from debt or injury where only the weight of
the state could bring a satisfactory ending. The court could
impose a solution on the parties, but increasingly after
1880 the parties worked out their own settlements under
the eyes of the court. Crowded calendars encouraged
judges to be flexible, to permit the litigants to do as much
for themselves as possible. The bench exerted enough
background pressure to keep them moving toward a settlement.

The flexibility of its machinery made the trial court an
essential institution. Legislation and high-court opinion
erected general doctrines by which the state could inter-
pose itself in conflicts resulting from debt or injury, but the
trial courts provided the process by which the state acted in
thousands of specific disputes that resembled one another
but whose circumstances required an individualized resolution.

Flexibility was purchased at the expense of efficiency.
The courts adjudicated thousands of variations on traditional themes in debt and injury litigation, but not as
quickly as they were presented. Far more radical routinization would have prevented a backlog, but it also would
have destroyed the semblance of individual consideration
that the public expected from the judicial branch of government. The legislature manufactured law wholesale, the

high court fashioned it for retail consumption, and the trial courts provided the final alterations for each consumer.

The inefficiency of trial courts should have been particularly annoying to a generation of reform-minded politicians and other public-spirited Bostonians who were obsessed with infusing efficiency and economy into governmental operations. The three decades after 1880 saw the heyday of the good-government movement in the Hub. The "goo-goos," among them many lawyers, advanced a number of ideas for streamlining the activities of the executive and legislative branches of the city government. Simply stated, they wished to take power from the wasteful, machine-dominated city council and concentrate it in the hands of a high-minded, tight-fisted Brahmin mayor and a merit-based civil service. Many of their ideas were incorporated in the new city charter of 1885 and implemented under reform mayor Nathan Matthews (1891-1895).[6]

.Little was done, however, to streamline the activities of the judicial branch of local government. The same mistrust of urban masses that encouraged men of property to attack the growing influence of the immigrant political machines in the executive and legislative branches made them reluctant to tinker with the judicial branch, which they regarded as a buffer against these new political forces. The delays and costs that annoyed men of means when they sued also protected them from the suits of others.[7]

Furthermore, the courts were by nature passive; that is, they waited for issues to be brought before them. In the late nineteenth and early twentieth centuries the scope of issues coming before the trial courts seemed rather narrow to reformers anxious to make an immediate impact. They lavished their attention on the executive and legislative branches, where they were able to initiate change in a variety of areas that interested them.

The speed with which the number of lawsuits multiplied annually meant that even a few years' delay in reforming

court procedures had serious consequences. While a complete overhaul of the judicial system was deferred, make-
shift repairs kept things moving; judges were added, out-
of-court settlements encouraged, informal and somewhat
arbitrary recovery schedules adopted. Fundamental
changes—removing certain classes of actions to administrative tribunals, levying defendants' costs on plaintiffs in nui-
sance suits, limiting the time for examination of witnesses,
limiting the right of appeal, and accepting less than
unanimous verdicts—were avoided. As a result, the judicial
process quickly ossified under a crushing caseload.[8]

The less efficient the trial courts became, the more often
they were bypassed by creditors and the injured. After
eight years of spectacular growth the number of suits filed
annually suddenly leveled off in 1898 and remained steady
until World War I. A saturation point had been reached.
The trial courts entertained the problems of about 20,000
plaintiffs a year. Other Bostonians sought relief through
the services of credit agencies and insurance companies,
enterprises that grew rapidly after 1900. The more often
the courts were bypassed in favor of other forms of relief,
the more marginal they appeared, and the less worthy they
seemed of public attention and investment.[9]

Measured by the standards of credit and insurance
agencies, the services of the trial courts were inefficient and
expensive, but that was usually the case when public and
private enterprise were compared. Credit and insurance
agencies chose their clientele, limited the amount of business they did, specialized in certain types of debt or injury,
and expanded their operations as business expanded. The
trial courts were not able to make such choices, at least not
easily.

The inability of the trial bench to determine the kind of
business it would entertain was its greatest handicap, but it
was also the characteristic that made the trial courts indis-
pensable urban institutions. When vehicular accidents
suddenly became a pressing problem in the late 1880s and

1890s, the trial courts were at hand to alleviate distress while legislators, high-court judges, and business executives debated long-term solutions. When new competition or new sources of potential profit drove retailers, wholesalers, bankers, brokers, landlords, or builders to extend credit unwisely, the trial courts were there to help reduce losses and promote discipline until credit-granting procedures were stabilized.

The trial courts settled a variety of urban problems arising from debt and from injury well enough to prevent chaos but badly enough to encourage the development of other means for dealing with them in the future. What they did and did not do had a subtle, but profound, effect on the growth of modern Boston.[10]

The trial courts had a direct influence on spatial manipulation through the thousands of real-estate matters brought before them. Housing in Boston was largely unregulated by statute. Builders, owners, buyers, and tenants traded in a free market. Boardinghouses, tenements, and single-family dwellings were provided by a host of petty entrepreneurs who risked their savings in hopes of profit. It was often necessary for these speculators to protect their investments by filing eviction petitions, rent claims, mechanic's liens, and petitions for the assessment of damage. The limited protection afforded by the trial courts provided landlords and builders with a degree of security in a risky market, encouraging them to supply the accommodations demanded by a swelling population.

The trial courts also influenced physical development in much the same manner, if not to the same extent, as did the street railways. The transit system spurred the building of residential communities outside the pedestrian city of 1850 by linking these new suburbs to the central business district and to one another. Similarly, the municipal and superior courts provided satisfactory legal connections among the individual sections of the metropolis. Creditors and debtors, victims and wrongdoers from various neighborhoods, suburbs, and satellite towns settled their differences in the centrally located courthouse on Pemberton Square under rules and in circumstances familiar to any lawyer they were likely to retain.

By ordering or encouraging thousands of settlements each year, the trial courts served as an essential disciplinary instrument. They disciplined directly by forcing debtors or those responsible for the injury of others to meet their obligations. However, by mitigating those obligations in many cases, the courts made it clear that each individual, not the state, was primarily responsible for his or her well-being. Financial and physical risks were taken with the knowledge that the law was not likely to provide full compensation for losses.

Losses occurred nevertheless, and, in thousands of personal-injury suits particularly, Bostonians learned to place precise dollar-and-cents values on themselves and their activities, to estimate the worth of a limb, of a spouse's company and service, of a reputation. Such estimates had been made before, but never so routinely by so many people. The routine of litigation, however, chipped away at the individuality of a Bostonian. The judicial process did not appraise particular loss but an abstract category of loss. In crowded dockets individual plaintiffs and defendants blended into an undifferentiated whole.

Production-line justice was not without its benefits, however. Boston drew its people from many cultures. Small-town Yankees, immigrants from two dozen countries, southern blacks, and, of course, native Bostonians were accustomed to various systems of justice. With the notable exception of black Bostonians, people participated in the judicial process as plaintiffs and defendants regardless of their ethnic antecedents. The thousands of suits in which these diverse people were involved, or of which they heard, homogenized their notions of law, if not of justice. That common understanding of one's legal rights and responsibilities was crucial in Boston's crowded society, where promiscuous contacts were multiplied and with them the possibilities for antisocial behavior.

Unanswered Questions

This study has suggested that the pattern of urban litigation in Boston varied according to several factors, including state and local law, court structure, the presence of certain industrial and commercial enterprises, the size and composition of the population and of the bar, and the deployment of consumer technologies. A combination of people and activities similar to those that produced Boston's lawsuits should have generated roughly the same litigation pattern elsewhere. The great eastern seaports of New York, Philadelphia, and Baltimore and the inland entrepôts of Chicago, St. Louis, and Cincinnati, which industrialized at about the same time as Boston (though in different ways) and, like the Hub, absorbed many newcomers from the surrounding countryside and overseas, could have experienced similar litigation patterns. The ethnic and racial mixtures in these communities differed, however. Did a greater number and proportion of blacks or of immigrants from lands where English and the common law were virtually unknown affect the use of trial courts?[11]

Did the inhabitants of southern cities such as Charleston and New Orleans employ civil litigation in ways that reflected the legacy of slavery, the reign of King Cotton, and the paucity of industry? How did the presence of one or two dominant industries or companies alter the litigation pattern? Holyoke, Massachusetts, for example, was governed by the same statutes and judicial opinions as Boston. The city was built with Boston's money and Irish immigrants. Its economy, however, was based almost entirely on paper and textile manufacture controlled by absentee owners, and its population was less than one-tenth that of the Hub City proper. To what use was civil litigation put in just such a small manufacturing city?[12]

Across the country in the late nineteenth and early twentieth centuries cities were nurtured by a variety of enterprises. Denver in the 1870s and 1880s became the metropolis of a great western mining and cattle empire. At the same time, livestock and grain turned prairie villages like Wichita into cities of 25,000 in a decade. The populations of these western boom towns included much smaller proportions of the foreign-born than did those of many cities of the East and Middle West. Did the homogeneity of population and of economic activity make these new communities less litigious?[13]

The timing as well as the manner of growth might have been important. Seattle, for example, began its period of initial development in the late 1890s, serving as the gateway to the Alaskan gold fields. Did Seattle's inhabitants take advantage of the judicial experiences of older metropolises?[14]

There is, moreover, evidence of the spread of urban patterns of litigation to rural areas. That is, the litigious characteristics of cities and small towns may have become less distinguishable as mass media and mass transportation bound urban and rural communities into one urban, industrial society.[15]

This list of questions is not exhaustive; it is intended merely to suggest how much we could learn from America's trial-court records. Time is short, however. Of little day-to-day value to bar and bench, these documents have disintegrated slowly or have been discarded to make room for newer cases. Much remains, but it will survive only through use. In this sense, daylight will be the most powerful preservative.

APPENDIXES

SOURCES AND SAMPLES

SOURCES

Sample cases were drawn from civil records of the Boston Municipal Court and of the Superior Court of Suffolk County. These records are maintained in two separate collections, dockets and papers.

The dockets are ledgers in which the clerks and their assistants entered the names of parties, their attorneys, the type of action (contract, tort, replevin, or some special petition), the sum of money claimed by the plaintiff (*ad damnum*), a list of documents submitted, intermediate and final decisions of the court, and the date on which judgment was executed. Dockets of the superior court also indicate whether or not a jury trial was demanded by either party. Trial by jury was not available in municipal court.

Papers comprise all documents filed with the clerk, including: motions for a variety of decisions by judges; depositions; interrogatories and answers to them; reports of auditors, assessors, referees, and masters; witness and jury lists; and declarations by plaintiffs and defendants. Assortments vary from one case to the next. In some actions only a plaintiff's declaration was filed. This, however, was the most important paper in a packet, for it stated a plaintiff's reasons for bringing suit and usually included specific information about the debt or injury in question. In a debt action, for example, a plaintiff's declaration normally stated the goods or services involved and their value. For injury lawsuits, a plaintiff's declaration usually specified the circumstances under which the harm was done, the nature of the injury, and the value of losses incurred. If a suit stemmed from an accident, for example, the declaration

stated where, when, and how the accident took place, the
physical and mental injuries allegedly sustained, the extent
of any property damage (for example, to a vehicle), the
cost of repairs, and the value of damage that could not be
repaired. Those defendants who did not default also filed a
declaration. Unfortunately, these documents usually contain nothing more than a blanket repudiation of the plaintiff's claims. Under Massachusetts law, defendants were
permitted to file general denials and present specific oral
defenses during trial.[1]

Oral arguments of plaintiffs and defendants were recorded by court-appointed stenographers; however, tran-
scripts were produced only when judges, jurors, or one of
the parties requested them. The parties had to pay for
their copies, which became their personal property; they
were not filed with official papers. Stenographic notes were
kept in books not filed with official papers. Some early-
nineteenth-century notebooks have survived in the vaults
of the municipal and superior courts, but those pertaining
to the late nineteenth and early twentieth centuries have
not. Lost with those notebooks is the courtroom drama, the
give-and-take of each trial.[2]

Without the oral pleadings of parties, the language of
judges, and the testimony of witnesses, precise dissection of
each case is impossible. The flesh is gone; only bones remain. As with the scattered relics found at an archaeologi-
cal site, the meaning of what survives lies not within each
fragment but in the relationship of fragments to one
another and to their surroundings. To connect those rem-
nants, to infuse those skeletal remains with life, it was
necessary to employ other sources. The most important
supplementary sources are the manuscript federal census
schedules of 1880 and 1900 and their indexes. Court records usually tell nothing more about litigants, lawyers,
judges, and jurors than their names. Even addresses, professional titles, and occupations of litigants normally are
not recorded. Fortunately, the lives of all but a few judges

are documented in various biographies. The manuscript census schedules provide background data on the far more obscure litigants and jurors, specifically: the individual's sex, age, race, ethnic origins, exact residence, and occupation. Lawyers, of course, are also listed in these schedules.[3]

Not all litigants were individuals; a number of partnerships and corporations were among them. Directories for Boston and surrounding communities were used to determine the nature of these businesses and their precise locations. Directories were also the source for business addresses of individuals, and they were used to confirm occupations. Where schedules and directories disagree about someone's vocation, the schedule listing was adopted, because schedules have been shown to be more reliable.[4]

Both sources have their biases. Census takers missed people who moved during enumeration. Underenumeration may have reached nearly 10 percent. Directories also failed to include many mobile individuals, which means that they often overlooked blacks, unskilled and semi-skilled laborers, immigrants, and those with less than $1,000 in taxable property. The bias against transients means that the data assembled here provides a more accurate description of Boston's settled population.[5]

A similar bias was built into *R. G. Dun's Mercantile Reference Book*, which was used to determine the assets and credit ratings of litigating businessmen or businesses. Dun's reference books were widely used throughout the United States, Canada, and Europe in the late nineteenth century but were often criticized for their inaccuracies. Credit information was compiled through a network of correspondents who interviewed those to be listed. If an interview could not be arranged, correspondents simply estimated the worth and reliability of an enterprise. There were certainly opportunities for bribery or revenge. More important, the Dun network often overlooked small businesses, at least during their first year or two in operation. Dun ratings, therefore, have been used in this study to provide suggestive rather than exact information. Those Boston-area enterprises listed by Dun in 1880 and 1900 with assets of $1,000 or more and a "good" or higher credit rating were considered "established." Those listed in the lowest asset category, less than $1,000, with a "fair" credit rating or none at all and those not listed were considered "marginal."[6]

Four additional sources provide valuable information about trial lawyers. *The Professional and Industrial History of Suffolk County* (Boston, 1894), Volume I, edited by William T. Davis, attempted to record every lawyer who had been admitted to the Suffolk bar through June 1892. Entries range from elaborate biographies to mere listings of years of admission to the bar. In most cases, however, an attorney's legal education is indicated. The Supreme Judicial Court of Massachusetts maintained a card file of all lawyers admitted to practice in the state; this was used to provide the date of admission for those lawyers not listed in the *Professional History*. Additional Harvard Law School alumni were identified from the quinquennial lists published by that institution. Unfortunately, such lists are not available for Boston University's law graduates. Prominent trial attorneys or firms were isolated from lesser lights by using *Hubbell's Legal Directory*. This reference claimed to list only "able and trustworthy" attorneys in cities and towns throughout the United States. Its compilers relied on recommendations of bankers and leading merchants. The ratings were, of course, subjective, but they at least indicate that a lawyer or firm was well known.[7]

SAMPLES

The random sample employed in this study, 1,445 cases, was large enough to provide a reliability of ±5 percent at a confidence level of 95 percent. In other words, 95 out of 100 times a sample of this magnitude reproduces the characteristics of the entire population being sampled with a ± 5 percent margin of error.[8]

Actually, four separate samples were collected at these reliability and confidence levels, one each from the dockets of the superior and of the municipal court for the year 1880, one from the dockets of the superior court for 1900, and one from the dockets of the municipal court for 1902. The municipal court dockets for 1900 have survived, but the papers relating to those cases have mysteriously disappeared, along with some 40,000 others from the years 1898, 1899, and 1901. This loss was not discovered until the data from the superior court had been collected. It was decided, therefore, to sample cases from the closest surviving year, 1902, and to treat them together with the superior court sample of 1900 as representative of litigation at the turn of the century.[9]

These four samples, sometimes referred to collectively in the text or notes as "the sample," are four snapshots of litigation in the late nineteenth and early twentieth centuries. It would have been possible to sample from each year of the 1880s, 1890s, and 1900s to produce a sort of motion picture instead of four stills. This might have revealed annual fluctuations and would have eliminated any eccentricities present in the litigation of 1880, 1900, or 1902. However, the process of linking the participants in lawsuits to individuals listed in the manuscript schedules of the United States census made that form of dynamic sampling impractical.[10]

Litigants presented the greatest tracing problems. Court records provide a name, a town or city of residence, and sometimes a suggestion of occupation by the nature of the lawsuit. Only petitions for eviction specify an address, and then only for the defendant. Often a litigant's full name is not provided. Initials replaced names, middle initials frequently were not recorded. Many plaintiffs and defendants had common surnames—Murphy, Smith, Brown. Moreover, the population of Boston was highly mobile in the late nineteenth and early twentieth centuries. Some litigants with easily identifiable names moved into or out of the court-recorded place of residence after the census was taken. Under these circumstances, identifying the litigants of 1880, 1900, or 1902 in the census schedules of 1880 or of 1900 was difficult enough. Identifying with some degree of certainty a substantial portion of litigants from other years would have been more an act of faith than of reason. The process would have been further confounded by the absence of the census schedules for 1890, which were destroyed by fire in 1921. Indeed, the destruction of those schedules prevented the sampling of cases filed in 1890, which would have created two additional snapshots. Attrition was a problem nevertheless. In only a few sample cases was all of the desired information compiled on plaintiffs, defendants, and their attorneys. Profiles of the participants did emerge in the aggregate, however.[11]

Because the observations made here rest on samples, standard statistical tests were employed throughout to determine significance when differences or similarities could be explained by sampling error. In instances where a major statement of fact is based on a sample, the sample size (N) is indicated. Two-sample proportions have been contrasted throughout the text and notes. Unless otherwise indicated, difference-of-proportion tests were performed and the null hypothesis rejected at the .05 level.

Statistical significance, however, was viewed as a matter of subjective judgment. Though calculated by precise means, levels of significance were considered together with corroborating or conflicting historical evidence of the traditional kind. A trend was not rejected if, for example, it did not meet the .05 level of significance in a t-test but did confirm the recollections of a trial lawyer. Statistical data and literary exposition were combined in the text and notes. Statistical tests supplemented, but did not supplant, historical judgments.[12]

CLASSIFICATION OF CASES

THE classification scheme employed in this study did not adhere strictly to distinctions that a lawyer would have made. Debt actions were considered largely matters of contract law, but not exclusively so. Injury actions were mostly torts, but also included were several nontortious causes. The groups reflect, in lay terms, distinct, if broad, areas of human activity. Judges, for example, considered a promissory note under the law of negotiable instruments and a refund under the law of sales, but both are products of commercial activity, of buying and selling goods. Courts treated slander under the law of torts and breach of marriage promise under the law of contracts, but both involve damage to someone's reputation.

In 1880, 78 percent of the 698 sample plaintiffs were suing for debt and 7 percent for injury. The remaining 15 percent were suing for miscellaneous or unknown reasons. The three figures for 1900 were: 70 percent, debt; 25 percent, injury; 5 percent, miscellaneous or unknown (sample N = 747).

For the purposes of this study, the types of actions considered as debt or injury were:

DEBT

Commercial Credit
  unpaid bill for items purchased or rented (open account)
  unpaid promissory note (for goods purchased or rented)
  unpaid promissory note (for money loaned)
  unpaid promissory note (unspecified)
  uncollectable check or bill of exchange
  unrepaid loan (unspecified)
  failure to purchase items ordered

   failure to deliver items purchased
   unsettled insurance claim
   unpaid premium or mortgage installment
   replevin
   refund or damages for inadequate goods or services
   partnership partition
   conversion (certain cases)
Emoluments
   unpaid wages or fees
   unpaid commission
   promise of employment withdrawn
Real Property
   ejectment (eviction)
   rent claim
   mechanic's lien on building
   assessment for damage or betterment to property

INJURY

Accidental Injury
   streetcar accident
   steam railroad accident
   other vehicular accident
   gas leak
   industrial accident (other than streetcar or railroad)
   other accidental injury
Malicious Injury
   fraud
   assault
   slander
   alienation of affection
   breach of marriage promise
   bastardy

MISCELLANEOUS

Special Petitions
   enforcement of previous judgment
   writ of protection
   complaint for costs
   other petitions

APPENDIX C

OCCUPATIONS AND ENTERPRISES

OCCUPATION was used for two purposes: to indicate socio-economic status in a rough way and to describe what litigants did for a living. Occupations were classified for the first purpose according to a scheme employed by Stephan Thernstrom and others (see below, occupational rankings). One modification was made regarding the distinction between major and petty proprietors. Thernstrom used assessment rolls to determine whether an individual had at least $1,000 in personal property or $5,000 in real estate, the dividing line between major and petty status. The tax records, however, do not state the taxpayer's address or occupation, which makes identification difficult. Here, assets listed in *R. G. Dun's Mercantile Reference Book* were substituted for assessments. Dun's listings were limited to proprietors and indicated the line of business, which made identification easier and presumably more certain. Individuals with $1,000 or more in assets were considered major proprietors; those with less than $1,000 were considered petty proprietors.[1]

One other modification was made regarding persons listed in Thernstrom's study as "manufacturer," "merchant," "proprietor or manager of a small business," and "self-employed artisan." The specific businesses in which these people were engaged were recorded in order to study the relationship between certain lines of enterprise and civil litigation (see below, Lines of Enterprise). In addition, certain occupations that did not exist in the period 1880-1900 were deleted from Thernstrom's list, which covers the period 1880-1970.[2]

OCCUPATIONAL RANKINGS

White-Collar Occupations

HIGH WHITE-COLLAR

Professionals

architect
chemist
clergyman
editor
engineer (except
   locomotive or
   stationary)

lawyer
pharmacist
physician
scientist
social worker
teacher
veterinarian

Major Proprietors, Managers, and Officials[3]

banker
broker
builder, contractor (with
  sufficient property)
corporation official
government official
  (upper ranks only)[4]
hotel keeper or manager

labor-union officer
manufacturer (see Lines
  of Enterprise below)
merchant (with sufficient
  property, see Lines of
  Enterprise below)
ship's captain

LOW WHITE-COLLAR

Clerks and Salesmen

accountant
agent
auctioneer
auditor
baggageman
bank teller
bill collector
bookkeeper
canvasser
cashier
clerk
collector

conveyancer
credit man
dispatcher
insurance adjuster or
  salesman
mail carrier
messenger
office boy
salesman
secretary
telegrapher
typist

Semiprofessionals

actor
artist
athlete
chiropodist
chiropractor
designer
dietician
draftsman
embalmer
entertainer
harbor pilot
journalist

librarian
musician
newspaperman
nurse
optician, optometrist
osteopath
photographer
surveyor
technician (medical, dental, electrical, etc.)
writer

Petty Proprietors, Managers, and Officials

foreman
huckster, peddler (see Lines of Enterprise below)
minor government official

proprietor or manager of a small business (see Lines of Enterprise below)
railroad conductor
self-employed artisan (see Lines of Enterprise below and note 3)

Blue-Collar Occupations

SKILLED[5]

baker
blacksmith
boilermaker
bookbinder
bricklayer, mason
carpenter, cabinetmaker
caulker
compositor, printer
confectioner
coppersmith
craneman, derrickman
electrician

engineer (locomotive or stationary)
engraver
fireman (locomotive)
furrier
glasier
goldsmith
jeweler
lithographer
machinist
master mariner, diver
mechanic

millwright
molder
painter
paperhanger
patternmaker
pianomaker
plasterer
plumber
roofer
saddler
shoemaker (except in fac-
tory; see semiskilled
workers below)
silversmith
slater
steamfitter
stonecutter
tailor, dressmaker
tinner
tool-and-die maker
upholsterer
watchmaker

SEMISKILLED AND SERVICE WORKERS

apprentice
barber, hairdresser
bartender
brakeman
constable, deputy sheriff
cook
cooper
deliveryman
elevator operator
factory operative
fireman (stationary or
    city)
fisherman
guard, watchman
hospital attendant
janitor
lineman, lamplighter
longshoreman
meatcutter
milkman
motorman
policeman
sailor
servant
soldier (except officers)
stevedore
switchman
teamster
waiter
welder

UNSKILLED LABORERS AND MENIAL SERVICE WORKERS

coachman
gardener
hostler, liveryman
laborer
lumberman
porter

MISCELLANEOUS

housewife
no occupation
student

The lines of enterprise that appear below were coded for litigants. Some of them apply only to corporate plaintiffs and defendants. Most, however, apply either to corporate or to self-employed, individual litigants. In the case of individuals, the assets attributed to them by *R. G. Dun's Mercantile Reference Book* determined whether they were placed in the high white-collar or low white-collar category of occupational rankings above (see note 3).

LINES OF ENTERPRISE

agricultural supplies
auction house
bakery
bank (corporate only)
barber shop
boots and shoes, retail
boots and shoes, wholesale
brushes
builder's supplies
business machines
carriages or bicycles
chemicals
clothing and fabric, retail
clothing and fabric, wholesale
coal and wood
commission merchant
confectionaries
crockery, china, glassware
department store
drugs, retail
drugs, wholesale
dry goods
electrical appliances

entertainment establishment
express company
farming
fish
florist
foundry
furniture and home furnishings
groceries, retail
groceries, wholesale
hardware
ice
insurance agency
insurance company
jewelry, retail
jewelry, wholesale
junk
laundry
leather or fur
liquor, retail
liquor, wholesale
metals
mill
musical instruments
notions

painting, paperhanging
paper
pawn shop
periodicals
printing, publishing
railroad
real estate
restaurant
rubber
school (private)
stable

steamship line
stoves, ranges, tinware
street railway
tea
ticket agency
tobacco, retail
tobacco, wholesale
toys
utility company
warehouse
woolens

The following miscellaneous litigants were also coded:
Archdiocese of Boston
church other than the Archdiocese of Boston
City of Boston
city or town other than Boston
club or fraternal order
Commonwealth of Massachusetts

THE BENCH

UNLESS otherwise noted, information about judges was obtained from *The Professional and Industrial History of Suffolk County*, volume I, edited by William T. Davis (Boston, 1894), a biographical dictionary of lawyers and judges.

1880

Superior Court

Lincoln F. Brigham, Chief Justice
Peleg Emory Aldrich
William Allen
John W. Bacon
Waldo Colburn
Francis H. Dewey
William S. Gardner
Robert C. Pitman
John P. Putnam
Julius Rockwell

Municipal Court

John Wilder May, Chief Justice
Joseph McKean Churchill
William J. Forsaith
William E. Parmenter

1900

Superior Court

Albert Mason, Chief Justice
John A. Aiken[1]

Charles U. Bell[2]
Robert R. Bishop
Caleb Blodgett
Daniel W. Bond[3]
Henry K. Braley
Justin Dewey
Franklin G. Fessenden
Francis A. Gaskill[4]
John H. Hardy
John Hopkins
Frederick Lawton[5]
Elisha B. Maynard
James B. Richardson
Henry N. Sheldon[6]
Edgar J. Sherman
William B. Stevens

Municipal Court

John Freeman Brown,[7] Chief Justice
George Z. Adams
John A. Bennett
John H. Burke
Henry S. Dewey
Frederick D. Ely
James P. Parmenter
William Sullivan[8]
George L. Wentworth

NOTES

CHAPTER ONE. Boston and Its Trial Courts

1. The quotation is from Lawrence M. Friedman, *A History of American Law* (New York, 1973), p. 573.

2. James Willard Hurst, *The Growth of American Law: The Law Makers* (Boston, 1950), pp. 149-150; Friedman, *History of American Law*, p. 339.

3. Criminal litigation in Boston's trial courts is the subject of William F. Kuntz's "Criminal Sentencing in Three Nineteenth-Century Cities: A Social History of Punishment in New York, Boston, and Philadelphia, 1830-1880" (Ph.D. diss., Harvard University, 1979). An older study of criminal litigation is Sam Bass Warner, *Crime and Criminal Statistics in Boston* (Cambridge, Mass., 1934). (A detailed discussion of the sources employed here is provided in Appendix A.)

4. The number of suits per capita was computed by dividing the number of Bostonians, male and female, 21 years of age or older in 1900 (359,673) by the number of civil cases entered that year (18,793). Source of the population: U.S. Census Office, *Abstract of the Twelfth Census of the United States, 1900* (Washington, D.C., 1902), pp. 100, 109, 112. Source of the civil actions: Dockets of the Superior Court of Suffolk County (Civil Branch) and Dockets of the Boston Municipal Court (Civil Branch). The total value of criminal fines was published in *Board of Police Report*, Mass. Doc. no. 49 (1900), pp. 88-89. (Throughout this study, *Massachusetts Public Documents* [1858-   ] are cited by title, number, and date.) The civil figure was estimated from a sample of cases for the year 1900 (N = 747). At least half of the superior court actions of 1900 (N = 370) were settled out of court, as were 15 percent of the municipal court actions (N = 377). The superior court figure was similar to those reported in several twentieth-century studies. See Hurst, *Growth of American Law*, p. 172. The property tax was published in Nathan Matthews, Jr., *The City Government of Boston* (Boston, 1895), p. 209.

5. Friedman, *History of American Law*, p. 336.

6. Roscoe Pound, *Harvard Law Review* 26 (1912-13):315, 317. On later analysis, see Hurst, *Growth of American Law*, pp. 170-171.

7. Examples of new books are: William W. Morrill, ed., *American Electrical Cases*, 6 vols. (Albany, 1894-97); James A. Webb, *The Law of Passenger and Freight Elevators* (St. Louis, 1896); William George, *The Law of Apartments, Flats, and Tenements* (New York, 1909); Andrew J. Nellis, *Street Railway Accident Law* (Albany, 1904); Waterman L. Williams, *The Liability of Municipal Corporations for Tort* (Boston, 1901). The first American treatise

on the legal problems of municipalities was John F. Dillon's *The Law of Municipal Corporations* (New York, 1872).

8. The value of substantive law for understanding the development of Boston is best illustrated by two works: Oscar and Mary Handlin, *Commonwealth, A Study of the Role of Government in the American Economy: Massachusetts, 1774-1861*, rev. ed. (Cambridge, Mass., 1969), and Leonard W. Levy, *The Law of the Commonwealth and Chief Justice Shaw* (Cambridge, Mass., 1957). Neither book is concerned primarily with the development of Boston, but both investigate the roles of the state legislature and supreme court in creating a favorable economic environment for venture capital in Massachusetts. Most of this capital came from Boston sources; its successful investment in the state was a stimulus to prosperity and growth in the Hub. Levy also touches on the problem of urban discipline when writing on fugitive slaves (chaps. 5-6), segregation (chap. 7), criminal law (chap. 11), and the police power (chap. 12). Only students of early American legal history have paid much attention to inferior-court records. For Boston, see *Records of the Suffolk County Court, 1671-1680* (Boston, 1933), published by the Colonial Society of Massachusetts.

9. During the past 25 years dozens of essays have opened new directions in urban history. Most of them are listed in Michael H. Ebner, *The New Urban History: Bibliography on Methodology and Historiography*, Council of Planning Librarians Exchange Bibliography no. 445 (Monticello, Ill., 1973), which also provides a concise summary of trends. On the new legal history, see James Willard Hurst, "Legal Elements in United States History," *Perspectives in American History* 5 (1971):3-92, and Michael S. Hindus and Douglas L. Jones, "The Social History of American Law: What It Is and Where to Begin" (paper presented at the sixth annual meeting of the American Society for Legal History, Philadelphia, October 23, 1976). Three principal historical studies of post-Revolutionary trial-court business have appeared during the last 40 years: Charles Clark and Harry Shulman, *A Study of Law Administration in Connecticut* (New Haven, 1937); Francis W. Laurent, *The Business of a Trial Court: 100 Years of Cases* (Madison, 1959); Lawrence M. Friedman and Robert V. Percival, "A Tale of Two Courts: Litigation in Alameda and San Benito Counties," *Law and Society Review* 10 (1975-76):267-301. In addition, William E. Nelson's *Americanization of the Common Law: The Impact of Legal Change on Massachusetts, 1760-1830* (Cambridge, Mass., 1975) draws heavily on lower-court records.

10. The proportion of suburbanites was estimated from a sample of litigants. See table 1.

11. *Revised Laws of Massachusetts* (1902), ch. 157, secs. 1-6, 24-25; ch. 160, secs. 2, 4, 55.

12. Ibid.; *Acts and Resolves of Massachusetts* (1883), ch. 223, sec. 1. Jury trials were available only in superior court.

13. *Revised Laws* (1902), ch. 156, secs. 3-5; ch. 162, secs. 1-7; ch. 163, sec. 1.

14. Hurst, *Growth of American Law*, pp. 115-117.

15. Court Dockets (1865-1917).

16. The sample confidence level = 95 percent: reliability = ± 5 percent. The sampling procedure is discussed in Appendix A.

17. Oscar Handlin, *Boston's Immigrants: A Study in Acculturation*, rev. ed. (Cambridge, Mass., 1959), pp. 1-9.

18. Ibid., pp. 9-12; Peter R. Knights, *The Plain People of Boston, 1830-1860* (New York, 1971), p. 84.

19. Handlin, *Boston's Immigrants*, pp. 72-82, 214-215; Knights, *Plain People of Boston*, p. 84.

20. Oscar Handlin, "The Modern City as a Field of Historical Study," in Oscar Handlin and John Burchard, eds., *The Historian and the City* (Cambridge, Mass., 1963), p. 8.

21. Handlin, *Boston's Immigrants*, pp. 13-15.

22. Ibid.; William H. Clark, *The History of Winthrop, Massachusetts, 1630-1952* (Winthrop, Mass., 1952), pp. 24-25; Elizabeth M. Herlihy, ed., *Fifty Years of Boston* (Boston, 1932), pp. 117-118; Walter M. Pratt, *Seven Generations: The Story of Prattville and Chelsea* (n.p., 1930), pp. 92-97; Benjamin Shurtleff, *History of the Town of Revere* (Boston, 1938), pp. 331-349.

23. Herlihy, ed., *Boston*, pp. 118-123; Pratt, *Seven Generations*, p. 95; Sam Bass Warner, Jr., *Streetcar Suburbs: The Process of Growth in Boston, 1870-1900* (Cambridge, Mass., 1962), p. 42.

24. Alfred D. Chandler, *Annexation of Brookline to Boston* (Brookline, 1880), pp. 15-24; Herlihy, ed., *Boston*, pp. 123-124; Warner, *Streetcar Suburbs*, pp. 163-165.

25. Minor charter revisions were made in 1854. See James M. Bugbee, *The City Government of Boston*, Johns Hopkins University Studies in Historical and Political Sciences, 5th ser., 3 (Baltimore, 1887), pp. 34-43; Matthews, *City Government of Boston*, pp. 167-173.

26. Bugbee, *City Government of Boston*, pp. 14-26; *Report of the Commission Appointed to Revise the City Charter*, City Doc. no. 3 (1875), pp. iii-iv. (Throughout this study, *Boston City Documents* [1834-] are cited by title, number, and date.) Social stratification and inequalities certainly existed in Boston, but they did not result in violent social upheaval. See James A. Henretta, *The Evolution of American Society, 1700-1815* (Lexington, Mass., 1973), pp. 96-97, and Allen Kulikoff, "The Progress of Inequality in Revolutionary Boston," *William and Mary Quarterly*, 3d ser. 28 (1971):375-412.

27. *Report*, City Doc. no. 3 (1875), p. v; Matthews, *City Government of Boston*, pp. 165, 167; Knights, *Plain People of Boston*, p. 84.

28. On spatial manipulation, see Walter Firey, *Land Use in Central Boston* (Cambridge, Mass., 1947); Henry-Russell Hitchcock, *A Guide to Boston Architecture, 1637-1954* (New York, 1954); Walter H. Kilham, *Boston after*

Bulfinch (Cambridge, Mass., 1946); Lloyd Rodwin, *Housing and Economic Progress: A Study of Housing Experiences of Boston's Middle-Income Families* (Cambridge, Mass., 1961); Warner, *Streetcar Suburbs;* Walter M. Whitehill, *Boston: A Topographical History*, rev. ed. (Cambridge, Mass., 1968). On discipline, see Roger Lane, *Policing the City: Boston, 1822-1885* (Cambridge, Mass., 1967); Marvin Lazerson, *Origins of the Urban School* (Cambridge, Mass., 1971); Donna Merwick, *Boston Priests, 1848-1910* (Cambridge, Mass., 1973); Warner, *Streetcar Suburbs.* Psychological adjustment is a subliminal concern of the works just cited, but it has been a more conscious interest of those who have focused on the intellectual and political history of Boston, dealing with concepts such as reform and nativism. See Arthur Mann, *Yankee Reformers in the Urban Age* (Cambridge, Mass., 1954); Barbara M. Solomon, *Ancestors and Immigrants: A Changing New England Tradition* (Cambridge, Mass., 1956); Geoffrey Blodgett, *The Gentle Reformers: Massachusetts Democrats in the Cleveland Era* (Cambridge, Mass., 1966), esp. chaps. 6 and 9. See also Handlin, "Modern City," pp. 7-20.

CHAPTER TWO. *Personae*

1. Samuel L. Powers, *Portraits of a Half Century* (Boston, 1925), p. 69; Matthews, *City Government of Boston*, p. 73.

2. In 1880 debt and injury accounted for 85 percent of the civil actions filed in the municipal and superior courts ($N = 698$). In 1900 the figure was 95 percent ($N = 747$). These figures do not include divorce suits. A detailed list of the actions included in each category and a discussion of the classification scheme is provided in Appendix B. Cf. Clark and Shulman, *Law Administration in Connecticut*, pp. 8-9; Laurent, *Trial Court*, pp. 46-51; Friedman and Percival, "Two Courts," pp. 280-281.

3. 1880 $N = 698$; 1900 $N = 747$. Such a change did not occur in rural Chippewa County, Wisconsin. Cf. Laurent, *Trial Court*, p. 220.

4. Sample sizes indicate that in 1880 approximately 730 plaintiffs ($N = 71$) and 600 defendants ($N = 54$) were female. In 1900 the figures were 3,300 plaintiffs ($N = 135$) and 1,700 defendants ($N = 60$).

5. Herlihy, ed., *Boston*, pp. 632, 633.

6. Women constituted 17 percent of all plaintiffs in industrial accident cases in 1900 ($N = 18$), but none of the plaintiffs in construction accident cases was female ($N = 6$). On justice for females, see Martha Strickland, "Women and the Forum," *Green Bag* 3 (1891):240-241.

7. $N = 363$ plaintiffs and 362 defendants in 1880; $N = 361$ plaintiffs and 304 defendants in 1900. Dependents are defined as nonboarders without occupations or with the occupation of housewife.

8. This classification scheme was adapted from Stephan Thernstrom, *The Other Bostonians: Poverty and Progress in the American Metropolis, 1880-*

1970 (Cambridge, Mass., 1973), Appendix B. Some modifications have been made here; an explanation of them is provided in Appendix C. Thernstrom also traces the problems of such a system and the objections voiced. He makes a sensible argument for the reality of a white-collar—blue-collar division in late-nineteenth-century Boston's occupational structure. Even a strong critic of this approach in twentieth-century research considers it meaningful for 1900. See Harry Braverman, *Labor and Monopoly Capital: The Degradation of Work in the Twentieth Century* (New York, 1974), pp. 296-297.

9. Only six plaintiffs and four defendants in the combined samples of 1880 and 1900 were black.

10. Observations on the status of ethnic groups are from Thernstrom, *Other Bostonians*, pp. 132-136.

11. Responsibility was divided as follows: 31 percent native, 42 percent foreign-born, and 27 percent children of the foreign-born. N = 70. Of the population of Boston, natives = 28 percent, foreign-born = 35 percent, and children of the foreign-born = 37 percent. U.S. Census Office, *Twelfth Census of the United States, 1900*, Vol. 1, *Population* (Washington, D.C., 1900), p. 188.

12. Five percent of the plaintiffs and 3 percent of the defendants in both 1880 and 1900 were 25 years of age or younger. N for 1880 = 217 plaintiffs and 247 defendants; N for 1900 = 293 plaintiffs and 235 defendants.

13. Similar increases in tortious litigation have been noted in urban and rural areas of America. These, however, have been associated with the widespread use of automobiles. Cf. Clark and Shulman, *Law Administration in Connecticut*, pp. 14, 166-176; Laurent, *Trial Court*, pp. 161, 170; Friedman and Percival, "Two Courts," pp. 280-281.

14. Reginald H. Smith, *Justice and the Poor* (Boston, 1919), pp. 112, 181. About 23 percent of the defendants acted as their own lawyers in 1880; only 4 percent of the plaintiffs did so. The 1900 percentages were 28 and 5.

15. The city directory of 1880 lists 1,150 lawyers with offices in Boston; the directory of 1900 lists 2,130, an 85-percent increase. On the skills of the advocate, see Margaret M. Elder, *The Life of Samuel J. Elder* (New Haven, 1925), p. 153; James P. Hall, "Practice Work in Law Schools," *Green Bag* 17 (1905):532; George R. Nutter, *Nathan Matthews* (Boston, 1928), pp. 14-15. On the division of labor, see "An English View of the American Bar," *Green Bag* 1 (1889):415. In the 1880 sample there were 1.38 cases per counsel; in the 1900 sample the figure was 1.20.

16. Albert Bushnell Hart, ed., *Commonwealth History of Massachusetts*, Vol. 5 (New York, 1930), p. 101. As late as 1915 only 47 women practiced law in the entire state of Massachusetts. See also Robert Grant, *Law and the Family* (New York, 1919), pp. 16-17; Robinson's Case, 131 Mass. 376

(1881); *Acts and Resolves of Massachusetts* (1882), ch. 139; Arthur E. Sutherland, *The Law at Harvard: A History of Ideas and Men, 1817-1967* (Cambridge, Mass., 1967), p. 319; Bar Association of the City of Boston, *Annual Report, 1916* (Boston, 1916), pp. 15-16. Boston University had admitted women law students since its founding in 1872. See Herlihy, ed., *Boston*, p. 632.

17. Ethnicity/race N for 1880 = 388; N for 1900 = 353. Only two black attorneys appeared in the samples, one each in 1880 and 1900. In 1880, 73 percent of all lawyers were solo practitioners; 26 percent were in two- or three-man partnerships (N = 503). The 1900 figures were 68 and 31 percent (N = 633). See also Albert Boyden, *Ropes-Gray, 1865-1940* (Boston, 1942), pp. 90, 93.

18. Figures refer to appearances by all attorneys, including multiple appearances by the same lawyer or firm. N for years of experience was 979 in 1880 and 1,264 in 1900. The attitudes of older lawyers were expressed in George P. Costigan, Jr., "The Proposed American Code of Legal Ethics," *Green Bag* 20 (1908):51; Percy Edwards, "Hustling in the Law," ibid. 4 (1892):292-294; Gilbert R. Hawes, "Literature and the Law," ibid. 6 (1899):234; review of Gleason Archer's *Law Office and Court Procedure* (Boston, 1910), by the editors of *Green Bag* 22 (1910):358.

19. Louis Brandeis to C. C. Langdell, Dec. 30, 1889, in Melvin I. Urofsky and David W. Levy, eds., *Letters of Louis D. Brandeis*, Vol. 1 (Albany, 1971), pp. 85-88; Herlihy, ed., *Boston*, pp. 496-497; Sutherland, *Law at Harvard*, pp. 162, 174-175, 179, 190; Friedman, *History of American Law*, p. 537; Hart, ed., *Massachusetts*, pp. 106-108.

20. Alfred Z. Reed, *Training for the Public Profession of the Law* (New York, 1921), p. 339.

21. Sutherland, *Law at Harvard*, pp. 168, 170-171, 180-182. Of the appearances by Harvard-trained lawyers in 1880 (N = 219), 60 percent were by those trained prior to Langdell's arrival. At the turn of the century only 10 percent had passed through Harvard before Langdell's tenure (N = 247).

22. Josef Redlich, *The Common Law and the Case Method in American University Law Schools* (New York, 1914), p. 18.

23. Charles Warren, *A History of the American Bar* (Boston, 1911), p. 557; Irving Browne, "The Lawyer's Easy Chair," *Green Bag* 6 (1894):93-94; Editorial, ibid. 1 (1889):123; "Oratory of the Bar," ibid. 5 (1893):428; Peter J. Hamilton, "Scholarship, the Handmaiden of the Lawyer," ibid. 15 (1903):159-161; Browne, "Easy Chair," ibid. 6 (1894):247; Roscoe Pound, "Dogs and the Law," ibid. 8 (1896):172-174; Percy Edwards, "A Serious Problem," ibid. 5 (1893):358; Browne, "Easy Chair," ibid. 7 (1895):482-483; Browne, "Easy Chair," ibid. 11 (1899):89; Browne, "Easy Chair," ibid. 5 (1893):245; Browne, "Easy Chair," ibid. 8 (1896):83.

24. Robert T. Swaine, *The Cravath Firm and Its Predecessors, 1819-1947*, Vol. 1 (New York, 1947), pp. 448-450.

25. Boyden, *Ropes-Gray*, pp. 28-29; Reed, *Training for the Law*, p. 339.

26. "Lawyers and Marriage," *Green Bag* 5 (1893):301; Francis L. Stetson, "The Lawyer's Livelihood," ibid. 21 (1909):45; Boyden, *Ropes-Gray*, pp. 77-79; *Annual Report of the Bureau of the Statistics of Labor*, Mass. Doc. no. 15 (1884); Richard Ames, "Suggestions from Law School Graduates as to Where and How to Began Practice," *Harvard Law Review* 27 (1914): 261; *Annual Report of the Bureau of the Statistics of Labor*, Mass. Doc. no. 15 (1902).

27. Boyden, *Ropes-Gray*, p. 92; Alpheus T. Mason, *Brandeis: A Free Man's Life* (New York, 1956), p. 691; Elder, *Life of Samuel Elder*, pp. 185, 241.

28. William T. Abbott, "The Trust Company—Not a Competitor of the Lawyer," *Illinois Law Review* 6 (1911):79; Friedman, *History of American Law*, pp. 549-550.

29. Horace W. Fuller, "Overcrowding the Profession," *Green Bag* 3 (1891):198-199; Irving Browne, "Easy Chair," ibid. 7 (1895):199; Guy C. Lee, "The Lawyer's Position in Society," ibid. 8 (1896):247-248; Charles F. Chamberlayne, "The Soul of the Profession," ibid., 18 (1906):397; David J. Brewer, "The Ideal Lawyer," *Atlantic Monthly* 98 (1906):587; William L. Marbury, "The Lawyer of Fifty Years Ago and the Lawyer of Today," *Green Bag* 24 (1912):64-74; Ashley Cockrill, "The Shyster Lawyer," *Yale Law Journal* 21 (1909):383; Elder, *Life of Samuel Elder*, p. 159; Joseph B. Moors, "Rufus Choate," *Green Bag* 15 (1903):399-406; George A. Torrey, *A Lawyer's Recollections In and Out of Court* (Boston, 1910), pp. 182-184; Powers, *Portraits*, pp. 70-72, 80; Friedman, *History of American Law*, p. 549.

30. Joseph A. Willard, *Half a Century with Judges and Lawyers* (Boston, 1895), pp. 78-79; Bar Association of the City of Boston, *Report . . . on the Possibility of Increasing the Usefulness of the Association* (Boston, 1885), p. 9; Records of the Council of the Boston Bar Association, Dec. 3, 1886, Dec. 7, 1909. Between 1910 and 1924 just over 5 percent of the newly admitted attorneys in Suffolk County joined the association. See the association's *Annual Report* (Boston, 1923-24), p. 25.

31. Friedman, *History of American Law*, p. 323; Judge Harvey R. Keeler to the editor, *Green Bag* 22 (1910):430-431. Unless otherwise noted, statistical statements about the bench were calculated from biographical sources listed in Appendix D. On the financial sacrifices of a judge, see *James Robert Dunbar, A Memorial* (Boston, 1916), p. 9.

32. N = 449.

33. James B. Richardson, *Address to the Graduating Class of the Evening Law School of the Young Men's Christian Association, June 7, 1905* (Boston, 1905), pp. 5, 7, 14, 18, 20-21; Edgar J. Sherman, *Recollections of a Long Life* (Boston, 1908), pp. 183-186.

34. Friedman and Percival have argued that in "highly technical, urban societies where people deal constantly with strangers" a lawsuit becomes "a cold-blooded matter, a matter of dollars and cents" in which the

aim of the court "is to handle some precise point of law or fact" ("Two Courts," pp. 269-270). Harmonious relationships among lawyers and judges may have worked against, and disharmonious ones for, the development of such impersonal adjudication.

35. *Revised Laws of Massachusetts* (1902), ch. 176, secs. 1, 36; Irving Browne, "Easy Chair," *Green Bag* 6 (1894):149. One researcher conducted an experiment on the reasoning ability of jurors; he concluded that "women did not learn anything more by discussion with peers and therefore" were "unfit for jury duty." See Hugo Muensterberg, "The Mind of the Juryman, With a Side-light on Women as Jurors," *Century* 86 (1913):711.

36. Willard, *Half Century*, pp. 80, 84; Charles E. Grinnell, "Beyond a Reasonable Doubt," *Green Bag* 9 (1897):102; John B. Phillips, "Modifications of the Jury System," ibid. 16 (1904):514-519; Alfred Russell, "The Jury System in Civil Cases," ibid. 3 (1891):499-451; A. Oakey Hall, "Trial by Newspaper," ibid. 6 (1894):308; Richardson, *Address*, pp. 10-11; William H. Cowles, "Has Trial by Jury in Civil Actions Been Abolished," *Green Bag* 19 (1907):341-342; Herlihy, ed., *Boston*, p. 493.

37. Albert C. Applegarth, "The Jury System and Its Critics," *Green Bag* 4 (1892):110-112; David J. Brewer, "The Jury," ibid. 14 (1902):69.

38. While gathering data on the superior court of 1900, this author found 31 jury lists filed with the 370 sample cases examined. The filing of jury lists with other case papers was not required apparently and occurred haphazardly. The 31 lists provided the names of 372 jurors.

39. *Revised Laws of Massachusetts* (1902), ch. 165; *Rules of the Superior Court* (Boston, 1874), pp. 14-15; *Rules of the Superior Court of Massachusetts* (n.p., 1900), pp. 14-15. Stenographic records are discussed in Appendix A. The findings of masters, referees, auditors, and assessors were accepted by the judges in every sample case (N = 18 in 1880; N = 31 in 1900).

40. W.B.W. to the editor, *Green Bag* 16 (1904):554.

CHAPTER THREE. Commercial Credit

1. Robert S. Lopez, "The Crossroads within the Wall," in Handlin and Burchard, eds., *The Historian and the City*, pp. 27-39; Lewis Mumford, *The City in History* (New York, 1961), pp. 70-73, 251, 254, 434-439.

2. Herlihy, ed., *Boston*, pp. 126, 168, 236; Hart, ed., *Massachusetts*, pp. 250, 420-422; *Changes in Conducting Retail Trade in Boston since 1874*, Mass. Doc. no. 15, pt. 1 (1899), pp. 34, 68.

3. Adna F. Weber, *The Growth of Cities in the Nineteenth Century* (New York, 1899), p. 241; Knights, *Plain People of Boston*, pp. 19-47; Thernstrom, *Other Bostonians*, pp. 10, 15-21.

4. *Retail Trade*, Mass. Doc. no. 15 (1899), pp. 41-42, 46; Milton Friedman and Anna J. Schwartz, *A Monetary History of the United States, 1867-1960* (New York, 1963), pp. 94-95; Daniel J. Boorstin, *The Americans: The Democratic Experience* (New York, 1973), pp. 97-101, 107-109.

5. *Retail Trade*, Mass. Doc. no. 15 (1899), pp. 34, 40, 45-46, 68; Frank Foxcroft, "The Boston Subway and Others," *New England Magazine*, n.s. 13 (1895):194; Boorstin, *Americans*, pp. 104-107.

6. *Retail Trade*, Mass. Doc. no. 15 (1899), pp. 45-46; Harold Barger, *Distribution's Place in the American Economy since 1869* (Princeton, 1955), p. 34.

7. Charles A. Meyer, *Mercantile Credits and Collections* (New York, 1919), chaps. 3 and 6; William A. Prendergast, *Credit and Its Uses* (New York, 1914), chaps. 9 and 10; Paul H. Nystrom, *The Economics of Retailing* (New York, 1915), p. 31. The mercantile agencies were criticized for providing incomplete and inaccurate information. See Appendix A for details.

8. Margin is the difference between the cost and the selling price of goods. The source for margins was Barger, *Distribution*, p. 81. Geographical distribution of Boston's liquor stores was determined by checking their addresses in the city directory against a list of streets and wards. The same procedure was followed for the other retail trades discussed.

9. *Retail Trade*, Mass. Doc. no. 15 (1899), pp. 34, 45-46; James E. Hagerty, *Mercantile Credit* (New York, 1913), p. 80. See above, note 8.

10. Turnover is the number of times a stock of merchandise is sold and replenished in a given period of time. See Barger, *Distribution*, p. 81; Nystrom, *Retailing*, p. 186; *Retail Trade*, Mass. Doc. no. 15 (1899), p. 46; Hagerty, *Mercantile Credit*, p. 81.

11. On the grocery business, see Mary Antin, *The Promised Land*, 2d ed. (Boston, 1969; orig. publ. Boston, 1912), pp. 195-196, 350-351.

12. *Retail Trade*, Mass. Doc. no. 15 (1899), p. 56; Boorstin, *Americans*, pp. 423-424.

13. *Retail Trade*, Mass. Doc. no. 15 (1899), pp. 54-55; Nystrom, *Retailing*, p. 186; Barger, *Distribution*, p. 81; Edwin R. A. Seligman, *The Economics of Installment Selling: A Study in Consumer's Credit*, 2 vols. (New York, 1927), 1:183-184; Meyer, *Mercantile Credits*, p. 5. Litigation for repossession was necessary under a conditional sales contract if the buyer refused to surrender the items or if a third party claimed ownership. This did not occur in any of the sample cases (N = 15). In these actions the furniture dealers recognized the defendant's title to the items but demanded the remainder of the purchase price.

14. *Retail Trade*, Mass. Doc. no. 15 (1899), pp. 49-51.

15. Ibid., p. 40; Arthur H. Cole, *The American Wool Manufacture*, 2 vols. (Cambridge, Mass., 1926), 1:137-139, 292-293; Barger, *Distribution*, p. 81; Nystrom, *Retailing*, p. 186.

16. *Retail Trade*, Mass. Doc. no. 15 (1899), p. 50; Seligman, *Installment Selling*, 1:207-212.

17. Barger, *Distribution*, pp. 33-34.

18. Stanley Baron, *Brewed in America: A History of Beer and Ale in the United States* (Boston, 1962), pp. 257-270; Barger, *Distribution*, p. 84.

19. Cole, *Wool Manufacture*, 1:139, 292-296, 2:136-144; Herlihy, ed., *Boston*, p. 183.

20. Willis N. Baer, *The Economic Development of the Cigar Industry in the United States* (Lancaster, Pa., 1933), p. 102; Meyer Jacobstein, *The Tobacco Industry in the United States* (New York, 1907), pp. 86, 89, 99; Barger, *Distribution*, p. 84.

21. National Wholesale Druggists' Association, *A History of the National Wholesale Druggists' Association* (New York, 1924), pp. 19, 27, 38-40.

22. David C. Smith, *History of Papermaking in the United States (1691-1969)* (New York, 1970), pp. 89, 153, 166-167, 220-221, 226; Lyman H. Weeks, *A History of Paper-Manufacturing in the United States, 1690-1916* (New York, 1916), p. 302.

23. Barger, *Distribution*, p. 33. In the late nineteenth century the promissory note was the chief instrument of debt and credit, according to Friedman, *History of American Law*, p. 468.

24. Albert O. Greef, *The Commercial Paper House in the United States* (Cambridge, Mass., 1938), pp. 96, 100-107; W. H. Kniffin, Jr., *Commercial Paper Acceptances and the Analysis of Credit Statements* (New York, 1918), pp. 3-4; Herlihy, ed., *Boston*, pp. 231-232; Hart, ed., *Massachusetts*, p. 343. Since only large banks could afford to make routine, detailed credit investigations (Greef, p. 106), consolidation into fewer, larger institutions should have reduced the amount of "bad" paper in circulation. According to the sample (N = 18 in 1880; N = 12 in 1900), there were approximately 138 note cases in 1880 and 209 of them 20 years later.

25. In 1880, 46 percent of the creditors were marginal operators (N = 144); in 1900 the figure was 43 percent (N = 143). The assets and credit ratings are drawn from the 1880 and 1900 editions of *R. G. Dun's Mercantile Reference Book* (New York). Assets do not include those unconnected with the business, nor do they include such invisible assets as the value of a liquor dealer's license. The $1,000 cutoff point was suggested by the fact that Dun did not specify the assets of a firm below $1,000. In other words, Dun considered them tenuous or marginal operations. Similarly, "fair" was the lowest credit rating given to a firm. See Appendix A.

26. There was little difference between the proportions for 1880 (N = 207) and 1900 (N = 156).

27. P. R. Earling, *Whom to Trust: A Practical Treatise on Mercantile Credits* (Chicago and New York, 1890).

28. Meyer, *Mercantile Credits*, pp. 66-70, 130, 141-142; Prendergast, *Credit*, chaps. 16 and 17.

29. N = 226 in 1880; N = 157 in 1900. In a replevin action the plaintiff claimed that the defendant had unlawful possession of his goods. He petitioned the court to replevy them, that is, order the defendant to return the items. In a conversion action the plaintiff asserted that the defendant had converted the plaintiff's property to his own use, to the plaintiff's damage, a tort. A detailed listing of the actions classified here as commercial litigation is provided in Appendix B.

30. Retail N = 65 in 1880, 64 in 1900. Wholesale N = 53 in 1880, 43 in 1900. Bankers and brokers N = 18 in 1880, 12 in 1900. In 1880 and 1900, four out of five notes were double-name obligations.

31. On the qualities of a good risk, see Meyer, *Mercantile Credits*, p. 7; Prendergast, *Credit*, pp. 226-227, 246; Seligman, *Installment Selling*, p. 144.

32. About five out of six retail suits were for sums of $25 or more in 1880 and 1900; about three out of four wholesale and banking actions were for sums of $100 or more. These figures represent the actual debt as stated in the bill of particulars. The formal claim, the *ad damnum*, was usually much higher. For sample sizes, see above, note 30.

33. About three out of four retail debts were for sums of $150 or less; about three out of five wholesale and banking suits were for amounts of $500 or less. These sums represent the actual debt, not the *ad damnum*. For sample sizes, see above, note 30.

34. Only 1 out of 10 plaintiffs recovered 100 percent of the sum owed. Only 1 out of 20 recouped less than 20 percent. In 9 out of 10 actions costs awarded did not exceed $25. These are collective figures for retail, wholesale, and banking lawsuits. N = 136 in 1880; N = 119 in 1900. On attorneys' fees, see below, Chapter Four, note 10.

35. For the margins, see Barger, *Distribution*, pp. 81, 84.

36. The three-month standard was suggested by Moorfield Storey, *The Reform of Legal Procedure* (New Haven, 1911), p. 28. One-fourth of the cases in 1880 (N = 226) continued for more than three months, as did one-third of the cases in 1900 (N = 157). Here and elsewhere in this study the termination date is: the date on which final judgment was entered, with or without a jury verdict, on default, on stipulation, or otherwise; the date on which a non-suit was declared; or the date on which a case was discontinued or withdrawn. Where a case was appealed, the date of termination after appeal is used in computation. Delay increasingly plagued other trial courts around the country in the late nineteenth and early twentieth centuries. Cf. Clark and Shulman, *Law Administration in Connecticut*, p. 37, and Friedman and Percival, "Two Courts," p. 291.

37. Cf. Gleason L. Archer, *Law Office and Court Procedure* (Boston, 1910), pp. 20-24. In 1880, 69 percent of the commercial cases were resolved in the municipal court (N = 226); in 1900, 79 percent (N = 157). The superior court's backlog was due to the growth of tortious litigation, which involved many lengthy trials. See Chapter Six.

38. Hagerty, *Mercantile Credit*, pp. 184, 225-226; Herlihy, ed., *Boston*, p. 162. The number of mercantile agencies and debt collectors was determined by consulting the business section of the city directory for 1900.

39. The actual number of cases was estimated from the samples.

40. In 1880, 27 percent of the plaintiffs' attorneys had practiced five years or less (N = 212). In 1900, the figure was 35 percent (N = 153).

41. In 1880 women brought 14 percent of the commercial lawsuits (N = 195), 23 percent in 1900 (N = 152). Similarly, in 1880 first- and second-generation immigrants initiated 42 percent of the commercial actions (N = 85); 20 years later the figure was 49 percent (N = 96).

CHAPTER FOUR. Emoluments

1. Louis Brandeis, "The Living Law," an address delivered before the Chicago Bar Association, Jan. 3, 1916, quoted in Mason, *Brandeis*, pp. 245-246.

2. Department of the Interior, U.S. Census Office, *Tenth Census of the United States, 1880*, Vol. 1, *Population*, p. 864, and *Twelfth Census of the United States: Special Reports on Occupations*, pp. 494-498. On the decline in the number of self-employed persons and the rise in the number of large employers, see Alexander Keyssar, "Men Out of Work: A Social History of Unemployment in Massachusetts, 1870-1916" (Ph.D. diss., Harvard University, 1977), chaps. 1 and 2.

3. On public transit, see Warner, *Streetcar Suburbs*, p. 56. The actual number of job transfers is beyond accurate reconstruction. These figures are a combination of the proportion of workers who left Boston between 1880 and 1890 and the proportion of workers who moved from one occupational level to another, as estimated by Thernstrom in *The Other Bostonians*, pp. 40, 53. These figures do not include workers who changed jobs without leaving the city or moving to a different occupational level. Thus, they are low estimates. According to Thernstrom's calculations, the rate of change for low manual occupations was even higher.

4. See the annual reports of the Massachusetts Bureau of the Statistics of Labor, 1880 to 1900, which were always numbered public document 15. Thousands of reports from Massachusetts and elsewhere in the United States were catalogued by the U.S. Bureau of Labor Statistics in an *Index of All Reports* (Washington, D.C., 1902).

5. Edward C. Kirkland, *Industry Comes of Age: Business, Labor, and Public Policy, 1860-1897* (New York, 1961), pp. 345-351; John R. Commons and John B. Andrews, *Principles of Labor Legislation*, rev. ed. (New York, 1927), pp. 71-72.

6. C. Wright Mills, *White Collar: The American Middle Classes* (New York, 1951), pp. 71-72.

7. Compare the number of wage claims with the number of claims for

unpaid debts made by businessmen in table 13 or with the claims for fees made by doctors and lawyers in table 17.

8. In 1880, N = 38; in 1900, N = 8.

9. Cf. Smith, *Justice and the Poor*, p. 17. In 1880, 84 percent of the sample cases were initiated in the municipal court; in 1900 all of the sample cases were. All but 1 of the 27 unappealed sample cases from the municipal court for both years were completed in three months or less.

10. Smith, *Justice and the Poor*, pp. 33, 85, 133, 135-136. In late-nineteenth-century Boston a typical charge for consultation was $3 to $5, for letter writing $2, for a title search $10 to $25, for examining a will $5, and for drawing up one $10 to $50. An established, though not particularly prominent attorney could have charged $10 to $25 for a day in court. See Boyden, *Ropes-Gray*, pp. 40-41, 53; Elder, *Life of Samuel Elder*, p. 160; Gleason L. Archer, *Ethical Obligations of the Lawyer* (Boston, 1910), pp. 223-229. A prominent attorney was one who appeared in *Hubbell's Legal Directory*. See Appendix A.

11. This range-of-costs estimate was based on the sample cases. The Boston Legal Aid Society estimated the average advance costs to be $3 at the turn of the century. See the Boston Legal Aid Society's *Annual Report 1902-03* (Boston, 1903), pp. 18, 20. On workingmen's incomes, see *Annual Report of the Bureau of the Statistics of Labor*, Mass. Doc. no. 15 (1884). In 1895, 13 percent of the wage earners in manufacturing in Boston earned less than $5 per week. An additional 42 percent earned between $5 and $10, and another 39 percent brought home between $10 and $15 per week. See Massachusetts Bureau of the Statistics of Labor, *Census of Massachusetts: 1895*, Vol. 5, *Manufactures* (Boston, 1895), p. 238.

12. Smith, *Justice and the Poor*, p. 17.

13. Blodgett, *Gentle Reformers*, pp. 128-140; *Revised Laws of Massachusetts* (1902), ch. 106, secs. 62, 63.

14. Boston Legal Aid Society, *Annual Report 1902-03*, p. 16; Smith, *Justice and the Poor*, pp. xiii, 57, 135-136.

15. An estimate derived from the samples indicates that there were 118 cases filed in superior court in 1880 (N = 16) and 48 in 1900 (N = 3). In the municipal court the corresponding figures were 295 (N = 22) and 170 (N = 5).

16. Arnold M. Paul, *Conservative Crisis and the Rule of Law: Attitudes of Bar and Bench, 1887-1895* (Ithaca, N.Y., 1960), pp. 104-158.

17. N = 38 in 1880; N = 8 in 1900. None of the sample cases from 1900 was prosecuted by an attorney who is listed in *Hubbell's Legal Directory*. See above, note 10.

18. See above, note 10. In 1900, 78 percent of the cases involved sums of $20 to $30. The victory rate in 1900 was only 50 percent; in 1880 it had been 66 percent.

19. Service workers were becoming a larger part of Boston's work force in the late nineteenth century. In 1880 there were approximately

20,000 Bostonians in service jobs; by 1900 there were over 67,000. See Department of the Interior, U.S. Census Office, *Tenth Census of the United States, 1880*, Vol. 1, *Population*, p. 864, and *Twelfth Census of the United States, 1900: Special Reports on Occupations*, pp. 494-498. Four of the eight sample plaintiffs of 1900 were domestic servants.

20. Ibid.

21. Donald E. Konold, *A History of American Medical Ethics, 1847-1912* (Madison, 1962), p. 63.

22. Konold, *Medical Ethics*, p. 63; Henry Blanchard, "Unpaid Medical Services," *Boston Medical and Surgical Journal* 85 (1871):1; "The Medical Black List," ibid. 87 (1872):361; "Remuneration in the Medical Profession," ibid. 79 (1868):92. Fifty-six percent of the claims were for 5 to 10 visits over a period of 6 to 12 months.

23. Blanchard, "Unpaid Medical Services," p. 1. Sixty-seven percent of the plaintiffs practiced in those areas in 1880 (N = 9). In the remaining suits doctors were suing patients who lived in other neighborhoods. A physician from the North End sued a patient from the West End, a doctor from the Back Bay sued a patient who had moved to Worcester, and so on.

24. Richard H. Shryock, *The Development of Modern Medicine* (Philadelphia, 1936), pp. 369-372.

25. Blanchard, "Unpaid Medical Services," pp. 1-3; Konold, *Medical Ethics*, p. 64.

26. On customary charges, see H. G. Clark, letters to the editor of the *Boston Medical and Surgical Journal* 102 (June 17, 1880):599-600; 103 (July 1, 1880):19-20. In 1880, 7 of the 9 sample suits were for sums of $20 to $25. In 1900, 4 of the 17 sample suits were for sums below $20. None of the cases in 1880 was appealed; two of the suits in 1900 were.

27. Twenty out of 24 sample cases filed for the first time (not on appeal) were brought in the municipal court. All but 1 of them were completed in three months or less. In none of the sample cases (N = 28) did a physician sue a patient residing in the ward where his office was located. The business section of the city directory was used to determine approximately how long a physician had practiced in Boston. Seventy-five percent of the doctors were listed in the directory for five years or more (N = 20).

28. A similar scarcity of malpractice suits has been observed among appellate cases brought in New England generally. Cf. Richard A. Posner, "A Theory of Negligence," *Journal of Legal Studies* 1 (1972):54.

29. The ratio of doctors and lawyers to the population of Boston in 1880 and 1900 was:

Year	Doctors	Lawyers
1880	1:392	1:316
1900	1:325	1:263

Source: city directory.

30. Roscoe Pound, *The Lawyer from Antiquity to Modern Times* (St. Paul, 1953), chap. 8; Smith, *Justice and the Poor*, pp. 228-229; E. M. Shepard, "Lawyers and Corporate Capitalization," *Green Bag* 18 (1906):601.

31. W. E. Glanville, "Legal Ethics," *Green Bag* 8 (1896):209-212; Costigan, "Proposed American Code of Legal Ethics," p. 51; Hawes, "Literature and the Law," p. 234; Edwards, "Hustling in the Law," pp. 292-294.

32. Bar Association of the City of Boston, "Record of the Discipline of Lawyers in Massachusetts, 1806-1942" (Boston, n.d.) (photocopied).

33. L. E. Chittenden, "Legal Reminiscences," *Green Bag* 7 (1895):364; Elder, *Life of Samuel Elder*, p. 159; Fuller, "Overcrowding the Profession," pp. 198-199.

34. After giving annual lectures on preventive law for many years, the Bar Association summarized the entire campaign in its *Annual Report* of 1920, pp. 19-34. See also Chittenden, "Legal Reminiscences," p. 364, and Smith, *Justice and the Poor*, pp. 20-27.

35. Archer, *Ethical Obligations*, pp. 124-126.

36. N = 20 in 1880. In 1900, 90 percent of the plaintiffs had practiced 10 years or less (N = 10). In 1880, 3 out of 20 lawyers were listed in *Hubbell's Legal Directory*; in 1900 no lawyer-plaintiff was.

37. The comparative skills of doctors and lawyers are discussed in Dietrich Rueschemeyer, "Lawyers and Doctors: A Comparison of Two Professions," in Vilhelm Aubert, ed., *Sociology of Law* (Baltimore, 1969), pp. 268-271; George F. Tucker, "Professional Remuneration," *Green Bag* 2 (1890):446; George F. Tucker, "The Accused," ibid. 4 (1892):55-56.

CHAPTER FIVE. A Place to Live

1. Robert Treat Paine, "The Housing Conditions in Boston," *Annals of the American Academy of Political and Social Sciences* 20 (1902):131. Dozens, perhaps hundreds, of books, pamphlets, and articles were written on the subject of housing in the late nineteenth and early twentieth centuries. Among those often referred to were: Charles Booth, *Life and Labour of the People in London*, Vol. 3 (London, 1902); Georges Picot, "L'Habitation ouvrière a Paris. Le Logement en garni," *Institut de France, Académie des Sciences et Politiques, Seances et travaux*, n.s. 53 (1900):664-686; Edward Bowmaker, *The Housing of the Working Classes* (London, 1895); Robert W. DeForest and Lawrence Veiller, *The Tenement House Problem*, 2 vols. (New York, 1903); W. S. McNeill, *Die Aufgaben der Stadtgemeinden in der Wohnungsfrage* (Berlin, 1902).

2. See Dwight Porter, *Report upon a Sanitary Inspection of Certain Tenement-House Districts in Boston* (Boston, 1888); *Annual Report of the Bureau of the Statistics of Labor: A Tenement House Census of Boston*, Mass. Doc. no. 15 (1891 and 1892); *Partial Report of the Special Committee . . . on Tenement Districts*, City Doc. no. 125 (1895); H. K. Estabrook, *Some Slums in*

Boston (Boston, 1897); Robert A. Woods, *The City Wilderness* (Boston, 1899), esp. chap. 4, and also his *Americans in Process* (Boston, 1903), chap. 4; R. F. Phelps, *South End Operatives and Their Residences* (Boston, 1903); *Report of the Commission . . . to Investigate Tenement-House Conditions in the City of Boston*, City Doc. no. 77 (1904); *Report of the Lodging-House Commission*, City Doc. no. 160 (1908).

3. Public funds were used to finance two waterworks and a subway between 1862 and 1894; see Matthews, *City Government of Boston*, pp. 140-153, 161-163. None of the works listed in note 2 above seriously considered the possibility of financing housing with public money. All of them concluded that stricter regulation was needed.

4. Matthews, *City Government of Boston*, p. 102; *Acts and Resolves of Massachusetts* (1902), ch. 419.

5. Paine, "Housing Conditions in Boston," pp. 128-130. The building laws dealt mainly with three subjects: overcrowding, drainage, and fireproofing. Fireproofing was closely regulated only after 1897. A turn-of-the-century survey by the Health Department showed that overcrowding and defective drainage were severe problems in 3 of the city's 25 wards, which contained 49 percent of the population living in tenements but only 9 percent of the total population. See *Report of the Tenement-House Commission*, City Doc. no. 77 (1904), Appendix A, table 1. In the early 1890s less than 10 percent of Boston's tenement families were listed as living in "poor" or "bad" sanitary conditions. See *Annual Report of the Bureau of the Statistics of Labor: A Tenement House Census*, Mass. Doc. no. 15 (1892), pp. 56-57. On the housing market, see Warner, *Streetcar Suburbs*, pp. 3-4.

6. Warner wrote of "regulation without laws" but recognized the importance of equitable covenants, that is, agreements to ensure homogeneity of structures and land use (*Streetcar Suburbs*, p. 122). These agreements provided a means of safeguarding the character of a neighborhood long before zoning was introduced. The legitimacy of such contracts was first established in the United States in a Massachusetts case, Parker v. Nightingale, 6 Allen 341 (1863), but not a single sample case involved such a covenant. Between the polar influences of informal regulation and regulation by new legal doctrines, such as equitable covenant, there existed the thousands of mundane legal adjustments discussed here.

7. On the proportion of rented homes, see Rodwin, *Housing and Economic Progress*, p. 46; Warner, *Streetcar Suburbs*, p. 9; *Annual Report of the Bureau of the Statistics of Labor: A Tenement House Census*, Mass. Doc. no. 15 (1891), p. 540. In all but two sections of Boston—West Roxbury and Lower Dorchester—the number of rented houses exceeded the number of those owned. Most areas of the city could have been called rental districts. However, these three districts had the highest ratios of rented to owned houses, as calculated from *Tenement House Census*, Mass. Doc. no. 15 (1891), pp. 528-538. On the low-rent character of the North and West

ends, see Oscar Handlin, *Boston's Immigrants*, p. 15. On the South End, see Albert B. Wolfe, *The Lodging House Problem in Boston* (Cambridge, Mass., 1913), chap. 2, and Woods, *City Wilderness*, pp. 1-2, 34-35. The Boston of 1870 experienced a population growth rate of 23 percent during the succeeding 10 years. In addition, annexation of Brighton, Charlestown, and West Roxbury in 1873 contributed another 21 percent to the official growth rate of the 1870s; see *Tenth Census of the United States, 1880*, Vol. 1, *Population*, p. 210. On the division of living space, see Woods, *Americans in Process*, pp. 38-39.

8. On the demand for housing, see Rodwin, *Housing and Economic Progress*, pp. 88-91, and Warner, *Streetcar Suburbs*, p. 4. Termination of tenancy was the subject of the *Revised Laws of Massachusetts* (1902), ch. 129, secs. 11, 12. On leases, see Smith, *Justice and the Poor*, pp. 13-14. For a good example of a clumsy, violent, do-it-yourself eviction, see Ciampa v. DiStasio, case no. 9241, Suffolk County Superior Court, Civil Business (1901).

9. In 1880, 90 percent of the tenants defaulted (N = 40); in 1900, 80 percent defaulted (N = 10). Only 20 percent of the tenants in either year retained defense counsel. The remaining 80 percent might have been too poor to hire a lawyer. However, at least one-third of them were white-collar or skilled blue-collar workers, who might have had the financial resources but lacked a good defense or the inclination to resist. On court costs and constables' fees, see *Revised Laws of Massachusetts* (1902), ch. 181, sec. 3.

10. About 14 percent of the plaintiffs represented themselves in ejectment actions in 1880 and 1900 (N = 50); only one landlord acted as his own attorney in a rent claim (N = 90). In the remaining sample cases—tenants' suits, builders' actions, and petitions for assessment of damage or betterment—no plaintiff was without a lawyer (N = 59).

11. Two ejectment specialists appeared in the 1880 sample. William A. Dame handled two-thirds of the sample ejectment actions in the North End (N = 9). Charles H. Fleming represented one-sixth (N = 24) of the landlords in the South End. Both men were about 40 years old; they and their parents were born in the United States; both maintained offices in the districts where the ejectments occurred, but neither resided in them.

12. Between 157,000 and 800,000 people entered Boston temporarily during the 1880s; see Thernstrom, *Other Bostonians*, p. 21. Only 35 percent of the 1880 sample cases (N = 40) were defaulted, and 43 percent took more than three months to conclude. Landlords won 80 percent of these actions. Only 15 percent resulted in partial recoveries. About 65 percent of the defendants in 1880 retained a lawyer.

13. In 1880, 70 percent of rent claims (N = 40) were in the $20 to $100 range. The rental periods represented by these amounts were estimated from the average rents listed in *Tenement House Census*, Mass. Doc.

no. 15 (1891), p. 575. See above, Chapter Four, note 10, concerning lawyers' financial interests in petty cases. See above, note 10, and the *Revised Laws of Massachusetts* (1902), ch. 181, on ejectments.

14. The growth rate for the 1870s was 23 percent (see above, note 7); for the 1880s, 23.6 percent; for the 1890s, 25.1 percent. See *Twelfth Census of the United States, 1900*, Vol. 1, *Population*, p. 430. On the citywide housing market, see Warner, *Streetcar Suburbs*, pp. 52-64, and Paine, "Housing Conditions in Boston," p. 124.

15. Woods, *Americans in Process*, chap. 3 and p. 115; Frederic A. Bushee, *Ethnic Factors in the Population of Boston* (New York, 1903), p. 30; Firey, *Land Use in Central Boston*, pp. 192-197; Warner, *Streetcar Suburbs*, p. 79; *Tenement House Census*, Mass. Doc. no. 15 (1891), pp. 529, 531. The minimum vacancy standard was assumed to be 4 percent. These districts were less crowded in the early 1890s than they had been in the 1850s. See Rodwin, *Housing and Economic Progress*, p. 199n.

16. Robert A. Woods and Albert J. Kennedy, *The Zone of Emergence: Observations of the Lower Middle and Upper Working Class Communities of Boston, 1905-1915*, abr. and ed. Sam B. Warner, Jr. (Cambridge, Mass., 1962), p. 136; Woods, *City Wilderness*, pp. 3-4, 37-38, 49-50, 55, 87-88. See also Wolfe, *Lodging House Problem*, pp. 109-114. On the vacancy rate, see *Tenement House Census*, Mass. Doc. no. 15 (1891), pp. 531-535. See also note 15 above. The population of the South End grew by about 37 percent between 1891 and 1901. In the same period the number of tenements rose by 73 percent. These figures were calculated from data in *Tenement House Census*, Mass., Doc. no. 15 (1891), pp. 528-529, and in *Report of the Tenement-House Commission*, City Doc. no. 77 (1904), Appendix A, table 1.

17. Of the sample rent claims at the turn of the century (N = 50), 80 percent were successfully prosecuted. About 44 percent of the defendants defaulted. Only 26 percent of the cases took more than three months to conclude. There were partial recoveries in 32 percent of them. See note 12 above for the 1880 figures.

18. Sixty-two percent of the defendants held white-collar jobs (N = 44).

19. Only one of the sample cases for 1880 and 1900 (N = 26) was defaulted without an appearance by the defendant. On third-party rights, see *Revised Laws of Massachusetts* (1902), ch. 197, secs. 4-5. About 70 percent of the builders' cases were debt actions (N = 26). A setoff is "a counter demand, which defendant holds against plaintiff, arising out of a transaction extrinsic of plaintiff's cause of action." A counterclaim is "a claim presented by a defendant in opposition to or deduction from the claim of the plaintiff" (*Black's Law Dictionary*, 4th ed. [1951]). These occurred in one-third of the sample suits. About 65 percent of the sample suits were withdrawn by the plaintiff or discontinued by the court for lack

of prosecution. Of the 11 cases in which judgments or agreements were recorded, only 4 resulted in a full recovery. None of the 8 sample liens was enforced, that is, the property was not sold to compensate the plaintiff.

20. Warner, *Streetcar Suburbs*, pp. 117-124.

21. Three-fourths of the suits brought in 1880 (N = 14) involved work in the Back Bay, Dorchester, Roxbury, and West Roxbury. Only two of them were claims for building an entire house; the rest were claims of subcontractors. Three-fourths of the 1900 suits (N = 12) were concerned with work done in these districts, and half of them involved the installation of plumbing. Three-fourths of the 1880 suits were for amounts ranging from $100 to $1,000. Two-thirds of the 1900 suits were for amounts ranging from $100 to $500. Only 18 percent of the builders (N = 26) had business assets of $1,000, and only one of the homeowners did. The annual income of the typical middle-class family that bought a new house in late-nineteenth-century Boston ranged from $700 to $1,200 per year, according to Rodwin, *Housing and Economic Progress*, p. 32. The prices paid by middle-income families for new houses were suggested in S. B. Reed, *House-Plans for Everybody* (New York, 1883), and Louis H. Gibson, *Convenient Houses* (New York, 1889). On contracting practices, see Leslie H. Allen, *Cost Accounting on Construction Work* (Boston, 1914), pp. 2-3; Henry Ericsson, *Sixty Years a Builder* (Chicago, 1942), pp. 253-254; Building Trades Employers' Association of Boston, *Rules for Estimating* (Boston, 1918), p. 3.

22. Warner, *Streetcar Suburbs*, pp. 31, 140; Matthews, *City Government of Boston*, pp. 83-85, 89-92, 94-95.

23. Appeals to the superior court were the subject of the *Revised Laws of Massachusetts* (1902), ch. 48, sec. 109. The 1880 sample (N = 3) indicates that there were about 22 petitions presented that year. The 1900 sample (N = 21) implies that 338 petitions were filed in that year.

24. About 50 percent of the petitioners for damages (N = 24) were small businesses or businessmen. The rest were a mixture of single women, clerks, blue-collar workers, and several banks. *Revised Laws of Massachusetts* (1902), chs. 48 and 50, dealt with assessments for betterment. Betterment N = 4 in 1880; N = 2 in 1900. On corruption in assessments, see Matthews, *City Government of Boston*, pp. 37-40.

25. Over half of the suits (N = 30) took two or three years to conclude. All of the 1880 suits (N = 7) were withdrawn, and 74 percent of the 1900 suits (N = 23) were resolved by written agreements to a compromise figure.

26. See Warner, *Streetcar Suburbs*, pp. 141-152, for a summary of the housing market factors.

27. Antin, *Promised Land*, pp. 301, 310-312.

28. About 68 percent of the landlords (N = 28) in the 1880 rent

claims did not live in the same ward as the defending tenant; in 1900 the figure was 80 percent (N = 39). The figure for ejectment actions in 1880 was 86 percent (N = 35), 90 percent in 1900 (N = 10). Only 1 of 26 builders in the sample resided in the same ward as the homeowner. Warner observed that the typical suburban builder-speculator built on land within two blocks of his own home (*Streetcar Suburbs*, p. 127). The buyer was not just a mortgagor but a new neighbor. For this reason builders were probably careful to check occupants' financial condition and were reluctant to litigate.

29. Jews and Italians living in the North and West ends were prominent among the real-estate owners and brokers in those sections (Woods, *Americans in Process*, pp. 112-113, 120). Woods also observed that the Jews and Italians there, though among the poorest residents of the city, had the least need for outside philanthropy (*Americans in Process*, p. 332), because the people of the ghetto liked to take care of their own affairs. Furthermore, data in *Tenement House Census*, Mass. Doc. no. 15 (1891), pp. 528-538, show that the North and West ends (excluding the fashionable and the black sections of Beacon Hill) had the highest proportions of landlords living in the buildings they owned. The North End and West End rate was about 12 percent, the South End rate was only about 5.5 percent. Suits brought by suburban landlords in 1880 accounted for 20 percent of the total (N = 80); in 1900 they accounted for 46 percent (N = 59).

30. In 1880, 74 percent (N = 72) of the plaintiffs were clerks, salespeople, small businessmen, or blue-collar workers; in 1900 the figure was 64 percent (N = 55). First- and second-generation immigrants constituted 32 percent of the plaintiffs (N = 60) in 1880, 68 percent in 1900 (N = 50). Women initiated 14 percent of the lawsuits in 1880 (N = 102), 34 percent in 1900 (N = 97).

CHAPTER SIX. Accidents

1. A. B. Pasternack, *private interview held in Philadelphia, May 1976.* The accident occurred in 1905.

2. Herlihy, ed., *Boston*, pp. 690-700.

3. On the growing complexity of negligence law, see Friedman, *History of American Law*, p. 409; Thomas G. Shearman and Amasa A. Redfield, *Treatise on the Law of Negligence*, 5th ed. rev. (New York, 1898), p. 276; Wex S. Malone, "The Formative Era of Contributory Negligence," *Illinois Law Review* 41 (1946):166-178.

4. Herlihy, ed., *Boston*, pp. 270, 721, 727; *Railroad Commissioners' Report*, Mass. Doc. no. 14 (1889), pp. 348-349; *Railroad Commissioners' Report*, Mass. Doc. no. 14 (1901), pp. 410-413.

NOTES TO CHAPTER SIX

5. On the growth of the lines, see *Railroad Commissioners' Report*, Mass. Doc. no. 14 (1881), pp. 90-91; *Railroad Commissioners' Report*, Mass. Doc. no. 14 (1889), pp. 348-349. See also *Report on Streetcar Blockades*, City Doc. no. 125 (1885).

6. Department of the Interior, U.S. Census Office, *Eleventh Census of the United States, 1890*, Bulletin 55, *The Relative Economy of Cable, Electric, and Animal Motive Power for Street Railways* (Washington, D.C., 1890), p. 8. *Railroad Commissioners' Report*, Mass. Doc. no. 14 (1901), pp. 405-409, shows the growth of the trolley system. See also note 4 above. Torrey, *A Lawyer's Recollections*, pp. 201-202, discusses speed in the horse age. On downtown traffic, see Boston Transit Commission, *Annual Report, 1899* (Boston, 1899), p. 7.

7. *Acts and Resolves of Massachusetts* (1871), ch. 381; *Rules and Regulations for the Running of Street-Cars*, City Doc. no. 31 (1879), pp. 1-3; *Boston City Ordinances* (Boston, 1879), ch. 59; *Annual Report of the Police Commissioners*, City Doc. no. 77 (1880), p. 211; *Boston City Ordinances* (Boston, 1906), ch. 47, secs. 57-61.

8. City Doc. nos. 125, 142, and 152 (1885); Blodgett, *Gentle Reformers*, p. 109; Herlihy, ed., *Boston*, p. 232.

9. Excessive speed was considered in Hanlon v. South Boston Horse R. Co., 129 Mass. 310 (1880). The supreme judicial court reversed itself in 1910 in Horsman v. Brockton & P. St. Ry. Co., 205 Mass. 519. Child trespassers were considered in Brightman v. Union St. Ry. Co., 167 Mass. 113 (1896). See also Herlihy, ed., *Boston*, p. 679. The recollection was Mary Antin's in *The Promised Land*, p. 266.

10. Robbins v. Springfield St. Ry. Co., 165 Mass. 30 (1895); Jordan v. Old Colony St. Ry. Co., 188 Mass. 124 (1905).

11. N = 2 in 1880; superior court N = 48 and municipal court N = 15 in 1900.

12. In the nineteenth century a cart was a "two-wheeled vehicle of lighter or more elegant make, with springs, drawn by one horse at a rapid pace" (*OED*). Herlihy, ed., *Boston*, pp. 691, 697, and *Board of Police Report*, Mass. Doc. no. 49 (1900), p. 93, deal with traffic problems. The number of cart-and-carriage torts was estimated from an N of 6 in 1880 and an N of 13 in 1900.

13. *Acts and Resolves of Massachusetts* (1894), ch. 548, sec. 23, created the Transit Commission. On its work, see George G. Crocker, "The Passenger Traffic of Boston and the Subway," *New England Magazine*, n.s. 19 (1899):523-541.

14. On the evolution of railroad and street-railway negligence doctrine, see Waterman L. Williams, *Statutory Torts in Massachusetts*, 2d ed. rev. (Boston, 1906), p. 141n, and Gustavus Hay, *The Law of Railroad Accidents in Massachusetts* (Boston, 1897). Railroad accident figures appeared in *Railroad Commissioners' Report*, Mass. Doc. no. 14 (1881), pp. 159, 163 and

Railroad Commissioners' Report, Mass. Doc. no. 14 (1901), appendix, pp. 142, 145.

15. Williams, *Statutory Torts*, p. 141n.

16. *Acts and Resolves of Massachusetts* (1881), ch. 199, and (1883), ch. 243. A list of the cases relating to the latter act may be found in the marginal notes of the *Revised Laws of Massachusetts* (1902), ch. 111, sec. 267.

17. The number of torts was estimated from an N of 0 in 1880 and an N of 8 in 1900. Herlihy, ed., *Boston*, pp. 248-249, discusses switching, and Matthews, *City Government of Boston*, p. 92, deals with grade crossings. These torts were transitory actions, that is, they were founded on a wrong that might have been committed anywhere and therefore could be brought in any jurisdiction where the injury alleged was considered wrongful.

18. *Gas Commissioners' Report*, Mass. Doc. no. 35 (1887), pp. 38, 46-47; *Gas and Electric Light Commissioners' Report*, Mass. Doc. no. 35 (1901), pp. 125-126, 133-135.

19. *Gas and Electric Light Commissioners' Report*, Mass. Doc. no. 35 (1901), pp. 85-99.

20. *Acts and Resolves of Massachusetts* (1885), ch. 314, created the Gas Commission. On gas regulation, see *Communication . . . Relative to Inspection of Gas Piping and Fixtures*, City Doc. no. 47 (1897), and *Boston City Ordinances* (1897), ch. 265. *Gas and Electric Light Commissioners' Report*, Mass. Doc. no. 35 (1901), describes a variety of accidents, pp. 85-99.

21. The 1880 sample did not include a single tort against a gas company. The number of actions filed in Boston at the turn of the century was estimated from an N of 19.

22. See Holly v. Boston Gaslight Co., 74 Mass. 123 (1857); Hunt v. Lowell Gaslight Co., 83 Mass. 343 (1861); Bartlett v. Boston Gaslight Co., 117 Mass. 533 (1875).

23. The number of cases was estimated from an N of 0 in 1880 and an N of 18 in 1900.

24. See Farwell v. Boston & Worcester R.R., 4 Metc. 49 (1842). See also Wex S. Malone, "The Genesis of Wrongful Death," *Stanford Law Review* 17 (1965):1067-1073.

25. *Acts and Resolves of Massachusetts* (1887), ch. 270.

26. The list of workmen's compensation cases may be found in the marginal notes of the *Revised Laws of Massachusetts* (1902), ch. 106, sec. 71. Cf. Lawrence M. Friedman and Jack Ladinsky, "Law and Social Change in the Progressive Era: The Law of Industrial Accidents," in Stanley N. Katz and Stanley I. Kutler, eds., *New Perspectives on the American Past*, Vol. 2 (Boston, 1969), pp. 118-189. They argue that the unpredictability of industrial-accident litigation ultimately led employers as well as employees to favor the transfer of workmen's compensation from the courts to administrative agencies, which made scheduled awards established by statute.

27. The actual number of cases was estimated from an N of 6 in 1880, 29 in 1900. See *Board of Police Report*, Mass. Doc. no. 49 (1900), p. 93, for a description of the accidents.

28. N = 15 for personal-injury suits, including property-damage claims; N = 11 for property-damage claims alone.

29. On the predominance of the street railway in urban transportation at the turn of the century, see Warner, *Streetcar Suburbs*.

30. The number of cases was estimated from an N of 14 in 1880, 151 in 1900.

Urbanizing Alameda County (Oakland), California, did not experience such a sharp increase in tortious litigation until the automobile became ubiquitous between 1910 and 1930. Cf. Friedman and Percival, "Two Courts," p. 281. At the end of the nineteenth century, however, Oakland was the hub of a community less intensively urbanized and industrialized than Boston. Compare the following statistics:

	Boston	Oakland
Population in 1900[a]	560,892	66,960
Miles of street railway track in 1902[b]	452	123
Number of street railway passengers in 1902[b]	228,000,000	17,000,000
Number of manufacturing establishments in 1900[c]	7,247	752
Average number of wage earners in 1900[c]	72,142	4,012

Sources: (a) U.S. Census Office, *Twelfth Census of the United States, 1900*, Vol. 1, *Population*, p. lxix; (b) Department of Commerce and Labor, Bureau of the Census, *Street and Electric Railways, 1902* (Washington, D.C., 1905), p. 24; (c) U.S. Census Office, *Abstract of the Twelfth Census of the United States, 1900*, pp. 352, 357.

31. In 1880 about 30 torts were filed in the municipal court and 90 in the superior court. In 1900 about 1,650 torts were filed in each court. These figures were estimated from the samples. Three out of four lower-court claims (*ad damnum*) were for $1,000 to $2,000 (N = 49). Three out of four claims before the superior bench were for $3,000 or more, three-fifths of them for at least $5,000 (N = 102). Just over half of the suits filed in the municipal court were completed in three months or less, whereas only one-fifth of the superior court cases were finished that quickly. About one-third of the lower tribunal's actions were terminated by a written agreement between the parties; in the higher court the figure was two-thirds. For the rates of appeal, see below, p. 114.

32. *Acts and Resolves of Massachusetts* (1866), ch. 279, sec. 9, set the $2,000 limit on municipal court claims. Lengthy proceedings in jury trials were discussed in Moorfield Storey's *Reform of Legal Procedure*, pp. 92-98. On settlements, see above, note 31. An appeal required the posting of a

$100 bond. See *Rules for Civil Business of the Municipal Court of the City of Boston* (Boston, 1891), p. 20.

33. Costs did not exceed $10 in 78 percent of the municipal court cases. About 62 percent of all negligence suits filed in both tribunals were finished in the superior court. This proportion included lower-court cases appealed to the superior bench or initiated before it, and it excluded those cases appealed to the supreme judicial court.

The courts below the superior level apparently did not function as proving grounds for torts in urban Alameda County, California, or in rural San Benito County, California, and Chippewa County, Wisconsin. There the percentage of cases appealed to superior courts was probably much smaller. Cf. Friedman and Percival, "Two Courts," p. 277; Laurent, *Trial Court*, pp. 189, 196.

34. N = 151. In New Haven, Connecticut, between 1919 and 1932, similarly small proportions of negligence suits were appealed to the state supreme court. Cf. Clark and Shulman, *Law Administration in Connecticut*, p. 44.

35. Forty-two percent of the findings by judges or juries were for the defendants, 58 percent for the plaintiffs (N = 19). Seventy out of 102 superior court personal-injury suits in the sample were terminated by a written agreement between the parties.

36. The *ad damnum* was between $5,000 and $25,000 in 60 percent of the cases (N = 102).

37. The *ad damnum* was not recovered in any of the sample cases from the superior or municipal courts (N = 151).

38. N = 94 for recoveries, N = 151 for initial claims (*ad damnum*). The award exceeded 10 percent of the *ad damnum* in only 14 percent of the cases.

In New Haven and Waterbury, Connecticut, during the 1920s, 77 percent of recoveries in negligence suits (other than those involving automobiles) were greater than $500. Cf. Clark and Shulman, *Law Administration in Connecticut*, p. 33.

39. Friedman and Ladinsky, "Law and Social Change," p. 189, recount similar results in New York and Wisconsin. Richard A. Posner, however, has suggested that between 1875 and 1905 judgments in accident cases nationwide were generally much larger and essentially adequate to meet the victims' needs, that is, to cover lost earnings and medical expenses as well as pain and suffering. Posner was referring mainly to severe injuries, for example, those involving loss of a limb. He also drew his evidence primarily from appellate cases, which he realized might have exaggerated the size of awards. See his "A Theory of Negligence," pp. 92–94.

40. N = 63 for street railways, N = 6 for express companies, N = 18 for workmen's compensation, N = 19 for gas companies, N = 8 for rail-

roads, and N = 29 for miscellaneous accidents. See Matthews, *City Government of Boston*, pp. 94-95, 161.

41. N = 151.

42. The figures are for the superior and the municipal courts. Adjudication was typically quicker in the lower tribunal. See above, note 31. On delay in the superior court, see Storey, *Reform of Legal Procedure*, pp. 51-52.

43. Three firms—Coakley and Coakley; Burns and Clarke; and Daggett, Young, and Jefferson—as well as two solo practitioners—John J. Scott and John H. Blanchard—represented 24 percent of the sample plaintiffs (N = 151). The Coakley firm appeard 13 times, the Burns firm 4 times, and the others 5 to 7 times. No other firms or solo practitioners appeared more than twice in the sample.

44. Friedman, *History of American Law*, pp. 422-423.

45. L. G. Smith, "The Evolution of the Ambulance Chaser," *Green Bag* 14 (1902):264.

46. F. B. Mackinnon, *Contingent Fees for Legal Services* (Chicago, 1964), p. 1, defines the term; Bar Association of the City of Boston, Records of the Council, minutes of a meeting held Mar. 13, 1897, deals with unmeritorious suits.

47. There were 25 streetcar accidents reported for 1880 in *Railroad Commissioners' Report*, Mass. Doc. no. 14 (1881), pp. 90-91. Twenty years later 1,700 accidents were recorded in *Railroad Commissioners' Report*, Mass. Doc. no. 14 (1901), pp. 410-413. In 1880, 15 torts against street railways were listed in the dockets; in 1900 there were about 1,400 such actions (estimated from an N of 63). The plaintiffs' attorneys were distributed by years at the bar as follows (N = 151): 27 percent, 1-5 years; 27 percent, 6-10 years; 24 percent, 11-15 years; 22 percent, 16 years or more. About 64 percent of the attorneys were Yankees (N = 53); the remainder were first- or second-generation immigrants of various antecedents. The proportion of immigrant lawyers was slightly greater in negligence cases than in lawsuits generally. Ten of the sample attorneys were listed in *Hubbell's Legal Directory*.

48. The occupational distribution of the plaintiffs was as follows (N = 73): 9 percent professionals and semiprofessionals; 3 percent major proprietors; 23 percent small businessmen (petty proprietors); 17 percent clerical and salespeople; 18 percent skilled blue-collar workers; 20 percent semiskilled blue-collar workers; 9 percent unskilled blue-collar workers. Nationality N = 58. In 1900, 72 percent of the people of Boston had parents born outside the United States. See U.S. Census Office, *Twelfth Census of the United States, 1900*, Vol. 1, *Population*, p. clxviii. Sex N = 148.

49. See Chapter Two, pp. 18-29.

50. Wages for motormen and conductors each accounted for about 19 percent of annual operating expenses at the turn of the century. Dam-

ages and legal expenses in connection with damages amounted to about 10 percent of annual operating expenses. Source: Department of Commerce and Labor, Bureau of the Census, *Street and Electric Railways, 1902*, p. 79.

51. Between 1892 and 1900 the number of personal life insurance policies in force in Massachusetts rose from 88,687 to 786,280. These figures do not include industrial policies. The amount of accident and liability insurance in force in the state rose from $185.5 million to $411.9 million during the same period. Separate figures for accident and liability insurance are not available. Although these figures are for the entire state, they suggest what occurred in Boston, the largest city in Massachusetts. Sources: *Report of the Insurance Commissioner*, Mass. Doc. no. 9 (1892), pp. xlviii-li; *Report of the Insurance Commissioner*, Mass. Doc. no. 9 (1900), pp. lvi-lix.

52. See Morton Keller, *The Life Insurance Enterprise, 1885-1910* (Cambridge, Mass., 1963), pp. 187-189. Keller does not specifically consider accident and liability insurance, but the scarcity of lawsuits in the Boston trial courts involving claims against companies selling those coverages (N = 1) indicates that similar settlement patterns prevailed throughout the insurance industry.

CHAPTER SEVEN. Malice

1. Not all categories of divorce involved the willful infliction of harm. See p. 126. In 1880 fraud, assault, slander, breach of marriage promise, bastardy, and alienation of affection were the grounds for 143 lawsuits (estimated from an N of 17); in 1900 the figure was 603 (estimated from an N of 28). In the earlier year 154 divorces were granted; at the turn of the century 415 divorce petitions were filed, 351 granted. Source: *Registration Report*, Mass. Doc. no. 1 (1900), pp. 112-113. In 1880 nearly 7,500 civil actions were filed with the superior and municipal courts; 20 years later the figure exceeded 19,000.

2. Thirteen of 15 sample actions for slander and alienation of affection were based on accusations of adultery.

3. The *Revised Statutes* of 1835 specified 2 acts of fraud punishable by fine or imprisonment, as did the *General Statutes* of 1860. The *Public Statutes* of 1882 listed 9 forms of criminal fraud, and the *Revised Laws* of 1902 specified 15. Cf. Lawrence M. Friedman, *Contract Law in America: A Social and Economic Case Study* (Madison, 1965), p. 156.

4. In 1880 there were 70 arrests for fraud, 50 in 1900. Sources: *Annual Report of the Police Commissioner*, City Doc. no. 77 (1880), pp. 6-8; *Board of Police Report*, Mass. Doc. no. 49 (1900), p. 44. The definition is from Edwin M. Schur, "Sociological Analysis of Confidence Swindling,"

in Marshall B. Clinard and Richard Quinney, eds., *Criminal Behavior Systems* (New York, 1967), p. 437.

5. Edwin H. Sutherland and Donald R. Cressey, *Principles of Criminology*, 7th ed. (New York, 1966), pp. 45, 682, deal with the prevalence of fraud. On the difficulties of proving fraud, see Commonwealth v. Drew, 19 Pick. 179 (1841); People v. Ashley, 267 P.2d 271.

6. Herlihy, ed., *Boston*, p. 234, discusses speculation in the 1890s. Four of five sample actions from 1900 were concerned with investment swindles. On equity and equity jurisdiction in Massachusetts, see Edwin H. Woodruff, "Chancery in Massachusetts," *Law Quarterly Review* 5 (1889): 370-386, and *Acts and Resolves of Massachusetts* (1883), ch. 223, secs. 1-2.

7. The number of assault cases was estimated from an N of 4 in 1880 and an N of 5 in 1900. The full and correct title of the tort is "assault and battery," the "unlawful touching of the person of another by the aggressor himself or by any other substance put in motion by him." See William Mack and Howard P. Nash, eds., *Cyclopedia of Law and Procedure*, 41 vols. (New York, 1901-1913), 3:1021.

8. There were 2,315 arrests for assault in 1880; in 1900 there were 2,565. Sources: *Annual Report of the Police Commissioner*, City Doc. no. 77 (1880), p. 6; *Board of Police Report*, Mass. Doc. no. 49 (1900), p. 42. Between 1880 and 1900 arrests for serious crimes increased by the following factors: murder, 4.0; manslaughter, 6.5; robbery, 2.3; rape, 2.3. The police force grew by a factor of 1.7. Traffic duties and special service at public events or in public buildings also increased during the 1880s and 1890s. Sources: *Annual Report of the Police Commissioner*, City Doc. no. 77 (1880), p. 10; *Board of Police Report*, Mass. Doc. no. 49 (1900), p. 9.

9. The quotation is from Roger Lane, "Urbanization and Criminal Violence in the 19th Century: Massachusetts as a Test Case," in Hugh D. Graham and Ted R. Gurr, eds., *The History of Violence in America* (New York, 1969), p. 478.

10. Not a single sample defendant defaulted (N = 19).

11. Plaintiff occupational N = 13. Fourteen of 16 sample defendants were from the white-collar or skilled blue-collar stratum.

12. For a summary of the marriage controversies, see Friedman, *History of American Law*, pp. 434-440. The quotations are from Smith, *Justice and the Poor*, p. 73.

13. Nelson Blake, *The Road to Reno: A History of Divorce in the United States* (New York, 1962), pp. 90-91, 134; William L. O'Neill, *Divorce in the Progressive Era* (New Haven, 1967), p. 27. Boston (Suffolk County) divorce figures appear above in note 1. The supreme judicial court also possessed jurisdiction in divorce, but few petitions were filed there. Divorce libels were civil actions heard in special sessions of the superior court and listed in separate dockets. They thus form their own statistical universe. The

annual volumes of cases for 1880 and 1900 are too small to sample. Accuracy would demand an analysis of each divorce action filed in each year. However, these two populations are slightly larger than the samples drawn from the regular civil sessions of the superior court for each year. Therefore, an accurate analysis of the divorce business would more than double the number of superior court cases to be considered. Because divorce has been more carefully scrutinized than other civil business of the courts over the past 100 years, the additional investment of time and money did not seem justifiable. I have relied on printed statistics and secondary materials for this discussion.

14. Three divorces were granted for imprisonment or impotency in 1880, 2 in 1900. In 1880 adultery and desertion were grounds for 104 divorces, 238 in 1900. Sources: *Registration Report*, Mass. Doc. no. 1 (1885), p. 62; *Registration Report*, Mass. Doc. no. 1 (1900), p. 112.

15. On collusive divorce, see Friedman, *History of American Law*, pp. 438-440. For Boston (Suffolk County) divorce statistics, see *Registration Report*, Mass. Doc. no. 1 (1900), pp. 112-113. To obtain a divorce on grounds of desertion the plaintiff had to show that the libelee left without justification, that he or she failed to cohabit for three consecutive years, and that there was no consent to separation. This was not difficult to establish if the divorce were uncontested. See *Public Statutes of Massachusetts* (Boston, 1882), ch. 146, sec. 1; Ford v. Ford, 143 Mass. 577 (1887); Bradley v. Bradley, 160 Mass. 258 (1893).

16. Smith, *Justice and the Poor*, p. 155; Grant, *Law and the Family*, p. 171.

17. N = 1 in 1880; N = 4 in 1900.

18. Mack and Nash, eds. *Cyclopedia of Law*, 5:1000, 1002-1003, 1005; Van Houten v. Morse, 162 Mass. 414 (1894); Harrison v. Swift, 13 Allen 144 (1866).

19. Only 15 percent of the divorce actions at the turn of the century were not pursued to a final decree. See *Registration Report*, Mass. Doc. no. 1 (1900), pp. 112-113. Each of the sample marriage-promise actions of 1900 ended by an agreement to judgment for neither party, or it was dismissed for lack of prosecution. Three out of four actions took four months to three years to conclude.

20. Estimating from an N of 5 in 1880 and an N of 3 in 1900, there were about 40 bastardy actions begun in the earlier year and 50 in the later one. On the quasi-criminal nature of bastardy, see Young v. Makepeace, 103 Mass. 50 (1869); *General Statutes of Massachusetts* (Boston, 1860), ch. 72, secs. 1, 4, 7; *Public Statutes* (1882), ch. 85, secs. 1, 4, 15. Odewald v. Woodsum, 142 Mass. 512 (1886), deals with efforts to attack the prosecutrix's character. The degree of guilt was at issue in Richardson v. Burleigh, 85 Mass. 479 (1852). Procedural imperfection is the subject of Hyde v. Chapin, 60 Mass. 64 (1850).

21. Preliminary hearings were prescribed by the *General Statutes*

(1860), ch. 72, sec. 1 and the *Public Statutes* (1882), ch. 85, sec. 1. The sample actions lasted from four months to three years; awards ranged from $50 to $150. The Boston Legal Aid Society's *Annual Report* (1910-1911), p. 10, claims that awards were usually calculated according to the father's ability to pay.

22. Herlihy, ed., *Boston*, p. 530.

23. Legal Aid Society, *Annual Report* (1910-1911), pp. 10-11.

24. Thirteen of 15 slander and alienation-of-affection suits were based on accusations of adultery. Eleven of those suits took four months to three years to conclude. By written agreement or for lack of prosecution, plaintiffs failed to recover in 13 of the lawsuits.

25. Plaintiffs' occupational N = 10. These figures do not include divorce, for which no sample was drawn; see above, note 13. Divorce was usually beyond the financial means of poor couples, who simply stopped living together or received a legal separation. See Robert Grant, *Fourscore: An Autobiography* (Boston, 1934), pp. 234-235; Hurst, *Growth of American Law*, p. 149; Smith, *Justice and the Poor*, p. 155.

CONCLUSION. At the Threshold of the Law

1. The traditional business of Boston's seventeenth-century trial courts is reflected in John Noble and J. F. Cronin, eds., *Records of the Court of Assistants of the Colony of Massachusetts Bay*, 3 vols. (Boston, 1901-1928). A handful of eighteenth-century cases survives in the care of Mr. Edward Bellafontaine, Director of the Social Law Library, Boston, Massachusetts. The record of litigation in the early nineteenth century is preserved in the dockets and papers of the civil branches of the Superior Court of Suffolk County and of the Boston Municipal Court.

2. In 1880, 54 percent of all debt actions were defaulted (N = 488); 20 years later the figure was 53 percent (N = 477).

Delays in all forms of action also became greater in Alameda and San Benito counties, California, and in New Haven and Waterbury, Connecticut. Cf. Friedman and Percival, "Two Courts," pp. 290-291; Clark and Shulman, *Law Administration in Connecticut*, pp. 35-42.

3. In 1880, 77 percent (N = 341) of the superior court cases were for debt, as were 81 percent (N = 357) of the municipal court actions. Twenty years later only 57 percent of the superior court cases were for debt, while 39 percent of the actions were for injury (N = 370). In the municipal court, however, debt still accounted for 76 percent of the lawsuits (N = 377). Note that the jury also became more popular in superior court trials concerned with debt. In 1880, 32 percent of the superior court debt actions employed a jury (N = 211); 20 years later the figure was 47 percent (N = 83). However, these superior court trials with a jury represented about the same proportion of all debt actions (12 percent) in 1900 as they had in 1880 (11 percent).

4. In 1900, 47 percent of superior court suits ended by a written agreement (N = 370); 20 years earlier the figure was 31 percent (N = 341). About 16 percent of the municipal court actions of 1880 (N = 357) ended by written agreement; at the turn of the century the figure was still only 17 percent (N = 377).

Written agreements (stipulations) also became more common in negligence suits in Chippewa County, Wisconsin. Studies of Connecticut and California, however, do not note any sharp rise in the popularity of written agreements. If anything, New Haven and Waterbury auto negligence suits suggest a decline in the number of formal compromises in the 1920s. Cf. Laurent, *Trial Court,* p. 61; Friedman and Percival, "Two Courts," pp. 284-285; Clark and Shulman, *Law Administration in Connecticut,* pp. 20-27.

5. On the advantages of specialization, see Barlow F. Christensen, *Lawyers for People of Moderate Means* (Chicago, 1970), p. 45.

6. Blodgett, *Gentle Reformers,* pp. 65-67, 159-160.

7. On distrust of the immigrant electorate, see ibid., pp. 141-171; Solomon, *Ancestors and Immigrants,* pp. 98-99, 175.

8. Storey, *Reform of Legal Procedure,* pp. 91-93, 170-192.

9. The number of cases filed annually was determined from the Superior Court Dockets (1898-1917) and Municipal Court Dockets (1898-1917). See Friedman, *History of American Law,* p. 335, on the image of the courts as marginally useful institutions.

10. Cf. Friedman and Percival, "Two Courts," pp. 299-300. They argue that society has "permitted" the court system to become slow and expensive because it is healthier for the economy to keep parties out of court "except as a last resort."

11. Ethnic and racial compositions were listed by the U.S. Census Office, *Abstract of the Twelfth Census of the United States, 1900,* pp. 103-108.

12. Constance McLaughlin Green, *Holyoke, Massachusetts: A Case History of the Industrial Revolution in America* (New Haven, 1939), pp. 18-65, 137-176.

13. Clyde L. King, *History of the Government of Denver* (Denver, 1911), pp. 93-101; Constance McLaughlin Green, *American Cities in the Growth of the Nation* (Tuckahoe, N.Y., 1957), pp. 143, 148-158; U.S. Census Office, *Twelfth Census of the United States, 1900,* Vol. 1, *Population,* p. 617.

14. Glenn Chesney Quiett, *They Built the West* (New York, 1934), pp. 469-473.

15. Friedman and Percival, "Two Courts," p. 301.

APPENDIX A. Sources and Samples

1. *Revised Laws of Massachusetts* (1902), ch. 173, secs. 24-26.
2. Ibid., ch. 165, sec. 85.

3. Detailed discussions of the federal manuscript census schedules and their indexes are W. Neil Franklin, comp., *Federal Population and Mortality Census Schedules, 1790-1890, in the National Archives and the States: Outline of a Lecture on Their Availability, Content, and Use* (Washington, D.C., 1971); Christine J. Felty, "Schedules of the Census of Population in 1900" (n.p., n.d.) (photocopied), available at the Federal Records Center, Waltham, Mass.; "Guide to the Soundex System," in *Federal Population Censuses, 1790-1890: A Catalog of Microfilm Copies of the Schedules* (Washington, D.C., 1972); Charles Stephenson, "Tracing Those Who Left: Mobility Studies and the Soundex Indexes to the U.S. Census," *Journal of Urban History* 1 (1974):73-84.

4. Good discussions of the directories and their flaws are Knights, *Plain People of Boston*, app. A; Thernstrom, *Other Bostonians*, pp. 280-288.

5. Ibid.

6. The weaknesses of Dun's rating system are the subject of Thomas F. Meagher, *The Commercial Agency "System" of the United States and Canada Exposed* (New York, 1876), and W. Y. Chinn, *The Mercantile Agencies against Commerce: Are We a Nation of Swindlers and Liars?* (New York, 1896). Early writers on commercial credit were aware of numerous other books and articles written in criticism of the mercantile agencies. See Nystrom, *Economics of Retailing*, p. 32, and Earling, *Whom to Trust*, pp. 300-301.

7. H. H. Hubbell, ed. and comp., *Hubbell's Legal Directory* (New York, 1881), p. 3, and *Hubbell's Legal Directory* (New York, 1899), p. 6. Hubbell listed fewer than 1 out of 10 Boston attorneys, which indicates that his directory was very selective.

8. Herbert Arkin and Raymond R. Colton, eds., *Tables for Statisticians* (New York, 1963), pp. 22-23; Hubert M. Blalock, Jr., *Social Statistics*, 2d ed. (New York, 1972), pp. 509-530.

9. The sizes of the four samples were: superior court of 1880, 341; municipal court of 1880, 357; superior court of 1900, 370; municipal court of 1902, 377. See Arkin and Colton, eds., *Tables for Statisticians*, p. 145.

10. Cf. Thernstrom, *Other Bostonians*, pp. 267-268.

11. Cf. ibid., p. 269, regarding tracing problems. See also Knights, *Plain People of Boston*, app. C, and *Federal Population and Mortality Census Schedules*, p. 86. In the 1880 samples 40 percent of the litigants and 62 percent of the lawyers were located in the census schedules. The corresponding figures for 1900 were 50 percent and 56 percent.

12. Two statements on the need to integrate new quantitative and traditional historical methods, which also review much of the literature on the subject, are Eric E. Lampard, "Two Cheers for Quantitative History: An Agnostic Foreword," in Leo F. Schnore, ed., *The New Urban History: Quantitative Explorations by American Historians* (Princeton, 1975), pp. 12-48, and Oscar Handlin, "The Capacity of Quantitative History," *Per-*

spectives in American History 9 (1975):7-26. See also Robert W. Fogel's reply to Oscar Handlin in ibid., pp. 29-32.

APPENDIX C. Occupations and Enterprises

1. Thernstrom, *Other Bostonians*, app. B. Similar schemes have been used by other historians. See Knights, *Plain People of Boston*, app. E; Kathleen Neils Conzen, *Immigrant Milwaukee, 1836-1860* (Cambridge, Mass., 1976), appendix. Both Thernstrom and Conzen discuss at length the shortcomings of this classification method and refer to several critical articles. Both conclude that no practical, superior scheme has been devised.

2. Cf. Thernstrom, *Other Bostonians*, pp. 290-291. Similar modifications were made by Conzen in *Immigrant Milwaukee*, pp. 234-237.

3. The self-employed were identified by means of the business section of the city directories. They were coded as major or petty proprietors, depending on assets.

4. Chief elected officers and appointive positions at the level of police captain or higher.

5. Apprentices are considered with "Semiskilled and Service Workers." For the self-employed, see note 3 above.

APPENDIX D. The Bench

1. *Memorial to Chief Justice Aiken* (n.d., Harvard Law Library).
2. *National Cyclopedia of American Biography*, 18:362.
3. Obituary, *Boston Transcript*, January 23, 1911.
4. *Who Was Who in America*, 1:443.
5. Ibid., 3:505.
6. *Proceedings . . . in Memory of Henry Newton Sheldon* (Boston, 1927).
7. Obituary, *Boston Transcript*, September 18, 1924.
8. Ibid., September 12, 1928.

WORKS CITED

PRIMARY SOURCES

In addition to the sources discussed in Appendix A, the following primary materials were employed.

Public Documents

Boston City Documents (1834-) and *Massachusetts Public Documents* (1858-) are listed by title, number, and date.

Annual Report of the Bureau of the Statistics of Labor. Mass. Doc. no. 15. 1884, 1902.

Annual Report of the Bureau of the Statistics of Labor: A Tenement House Census of Boston. Mass. Doc. no. 15. 1891, 1892.

Annual Report of the Police Commissioner. City Doc. no. 77. 1880.

Board of Police Report. Mass. Doc. no. 49. 1900.

Boston Transit Commission. *Annual Report, 1899.* Boston, 1899.

Changes in Conducting Retail Trade in Boston since 1874. Mass. Doc. no. 15. Part 1. 1899.

Communication . . . Relative to Inspection of Gas Piping and Fixtures. City Doc. no. 47. 1897.

Department of Commerce and Labor, Bureau of the Census. *Street and Electric Railways, 1902.* Washington, D.C., 1905.

Department of the Interior, U.S. Census Office. *Eleventh Census of the United States, 1890.* Bulletin 55. *The Relative Economy of Cable, Electric, and Animal Motive Power for Street Railways.* Washington, D.C., 1890.

——. *Tenth Census of the United States, 1880.* Vol. 1: *Population.* Washington, D.C., 1880.

Gas and Electric Light Commissioners' Report. Mass. Doc. no. 35. 1901.

Gas Commissioners' Report. Mass. Doc. no. 35. 1887.

Massachusetts Bureau of the Statistics of Labor. *Census of Massachusetts, 1885*. Vol. 2: *Manufactures, the Fisheries, and Commerce*. Boston, 1885.

———. *Census of Massachusetts: 1895*. Vol. 5: *Manufactures*. Boston, 1895.

Partial Report of the Special Committee . . . on Tenement Districts. City Doc. no. 125. 1895.

Railroad Commissioners' Report. Mass. Doc. no. 14. 1881, 1889, 1901.

Registration Report. Mass. Doc. no. 1. 1885, 1900.

Report of the Commission Appointed to Revise the City Charter. City Doc. no. 3. 1875.

Report of the Commission . . . to Investigate Tenement-House Conditions in the City of Boston. City Doc. no. 77. 1904.

Report of the Insurance Commissioner. Mass. Doc. no. 9. 1892, 1900.

Report of the Lodging-House Commission. City Doc. no. 160. 1908.

Report on Streetcar Blockades. City Doc. no. 125. 1885.

U.S. Bureau of Labor Statistics. *Index of All Reports*. Washington, D.C., 1902.

U.S. Census Office. *Abstract of the Twelfth Census of the United States, 1900*. Washington, D.C., 1902.

———. *Twelfth Census of the United States, 1900*. Vol. 1: *Population*. Washington, D.C., 1900.

———. *Twelfth Census of the United States: Special Reports on Occupations*.

Contemporary Lawyers' Observations

Abbot, William T. "The Trust Company—Not a Competitor of the Lawyer." *Illinois Law Review* 6(1911): 75-80.

Ames, Richard. "Suggestions from Law School Graduates as to Where and How to Begin Practice." *Harvard Law Review* 27(1914):260-267.

Applegarth, Albert C. "The Jury System and Its Critics." *Green Bag* 4(1892):110-112.

Archer, Gleason L. *Ethical Obligations of the Lawyer*. Boston, 1910.

――――. *Law Office and Court Procedure*. Boston, 1910. Bar Association of the City of Boston. *Annual Report, 1916*. Boston, 1916.

――――. "Record of the Discipline of Lawyers in Massachusetts, 1806-1942." Boston, n.d. (photocopied). At the Boston Bar Association, Boston, Mass.

――――. Records of the Council of the Boston Bar Association, 1885-1926. At the Boston Bar Association, Boston, Mass.

――――. *Report . . . on the Possibility of Increasing the Usefulness of the Association*. Boston, 1885.

Boston Legal Aid Society. *Annual Report, 1902-03*. Boston, 1903.

Brewer, David J. "The Ideal Lawyer." *Atlantic Monthly* 98(1906):587.

――――. "The Jury." *Green Bag* 14(1902):67-69.

Browne, Irving. "The Lawyer's Easy Chair" (column). *Green Bag* 5(1893):245; 6(1894):93-94, 149, 247; 7(1895):199, 482-483; 8(1896):83; 11(1899):89.

Chamberlayne, Charles F. "The Soul of the Profession." *Green Bag* 18(1906):396-401.

Chittenden, L. E. "Legal Reminiscences." *Green Bag* 7(1895):364-367.

Cockrill, Ashley. "The Shyster Lawyer." *Yale Law Journal* 21(1909):383.

Costigan, George P., Jr. "The Proposed American Code of Legal Ethics." *Green Bag* 20(1908):57-71.

Cowles, William H. "Has Trial by Jury in Civil Actions Been Abolished?" *Green Bag* 19(1907):340-351.

Edwards, Percy. "Hustling in the Law." *Green Bag* 4(1892):292-294.

――――. "A Serious Problem." *Green Bag* 5(1893):355-358.

Elder, Margaret M. *The Life of Samuel J. Elder*. New Haven, 1925.

"An English View of the American Bar." *Green Bag* 1(1899):414-416.

Fuller, Horace W. "Overcrowding the Profession." *Green Bag* 3(1891):198-199.

Glanville, W. E. "Legal Ethics." *Green Bag* 8(1896):209-212.

Grant, Robert. *Fourscore: An Autobiography*. Boston, 1934.

——. *Law and the Family*. New York, 1919.

Grinnell, Charles E. "Beyond a Reasonable Doubt." *Green Bag* 9(1897):97-103.

Hall, A. Oakey. "Trial by Newspaper." *Green Bag* 6(1894): 308-310.

Hall, James P. "Practice Work in Law Schools." *Green Bag* 17(1905):528-532.

Hamilton, Peter J. "Scholarship, the Handmaiden of the Lawyer." *Green Bag* 15(1903):159-161.

Hawes, Gilbert R. "Literature and the Law." *Green Bag* 6(1899):234-237.

James Robert Dunbar, A Memorial. Boston, 1916.

"Lawyers and Marriage." *Green Bag* 5(1893):301-302.

Lee, Guy C. "The Lawyer's Position in Society." *Green Bag* 8(1896):246-251.

Marbury, William L. "The Lawyer of Fifty Years Ago and the Lawyer of Today." *Green Bag* 24(1912):64-74.

Moors, Joseph B. "Rufus Choate." *Green Bag* 15(1903): 399-406.

Muensterberg, Hugo. "The Mind of the Juryman, With a Side-light on Women as Jurors." *Century* 86(1913): 711.

Nutter, George R. *Nathan Matthews*. Boston, 1928.

"Oratory of the Bar." *Green Bag* 5(1893):428.

Phillips, John B. "Modifications of the Jury System." *Green Bag* 16(1904):514-519.

Pound, Roscoe. "The Administration of Justice in the Modern City." *Harvard Law Review* 26(1912-13):302-328.

———. "Dogs and the Law." *Green Bag* 8(1896):172-174.

Powers, Samuel L. *Portraits of a Half Century*. Boston, 1925.

Richardson, James B. *Address to the Graduating Class of the Evening Law School of the Young Men's Christian Association, June 7, 1905*. Boston, 1905.

Russell, Alfred. "The Jury System in Civil Cases." *Green Bag* 3(1891):449-451.

Shepard, E. M. "Lawyers and Corporate Capitalization." *Green Bag* 18(1906):601-613.

Sherman, Edgar J. *Recollections of a Long Life*. Boston, 1908.

Smith, L. G. "The Evolution of the Ambulance Chaser." *Green Bag* 14(1902):264.

Smith, Reginald H. *Justice and the Poor*. Boston, 1919.

Stetson, Francis L. "The Lawyer's Livelihood." *Green Bag* 21(1909):45-57.

Storey, Moorfield. *The Reform of Legal Procedure*. New Haven, 1911.

Strickland, Martha. "Women and the Forum." *Green Bag* 3(1891):240-243.

Torrey, George A. *A Lawyer's Recollections In and Out of Court*. Boston, 1910.

Tucker, George F. "The Accused." *Green Bag* 4(1892):153-156.

———. "Professional Remuneration." *Green Bag* 2(1890):446-447.

Urofsky, Melvin I., and Levy, David W. *Letters of Louis D. Brandeis*. Vol. 1. Albany, 1971.

Willard, Joseph A. *Half a Century with Judges and Lawyers*. Boston, 1895.

Woodruff, Edwin H. "Chancery in Massachusetts." *Law Quarterly Review* 5(1889):370-386.

Other Contemporary Observations

Allen, Leslie H. *Cost Accounting on Construction Work*. Boston, 1914.

Antin, Mary. *The Promised Land*. 2d ed. Boston, 1969. Orig. publ. Boston, 1912.

Blanchard, Henry. "Unpaid Medical Services." *Boston Medical and Surgical Journal* 85(1871):1-3.

Bugbee, James M. *The City Government of Boston*. Johns Hopkins University Studies in Historical and Political Science. 5th ser. Vol. 3. Baltimore, 1887.

Building Trades Employers' Association of Boston. *Rules for Estimating*. Boston, 1918.

Chandler, Alfred D. *Annexation of Brookline to Boston*. Brookline, 1880.

Colonial Society of Massachusetts. *Records of the Suffolk County Court, 1671-1680*. Boston, 1933.

Crocker, George G. "The Passenger Traffic of Boston and the Subway." *New England Magazine*, n.s., 19(1899):523-541.

Ericsson, Henry. *Sixty Years a Builder*. Chicago, 1942.

Estabrook, H. K. *Some Slums in Boston*. Boston, 1897.

Foxcroft, Frank. "The Boston Subway and Others." *New England Magazine*, n.s., 13(1895):193-210.

Gibson, Louis H. *Convenient Houses*. New York, 1889.

Matthews, Nathan, Jr. *The City Government of Boston*. Boston, 1895.

"The Medical Blacklist." *Boston Medical and Surgical Journal* 87(1872):361-362.

Noble, John, and Cronin, J. F., eds. *Records of the Court of Assistants of the Colony of Massachusetts Bay*. 3 vols. Boston, 1901-28.

Paine, Robert Treat. "The Housing Conditions in Boston." *Annals of the American Academy of Political and Social Science* 20(1902):121-136.

Phelps, R. F. *South End Operatives and Their Residences*. Boston, 1903.

Porter, Dwight. *Report upon a Sanitary Inspection of Certain Tenement-House Districts in Boston*. Boston, 1888.

Reed, S. B. *House-Plans for Everybody*. New York, 1883.

"Remuneration in the Medical Profession." *Boston Medical and Surgical Journal* 79(1868):83-93.

Wolfe, Albert B. *The Lodging House Problem in Boston*. Cambridge, Mass., 1913.

Woods, Robert A. *Americans in Process*. Boston, 1903.
———. *The City Wilderness*. Boston, 1899.
Woods, Robert A., and Kennedy, Albert J. *The Zone of Emergence: Observations of Lower Middle and Upper Working Class Communities of Boston, 1905-1915*. Abridged and edited by Sam B. Warner, Jr. Cambridge, Mass., 1962.

Massachusetts and Boston Statutes and Rules

Acts and Resolves of Massachusetts. Published annually. 1802-.
Boston City Ordinances. Boston, 1879, 1897, 1906.
General Statutes of Massachusetts. Boston, 1860.
Public Statutes of Massachusetts. Boston, 1882.
Revised Laws of Massachusetts. 3 vols. Boston, 1902.
Revised Statutes of Massachusetts. Boston, 1835.
Rules and Regulations for the Running of Street-Cars. City Doc. no. 31. 1879.
Rules for Civil Business of the Municipal Court of the City of Boston. Boston, 1879, 1891.
Rules of the Superior Court. Boston, 1874.
Rules of the Superior Court of Massachusetts. N.p., 1900.

Secondary Works

Interpretations of Legal Doctrine, 1880-1900

Dillon, John F. *The Law of Municipal Corporations*. New York, 1872.
Friedman, Lawrence M. *Contract Law in America: A Social and Economic Case Study*. Madison, 1965.
———. *A History of American Law*. New York, 1973.
George, William. *The Law of Apartments, Flats, and Tenements*. New York, 1909.
Gilbert, Frank B., ed. *Street Railway Reports*. Albany, 1904.
Hay, Gustavus. *The Law of Railroad Accidents in Massachusetts*. Boston, 1897.
Hurst, James Willard. *The Growth of American Law: The Law Makers*. Boston, 1950.

Levy, Leonard W. *The Law of the Commonwealth and Chief Justice Shaw*. Cambridge, Mass., 1957.

Mack, William, and Nash, Howard P., eds. *Cyclopedia of Law and Procedure*. 41 vols. New York, 1901-13.

Malone, Wex S. "The Formative Era of Contributory Negligence." *Illinois Law Review* 41(1946):166-178.

———. "The Genesis of Wrongful Death." *Stanford Law Review* 17(1965):1067-1073.

Morrill, William W., ed. *American Electrical Cases*. 6 vols. Albany, 1894-97.

Nellis, Andrew J. *Street Railway Accident Law*. Albany, 1904.

Paul, Arnold M. *Conservative Crisis and the Rule of Law: Attitudes of Bar and Bench, 1887-1895*. Ithaca, N.Y., 1960.

Shearman, Thomas G., and Redfield, Amasa A. *Treatise on the Law of Negligence*. 5th ed. rev. New York, 1898.

Webb, James A. *The Law of Passenger and Freight Elevators*. St. Louis, 1896.

Williams, Waterman L. *The Liability of Municipal Corporations for Tort*. Boston, 1901.

———. *Statutory Torts in Massachusetts*. 2d ed. rev. Boston, 1906.

Background

Abrams, Richard M. *Conservatism in a Progressive Era: Massachusetts Politics, 1900-1912*. Cambridge, Mass., 1964.

Baer, Willis N. *The Economic Development of the Cigar Industry in the United States*. Lancaster, Pa., 1933.

Barger, Harold. *Distribution's Place in the American Economy since 1869*. Princeton, 1955.

Baron, Stanley. *Brewed in America: A History of Beer and Ale in the United States*. Boston, 1962.

Blake, Nelson. *The Road to Reno: A History of Divorce in the United States*. New York, 1962.

Blodgett, Geoffrey. *The Gentle Reformers: Massachusetts Democrats in the Cleveland Era*. Cambridge, Mass., 1966.

Boorstin, Daniel J. *The Americans: The Democratic Experience*. New York, 1973.

Boyden, Albert. *Ropes-Gray, 1865-1940*. Boston, 1942.

Braverman, Harry. *Labor and Monopoly Capital: The Degradation of Work in the Twentieth Century*. New York, 1974.

Bushee, Frederic A. *Ethnic Factors in the Population of Boston*. New York, 1903.

Christensen, Barlow A. *Lawyers for People of Moderate Means*. Chicago, 1970.

Clark, Charles, and Shulman, Harry. *A Study of Law Administration in Connecticut*. New Haven, 1937.

Clark, William H. *The History of Winthrop, Massachusetts, 1630-1952*. Winthrop, Mass., 1952.

Cole, Arthur H. *The American Wool Manufacture*. 2 vols. Cambridge, Mass., 1926.

Commons, John R., and Andrews, John B. *Principles of Labor Legislation*. Rev. ed. New York, 1927.

Conzen, Kathleen Neils. *Immigrant Milwaukee, 1836-1860*. Cambridge, Mass., 1976.

Earling, P. R. *Whom to Trust: A Practical Treatise on Mercantile Credits*. Chicago and New York, 1890.

Ebner, Michael H. *The New Urban History: Bibliography on Methodology and Historiography*. Council of Planning Librarians Exchange Bibliography no. 445. Monticello, Ill., 1973.

Firey, Walter. *Land Use in Central Boston*. Cambridge, Mass., 1947.

Friedman, Lawrence M., and Ladinsky, Jack. "Law and Social Change in the Progressive Era: The Law of Industrial Accidents." In Stanley N. Katz and Stanley I. Kutler, eds., *New Perspectives on the American Past*. Vol. 2. Boston, 1969.

Friedman, Lawrence M., and Percival, Robert V. "A Tale of Two Courts: Litigation in Alameda and San Benito Counties." *Law and Society Review* 10(1975-76):267-301.

Friedman, Milton, and Schwartz, Anna J. *A Monetary History of the United States, 1867-1960*. New York, 1963.

Greef, Albert O. *The Commercial Paper House in the United States*. Cambridge, Mass., 1938.

Green, Constance McLaughlin. *American Cities in the Growth of the Nation*. Tuckahoe, N.Y., 1957.

———. *Holyoke, Massachusetts: A Case History of the Industrial Revolution in America*. New Haven, 1939.

Hagerty, James E. *Mercantile Credit*. New York, 1913.

Handlin, Oscar. *Boston's Immigrants: A Study in Acculturation*. Rev. ed. Cambridge, Mass., 1959.

———. "The Modern City as a Field of Historical Study." In Oscar Handlin and John Burchard, eds., *The Historian and the City*. Cambridge, Mass., 1963.

———, and Handlin, Mary F. *Commonwealth, a Study of the Role of Government in the American Economy: Massachusetts, 1774-1861*. Rev. ed. Cambridge, Mass., 1969.

Hart, Albert Bushnell, ed. *Commonwealth History of Massachusetts*. Vol. 5. New York, 1930.

Henretta, James, A. *The Evolution of American Society, 1700-1815*. Lexington, Mass., 1973.

Herlihy, Elizabeth M., ed. *Fifty Years of Boston*. Boston, 1932.

Hindus, Michael S., and Jones, Douglas L. "The Social History of American Law: What It Is and Where to Begin." Paper presented at the sixth annual meeting of the American Society for Legal History, Philadelphia, October 23, 1976.

Hitchcock, Henry-Russell. *A Guide to Boston Architecture, 1637-1954*. New York, 1954.

Hurst, James Willard. "Legal Elements in United States History." *Perspectives in American History* 5(1971):3-92.

Jacobstein, Meyer. *The Tobacco Industry in the United States*. New York, 1907.

Keller, Morton. *The Life Insurance Enterprise, 1885-1910*. Cambridge, Mass., 1963.

Keyssar, Alexander. "Men Out of Work: A Social History of Unemployment in Massachusetts, 1870-1916." Ph.D. diss., Harvard University, 1977.

Kilham, Walter H. *Boston after Bulfinch*. Cambridge, Mass., 1946.

King, Clyde L. *History of the Government of Denver*. Denver, 1911.

Kirkland, Edward C. *Industry Comes of Age: Business, Labor, and Public Policy, 1860-1897*. New York, 1961.

Kniffin, W. H., Jr. *Commercial Paper Acceptances and the Analysis of Credit Statements*. New York, 1918.

Knights, Peter R. *The Plain People of Boston, 1830-1860*. New York, 1971.

Konold, Donald E. *A History of American Medical Ethics, 1847-1912*. Madison, 1962.

Kulikoff, Allen. "The Progress of Inequality in Revolutionary Boston." *William and Mary Quarterly*, 3d ser., 28(1971):375-412.

Kuntz, William F., II. "Criminal Sentencing in Three Nineteenth-Century Cities: A Social History of Punishment in New York, Boston, and Philadelphia, 1830-1880." Ph.D. diss., Harvard University, 1979.

Lane, Roger. *Policing the City: Boston, 1822-1885*. Cambridge, Mass., 1967.

————. "Urbanization and Criminal Violence in the 19th Century: Massachusetts as a Test Case." In Hugh D. Graham and Ted R. Guff, eds., *The History of Violence in America*. New York, 1969.

Laurent, Francis W. *The Business of a Trial Court: 100 Years of Cases*. Madison, 1959.

Lazerson, Marvin. *Origins of the Urban School*. Cambridge, Mass., 1971.

Lopez, Robert S. "The Crossroad Within the Wall." In Oscar Handlin and John Burchard, eds., *The Historian and the City*. Cambridge, Mass., 1963.

Mackinnon, F. B. *Contingent Fees for Legal Services*. Chicago, 1964.

Mann, Arthur. *Yankee Reformers in the Urban Age*. Cambridge, Mass., 1954.

Marshall, Leon C., and Marquand, Elva L. *Unlocking the Treasuries of the Trial Courts*. Baltimore, 1933.

Mason, Alpheus T. *Brandeis: A Free Man's Life*. New York, 1956.

Merwick, Donna. *Boston Priests, 1848-1910*. Cambridge, Mass., 1973.

Meyer, Charles A. *Mercantile Credits and Collections*. New York, 1919.

Mills, C. Wright. *White Collar: The American Middle Classes*. New York, 1951.

Mumford, Lewis. *The City in History*. New York, 1961.

National Wholesale Druggists' Association. *A History of the National Wholesale Druggists' Association*. New York, 1924.

Nelson, William E. *Americanization of the Common Law: The Impact of Legal Change on Massachusetts, 1760-1830*. Cambridge, Mass., 1975.

Nystrom, Paul H. *The Economics of Retailing*. New York, 1915.

O'Neill, William L. *Divorce in the Progressive Era*. New Haven, 1967.

Posner, Richard A. "A Theory of Negligence." *Journal of Legal Studies* 1(1972):29-96.

Pound, Roscoe. *The Lawyer from Antiquity to Modern Times*. St. Paul, 1953.

Pratt, Walter M. *Seven Generations: The Story of Prattville and Chelsea*. N.p., 1930.

Prendergast, William A. *Credit and Its Uses*. New York, 1914.

Quiett, Glenn Chesney. *They Built the West*. New York, 1934.

Redlich, Josef. *The Common Law and the Case Method in American University Law Schools*. New York, 1914.

Reed, Alfred Z. *Training for the Public Profession of the Law*. New York, 1921.

Riggleman, John R. "Building Cycles in the United States, 1875-1932." *Journal of the American Statistical Association* 28(1933):176-185.

Rodwin, Lloyd. *Housing and Economic Progress: A Study of Housing Experiences of Boston's Middle-Income Families*. Cambridge, Mass., 1961.

Rueschemeyer, Dietrich. "Lawyers and Doctors: A Comparison of Two Professions." In Vilhelm Aubert, ed., *Sociology of Law*. Baltimore, 1969.

Schur, Edwin M. "Sociological Analysis of Confidence Swindling." In Marshall B. Clinard and Richard Quinney, eds., *Criminal Behavior Systems*. New York, 1967.

Seligman, Edwin R. A. *The Economics of Installment Selling: A Study in Consumer's Credit*. 2 vols. New York, 1927.

Shryock, Richard H. *The Development of Modern Medicine*. Philadelphia, 1936.

Shurtleff, Benjamin. *History of the Town of Revere*. Boston, 1938.

Smith, David C. *History of Papermaking in the United States (1691-1969)*. New York, 1970.

Solomon, Barbara M. *Ancestors and Immigrants: A Changing New England Tradition*. Cambridge, Mass., 1956.

Sutherland, Arthur E. *The Law at Harvard: A History of Ideas and Men, 1817-1967*. Cambridge, Mass., 1967.

Sutherland, Edwin H., and Cressey, Donald R. *Principles of Criminology*. 7th ed. New York, 1966.

Swaine, Robert T. *The Cravath Firm and Its Predecessors, 1819-1947*. Vol. 1. New York, 1947.

Thernstrom, Stephan. *The Other Bostonians: Poverty and Progress in the American Metropolis, 1880-1970*. Cambridge, Mass., 1973.

Warner, Sam Bass. *Crime and Criminal Statistics in Boston*. Cambridge, Mass., 1934.

Warner, Sam Bass, Jr. *Streetcar Suburbs: The Process of Growth in Boston, 1870-1900*. Cambridge, Mass., 1962.

Warren, Charles. *A History of the American Bar*. Boston, 1911.

Weber, Adna F. *The Growth of Cities in the Nineteenth Century*. New York, 1899.

Weeks, Lyman H. *A History of Paper-Manufacturing in the United States, 1690-1916*. New York, 1916.

Whitehill, Walter M. *Boston: A Topographical History*. Rev. ed. Cambridge, Mass., 1968.

INDEX

accidents, *see* injury
ad damnum, 115, 137, 139
"The Administration of Justice in the Modern City," 5
alienation of affection, 122, 130
ambulance chasers, 118
American Annual Digest, 34
American Medical Association (AMA), attitude toward debt, 77
American Tobacco Company, 59
appeals, 113, 114, 115
assault, 122, 124, 125
assessors, 42, 93
assigned counsel, 30
Associated Charities, 129, 130
assumption of risk, *see* tort law
auditors, 42-43

Back Bay, 91, 101
Baltimore, 147
bankers, 60, 63
bankruptcy, 7, 10
Bar Association of the City of Boston, 30, 37, 79, 80, 116, 118
bastardy, 122, 128-130
betterment, petitions for, 92-93
blacks, 24, 31, 146
Board of Gas Commissioners, 108
Board of Survey, 91-92
Boston: annexations, 14; becomes an entrepôt, 11-13, 49-50, 133, 145-147; political change, 13-16, 143; population, 13, 15, 16, 50, 87, 133; as subject of study, 6
Boston Chamber of Commerce, 65
Boston Elevated Railway, 115-116
Boston Legal Aid Society, 73, 127, 130

Boston University Law School, 31, 32, 38, 39, 154
Brandeis, Louis, 35-36, 67
breach of contract, 62
breach of marriage promise, 122, 127-128
Brighton, 7, 14
Brookline, 14, 101
builders, as plaintiffs, 90-91
building code, 83,182n5

Cambridge, 14
Canadians, English-speaking, 24, 88
cart-and-carriage lawsuits, 105-106, 112-113
case method, 32, 33
census schedules, 152-153
chancery, *see* equity
Charleston, 147
Charlestown, 7, 14
Chelsea, 7, 13, 14
Chicago, 147
Choate, Rufus, 36
Cincinnati, 147
city council, 102, 104, 108
city directories, 153
city government, as defendant, 92-93, 116, 119
city solicitor, 93, 116
civil litigation: accidents, 104-105, 108, 112, 113-119, 133, 134, 135, 144-145; changes in pattern, 17, 133; collective meaning, 4; commercial, 52-66; delay, 64, 72, 77, 86, 93, 117, 134-136, 137, 138, 140; distance factor, 76, 77, 94-95, 128, 145-146; ex-

civil litigation (*cont.*)
    pense of, 63, 64, 70-72, 86, 87,
      114, 118, 136, 138, 140; recov-
      eries, 45, 53, 62-64, 70-71, 77,
      86, 89, 93, 115, 125, 127, 128,
      129, 130, 136, 138, 139-140; re-
      lationship to society, 4, 6, 44-45,
      52, 91, 133, 140, 142-148; re-
      muneration through, 4, 80-81;
      as a safety valve, 130-131, 140;
      study of, 4-6, 151-152, 157-158;
      volume, 4, 6, 10, 17, 65, 73, 74,
      75, 77, 84, 88-89, 92-93, 105,
      106, 109, 112, 113, 122, 123,
      124, 128, 133, 134, 135, 144
clerks, *see* court clerks
clothiers, 56-57, 58
commercial paper, *see* promissory
    notes
conditional sales contract, 56,
    175n13
contingent fees, 118, 125, 135, 141
contributory negligence, 101,
    104-105, 135
conversion, 62, 177n29
corporations, 17-18, 21, 118, 141,
    153
counterclaims, 90, 184n19
court clerks, 3, 7, 43
court costs, 63, 71, 86, 114, 118. *See
    also* civil litigation, expense of
courthouse, 17, 18
court records, 4, 5, 6, 17, 148,
    151-152, 157-158
courts: district, 7, 129; federal, 8,
    10, 11; probate, 7, 127. *See also*
    judges; Municipal Court of the
    City of Boston; Superior Court
    of Suffolk County; Supreme
    Judicial Court of Massachusetts
credit, 49, 51, 52, 53, 57-60, 133,
    145; installment, 55, 56. *See also*
    mercantile (credit) references
    and agencies

crime and criminal law, 3, 122-126,
    128

damage, petitions for, 92-93
Davis, William T., 154, 165
debt: and age, 29; as a cause of ac-
    tion, 7, 17, 29, 133, 134, 135,
    157-158; and ethnicity, 27-28;
    and occupation, 20-24, 60-61
debt collection through litigation,
    62-66, 135, 138
defendants: age, 28-29, 45; black,
    24; corporations as, 17-18, 21,
    28, 118, 141; ethnicity, 24-28,
    45; self-representation, 30; sex
    ratios, 18-20, 45; white-collar
    and blue-collar, 20-24, 45, 61,
    89, 125, 141, 159-164. *See also*
    civil litigation
Democratic party, 72
Denver, 148
deputy sheriffs, 43-44
Dickson and Knowles (law firm),
    116
divorce and divorce laws, 7, 8, 122,
    126-127, 130
Dorchester, 7, 14, 91
druggists, wholesale, 59

East Boston, 7
education, legal, *see* legal education
ejectment, *see* evictions
Elder, Samuel J., 36
electricity, 108
eminent domain, 92-93
Employers' Liability Act, 110, 111
employment, 67-69, 178n3
equitable covenants, 182n6
equity, 7, 8, 123-124
Essex County, 7
evictions, 84-89
express companies, 116

Farnham, Frank A., 116

fellow-servant rule, *see* tort law
foreclosure, 90-91
fraud, 122-124, 125
furniture dealers, 51, 55-56

gas, 91-92, 108-109, 116
good government movement, 143
Greater Boston, 6, 7, 10, 49
grocers, 51, 53-55

Harbison, Robert, 116
Harvard Law School, 30, 31, 32, 33, 38, 39, 116, 154
Holyoke, Mass., 147
housing conditions, 82-84, 87-88, 90-91, 93-95
"The Housing Conditions in Boston," 82
Hubbell's Legal Directory, 154
Hurlburt, Jones, and Cabot (law firm), 116
Hyde and Baxter (law firm), 116
Hyde Park, 14

immigrants, 14, 118, 143. *See also* Canadians, English-speaking; defendants, ethnicity; Irish; Italians; Jews; judges, background; juries, social makeup; lawyers, ethnic bars; plaintiffs, ethnicity
industrial accidents, 19, 109-111
injury: and age, 29; as a cause of action, 17, 29, 99, 101, 105, 108, 109-110, 112, 133, 134, 158; and ethnicity, 27-28; leveling effect between sexes, 18-20; and occupation, 19-24, 109-112
inside contracting, 68
installment sales, 55, 56
insurance and insurance companies, 120-121, 139, 144
Irish, 24, 25-27, 37, 88
Italians, 24, 37, 88, 186*n*29

Jews, 24, 37, 88, 186*n*29
judges: background, 37-39; estrangement from the bar, 39-40; power to comment on evidence, 41; roles and attitudes, 30-31, 39-40, 91, 93, 114-115, 117, 127, 135, 136, 142, 173*n*34; salaries, 38; selection, assignment, and tenure, 3, 4, 7, 38, 165-166. *See also* courts; juries; lawyers
judgments, 45, 115
juries: criticized, 40, 41; defended, 41; instructions to, 41; selection, 40, 41; social makeup, 40, 41, 42, 135; women excluded from, 20, 30-31, 40

labor and labor law, 68, 72, 73-74
landlord and tenant, 83-89
Langdell, Christopher C., 32, 33
law: in action and in theory, 3, 5; commercialization of, 36, 78; preventive, 79, 102-104, 106, 120
lawyers: admission to the bar, 31, 37, 78; backgrounds, 31, 37, 44-46, 78-79, 116; black, 31; discipline, 37, 79; ethics, 36, 37, 71, 74, 78, 118-119, 141; ethnic bar, 31, 37, 44-46, 119; experience, 31, 36, 37-38, 65, 74, 79, 116, 117, 119; firms and partnerships, 31, 35; income, 35-36, 37, 65, 70-71, 74, 79, 141-142, 179*n*10; as plaintiffs, 75, 78-81; prominent, 35, 36, 37, 45-56, 65, 74, 78-80, 116; public image, 78-80; size of bar, 30, 31, 75, 78, 141, 180*n*29; solo practitioners, 31, 35; specialists, 30, 31, 35, 86, 115, 116-117, 130, 137; women, 20, 30-31; Yankee, 31, 45-46, 116, 119. *See also* legal education
legal education, 31, 32, 37

legal literature, 5, 34, 35, 37
legal profession, *see* lawyers
legal separation, 127
liquor dealers, 52-53, 54, 57-58
literature, *see* legal literature
litigants, suburban, 6, 94-95, 108. *See also* civil litigation, distance factor; defendants; plaintiffs
litigation, *see* civil litigation
lodging houses, 88

malpractice, medical, 78
marriage, *see* matrimony
Massachusetts, 12, 59, 73, 107
masters (in chancery), 42-43
matrimony, 122, 126-130
Matthews, Nathan, 116, 143
Matthews and Thompson (law firm), 116
mechanic's lien, 90
medical blacklist of debtors, 77
medical ethics toward debt, 76-77
mercantile (credit) references and agencies, 51-52, 65, 138-139, 144
Middlesex County, 7, 14
mortgages, 90-91
municipal corporations, 5. *See also* city solicitor
Municipal Court of the City of Boston: jurisdiction, 7, 10, 86, 113, 124, 133; specializes in debt litigation, 64, 70, 86, 136; speed of litigation in, 64, 70, 77-78, 86, 113-114, 134, 136

National Association of Credit Men, 65
negligence, *see* contributory negligence
negotiable instruments, *see* promissory notes
New Orleans, 147
New York City, 147

New York, New Haven, and Hartford Railroad, 116
Norfolk County, 7, 14
North End, 13, 83, 85, 87

paper manufacturers, 59-60
periodicals, legal, *see* legal literature
Philadelphia, 147
physicians, as litigants, 75-78
piecework system, 68
plaintiffs: age, 28-29, 45; black, 24; ethnicity, 24-28, 45, 65, 95, 119; self-representation, 30, 86; sex ratios, 18-20, 45, 65, 95, 119; white-collar and blue-collar, 20-24, 45, 60-61, 95, 119, 125, 127, 130, 140-141, 159-164. *See also* civil litigation
Plymouth County, 7
police, 73, 104, 123, 124, 125
Portuguese, 88
Pound, Roscoe, 5
probate court, 7, 10
Professional and Industrial History of Suffolk County, 154, 165
profit sharing, 68
promissory notes, 57, 60, 62, 63
property damage, 112-113, 133

railroads, *see* steam railroads; street railways
referees, 42-43
reform, legal, 143-144
rent claims, 86-89
replevin, 62, 177n29
Republicans, 72
reports, case, 34
retail trade, changes in, 50-52
Revere, 7, 13
R. G. Dun's Mercantile Reference Book, 153-154, 176n25
Ropes-Gray (law firm), 31, 35
routinization of legal procedure,

113, 136-137, 142, 146
Roxbury, 7, 14, 83, 85, 88, 91

St. Louis, 147
sample of cases, 10n, 11, 154-156,
    157-158, 193n13
Seattle, 148
setoffs, 90, 184n19
settlements, 73, 90, 113, 115, 118,
    125, 128, 136, 142
slander, 122, 130
South Boston, 7
South End, 76, 83, 85, 88, 93
specialization, see lawyers; Munici-
    pal Court of the City of Boston;
    Superior Court of Suffolk
    County
steam railroads, lawsuits against,
    107-108
stenographers, 34, 44, 152
street railways: accident rates, 101,
    112; as defendants, 105, 113;
    development of, 51, 68, 87,
    91-92, 101-102, 140; regulation
    of, 5, 91-92, 102-104, 106
streets, laying out of, 91-92
Superior Court of Suffolk County:
    jurisdiction, 7, 8, 10, 92, 114,
    123-124, 126, 129, 133; spe-
    cializes in injury litigation, 114,
    115, 117, 123-124, 136; speed of
    litigation in, 64, 70, 77-78, 93,
    117, 129, 134, 136
Supreme Judicial Court of Mas-
    sachusetts, 7-8, 11, 79, 101, 104,
    105, 109, 110, 111, 114, 154
sweatshops, effect of laws against,
    87-88

taxes, property, 4, 14, 93
telephones, 34-35, 37
Thernstrom, Stephan, 159
tobacco dealers, 58-59
tort law, 3, 101, 116, 127, 135, 136;

assumption of risk, 110; con-
    tributory negligence, 101;
    fellow-servant rule, 110; wrong-
    ful death actions, 107, 110
Transit Commission, 106
trial courts: constituency, 3, 6, 49,
    140-142, 146, 147; organization,
    3, 4, 6, 7; as social institutions, 3,
    142-148. See also civil litigation;
    Municipal Court of the City of
    Boston; Superior Court of Suf-
    folk County
typewriters, 34-35, 37

urbanization, 5, 6, 16, 87, 100,
    145-147, 148, 189n30
urban market, 49-52, 133

wage claims, 69-75
weekly-wage laws, 73, 74
West End, 83, 85, 87, 94
West End Street Railway, 101, 116
West Roxbury, 7, 14, 91
Whitney, Henry M., 101, 104
wholesalers, 52, 57-60, 63
Whom to Trust, 61
Wichita, 148
Winthrop, 7, 13
women; disadvantages before the
    law, 20, 30-31; excluded from
    juries, 20, 30-31, 40; as stenog-
    raphers, 44. See also defendants;
    divorce and divorce laws; mat-
    rimony; plaintiffs
Woods, Robert A., 88
wool merchants, 58
workmen's compensation, 107,
    109-112, 116
wrongful death, see tort law

Yankees, see defendants, ethnicity;
    judges, background; juries, so-
    cial makeup; lawyers, Yankee;
    plaintiffs, ethnicity

Library of Congress Cataloging in Publication Data

Silverman, Robert, 1947-
    Law and urban growth.

    Bibliography: p.
    Includes index.
    1.   Justice, Administration of—Massachusetts—
Boston—History.   2.   Law—Massachusetts—Boston—
History and criticism.   3.   Boston—History—1865-
I.   Title.
KFX1133.5.S54   347.744'61   80-7553
ISBN 0-691-04677-8

GPSR Authorized Representative: Easy Access System Europe - Mustamäe tee
50, 10621 Tallinn, Estonia, gpsr.requests@easproject.com

www.ingramcontent.com/pod-product-compliance
Lightning Source LLC
Chambersburg PA
CBHW050430280326
41932CB00013BA/2062